ARTHUR C. CLARKE'S MYSTERIES

JOHN FAIRLEY AND SIMON WELFARE

FOREWORD BY ARTHUR C. CLARKE

 Prometheus Books

59 John Glenn Drive
Amherst, New York 14228-2197

First published in this format in 1998 by
Michael O'Mara Books Limited
9 Lion Yard
Tremadoc Road
London SW4 7NQ

Arthur C. Clarke's *Mysterious World*
First published in Great Britain in 1980 by HarperCollins

Arthur C. Clarke's *World of Strange Powers*
First published in Great Britain in 1984 by HarperCollins

Arthur C. Clarke's *Chronicles of the Strange and Mysterious*
First published in Great Britain in 1987 by HarperCollins

Published 2000 by Prometheus Books

Inquiries should be addressed to
Prometheus Books
59 John Glenn Drive
Amherst, New York 14228–2197
VOICE: 716–691–0133, ext. 207
FAX: 716–564–2711
WWW.PROMETHEUSBOOKS.COM

04 03 02 01 00   5 4 3 2 1

Library of Congress Cataloging-in-Publication Data

Fairley, John, 1940–
    Arthur C. Clarke's mysteries / John Fairley and Simon Welfare ; foreword by
Arthur C. Clarke.
        p. cm.
    Includes index.
    ISBN 1–57392–833–X (alk. paper)
    1. Curiosities and wonders. I. Welfare, Simon.

AG243 .F328 2000
301.02—dc21   00–044141
                                                                                      CIP

Printed in the United States of America on acid-free paper

CONTENTS

FOREWORD

Looking back at the manifold mysteries that first engaged Simon, John and myself, twenty years ago (I can hardly believe it!), I am acutely aware that some of the most intriguing ones are as baffling as ever. Who built the vitrified forts of Scotland, or made the stone balls of Costa Rica? The answers are unlikely to be earth-shattering, but I really would like to know them. And I would never have imagined, twenty years ago, that UFOs would not only still be with us, but would be flourishing as never before. Although I am still an (almost) complete sceptic, I'm really beginning to wonder if something is happening 'Out There'. But I simply refuse to believe we are continually visited by alien spacecraft. After all this time, at least some equivalents of number-plates, windscreen wipers, or rear-lights would have fallen off, and we would have undeniable, concrete evidence . . .

And to me, the lack of photographic evidence is the most convincing argument. In 1972, a spectacular meteor went right across the western United States in broad daylight. There was of course no warning, yet many cameras recorded it, even though the event lasted only seconds. So hundreds of UFOs should have been clearly captured on film by this time, if they are as common as the believers maintain. Yet, I've never seen a single convincing photograph – they are either out of focus or obvious fakes, though nowadays anyone with a computer can make a very good UFO! And did none of the 'contactees' happen to have cameras with them? Really . . .

One subject which has become of much greater importance since we discussed it – indeed the US Congress has a hearing on it even as I dictate these words! – is the danger of asteroid or comet impacts. It is now generally realized that these have played a vital role in the development of life on earth. Indeed, we might not be here, if a convenient asteroid had not triggered the extinction of the dinosaurs sixty-five million years ago, and thus given an opportunity for an unprepossessing rat-like mammal to go on to greater things. And I am delighted that the name Spaceguard, which I coined in *Rendezvous with Rama*, a quarter of a century ago, has now been widely accepted for the programme to deal with this danger.

The search for life on other worlds is also gaining respectability and serious attention is being paid to the possibility of artefacts being left in the solar system by visitors from elsewhere. One enigma is the so-called Mars Face – a striking formation looking up at the stars from the Martian deserts. Although recent close-ups from the Mars Surveyor make it seem more probable that it is perfectly natural, there are still some curiously shaped objects in its vicinity. If I had to put any money on it, I would bet 90 pence in the pound that there has been life on Mars in the past, when its climate was more benign, and 10 pence that it's still hanging on in some warm, wet oasis, like the oceans which we now believe underlie the ice fields of Europa. The close-ups of this giant moon of Jupiter show the most extraordinary patterns, and in one place there is a straight line, hundreds of miles long, running right across the ice floes. To me it looks completely artificial, but I'm afraid it will probably turn out to be some extraordinary natural phenomenon. Intelligent life on Europa does seem too much to ask for – but the possibility of some life-forms beneath that ice shield is very real.

Finally, let me release one of the largest bees buzzing around in my bonnet – so-called Cold Fusion. It surfaced just about ten years ago with the announcement that two scientists had succeeded in creating energy in the laboratory with just simple equipment. After the initial furore, the whole subject was laughed out of court, but in the last few years these experiments, and even more advanced ones, have been repeated in scores of laboratories. I now have no doubt that we are about to tap new sources of energy – though fusion may not always be involved.

So that's the biggest mystery on my horizon at the moment.

Sir Arthur C Clarke

May 1998

INTRODUCTION

This book stems from a tale told to us by chance. A story that lingered in the mind and stays there still.

In 1972, we were filming with Arthur C Clarke on his favourite beach in Sri Lanka, the beautiful tropical island, which, almost twenty years earlier, had become his adopted home. We were making a documentary for British television, the first to record Arthur's achievements and to allow him to present, to a mass audience, his visions of the future. There was plenty of material: his science fiction like *2001 – A Space Odyssey* and *Childhood's End*, his predictions (infuriatingly accurate) of the technology of the years ahead, and his revelatory work that had made communications satellites possible. But we also hoped that he would offer us new thoughts upon which to ponder, and so we allowed space in the schedule for him to surprise us. This was almost a disastrous move. During one interview in the spectacular ruins of an ancient city, no one noticed a venomous snake slinking purposefully towards the famous author. The creature was about to strike when the cameraman, whose concentration had thankfully slipped for the briefest of moments, shouted a warning. Everyone scattered and waited, cowering behind the time-worn stones until the danger had passed.

However, our rather loose filming schedule also brought dividends. In search of exotic locations, we had travelled along the coast road, south from Sri Lanka's capital, Colombo, to Unawatuna beach. Arthur had discovered this spectacular horseshoe of palm-fringed golden sand soon after arriving on the island and rented a bungalow there.

One morning we found him sitting on a rock at the edge of the sea. Three huge lizards basked sluggishly nearby. Out amidst the gentle breakers of the Indian Ocean, straw-hatted fishermen perched on poles, languidly amassing the day's catch. The cameraman stuck the legs of the tripod deep into the warm sand, and soon film was spooling through the camera. Arthur's gaze was fixed on the horizon, a milky line beneath an azure sky. Beyond that, he told us, lay sea, unbroken all the way to Antarctica – and countless mysteries. Of these, the most spectacular of all was the great sea serpent.

> I think there's something in this, except that it probably isn't a serpent and it's probably not a single creature but a whole series of sea beasts, very large and perhaps very shy. We're realizing now that some of the old stories have a basis in truth, and one of them, about a giant octopus, is relevant to where we are today.
>
> About 100 years ago, a 150-ton schooner called *The Pearl* sailed round this headland from Galle harbour, just about two miles from here, and was becalmed in the Bay of Bengal.
>
> A P & O liner was passing at the time, and the people on the liner saw the schooner becalmed and this dark mass in the water. Foolishly, they fired shots at the dark mass which moved towards the schooner and, according to their description, "coalesced" round *The Pearl* and capsized her.
>
> This story was published in *The Times* of London, which is not prone to sensationalism. But the problem has always been that, if it was an octopus that sank *The Pearl* – and that's the creature that best fits the description given by the passengers on the liner – it would have been far larger than any previously recorded.
>
> Well, we've recently discovered that a sea monster washed up in Florida at the end of the nineteenth century has been identified from pieces kept in a museum as an octopus. Now the largest known octopus at the moment is about thirty feet across the tentacles. This one was apparently 200 feet from tentacle tip to tentacle tip, so the sea does probably hold much larger creatures than have ever come out of it.

Years later, when we were planning a documentary series exclusively devoted to mysteries, we remembered the sequence we had filmed on Unawatuna beach. The programmes needed a presenter. He or she would have to be able to speak with authority, and that meant that they had to know something about all the subjects we planned to tackle. Could it be, we wondered, that this acclaimed communicator of both science fact and science fiction was also a mystery buff?

We did not have to wait long to find out. By chance, Arthur was passing through London the following week. Over the first of many cups of his beloved milky, sugar-swamped tea, he treated us to tales even more exotic than the story of *The Pearl*: in Baghdad, he had been told, there was a battery dating from prehistoric times; a scientist friend claimed to have found a way of listening to sounds made centuries before; and one of his opponents in his daily games of table tennis at the Otters Swimming Club back home in Sri Lanka had almost been slapped on the head by a fish that had fallen from a clear blue sky...

And so our television series, *Arthur C Clarke's Mysterious World*, was born. There was, of course, an episode on sea monsters, and one on those other shadowy creatures, the Yeti and Bigfoot. At Stonehenge, we watched the sun rise on midsummer morning over those ancient stones which have puzzled investigators since long before the establishment of archaeology as a science. At Loch Ness, we interviewed eyewitnesses, all with apparently impeccable credentials, who were certain they had spotted the famous monster, and penetrated some rather scary research institutes in the then Soviet Union to investigate the Great Siberian Explosion of 1908. Meanwhile, from his hi-tech study in Colombo, Arthur offered us a non-stop stream of ideas, newspaper cuttings and references to obscure books and scientific papers.

As the months of research wore on, we realized that we would never be able to cram all the extraordinary stories we had come across into the television series. And so it was that *Mysterious World* spawned a book and another series, *Arthur C Clarke's World of Strange Powers*. They, in their turn, produced not one, but two, further books – our pile of fascinating mysteries had grown into a mountain!

And then something strange happened. The conventional wisdom, that books outlast TV programmes, was confounded. *Mysterious World* and *Strange Powers* have been running for more than a decade in America and Europe, mainly on the Discovery cable and satellite channels, yet the books that accompany them have been hard to find. And that is why we have compiled this omnibus edition of the most baffling mysteries featured in them.

To our surprise, little has changed since our original investigations. The giant octopus has perhaps been sighted but never captured, the Yeti remains as elusive as ever, the trilithons of Stonehenge keep their age-old secrets. Thanks to the *X-files*, the paranormal has become fashionable, but still no one can say for sure whether the dead can speak to us, if poltergeists exist or whether prophets really do see the future. A few hoaxes have been claimed, among them the 'surgeon's' photograph of the Loch Ness monster and the weird Bigfoot movie, but proof, even of human trickery, has remained elusive.

Even rarer than the original books, are the posters which were displayed in bookshops to mark their publication. They contain two quotes from Arthur C Clarke. The first is an invitation:

> The Universe is such a strange and wonderful place that reality will always outrun the wildest imagination.

The second is a warning:

> At a generous assessment, approximately half this book is nonsense. Unfortunately, I don't know which half, and neither does anyone else.

We believe they are all you need to guide you, as you cross the threshold into the Mysterious World . . .

John Fairley and Simon Welfare
August 1998

THE BEASTS THAT HIDE
FROM MAN

THE MISSING APE MAN

Mysterious footprints have travelled from the high peaks of the Himalayas, the mountains of Georgia and of northwest America and Canada, into the imaginations of thousands of scientists, zoologists, mountaineers, and showmen, whose dream is to find the 'Missing Link', the half ape half man of countless fabulous tales. In the process, these prints have trampled on many reputations, launched huge expeditions and parted fortunes from otherwise shrewd businessmen.

The names of the mysterious creature are the stuff of the most ludicrous tall stories: the 'Abominable Snowman', 'Bigfoot', the Russian 'Man of the Mountains', and its description belongs to the world of nursery rhyme: seven, eight, nine feet tall, vile and ugly of face, covered in long hair, strong enough to wring the necks of full-grown cattle, fast enough to outrun man or dog, or, in Russia, even a horse, attacking young virgins and battering men to death with a club.

On the other hand, Lord Hunt, leader of the expedition that first conquered Mount Everest, believes that such a creature may exist. In 1978, he and his wife found and photographed convincing tracks in the Himalayas. In America, Dr Grover Krantz of Washington State University is also convinced of the reality of Bigfoot, or the sasquatch as it is called by the North American Indians. In 1978, the University of British Columbia organized an academic conference in which thirty-five separate papers of analysis and speculation were on offer, from universities all over the world. In Tbilisi, Georgia, there is a whole department devoted to the search for the Neanderthal 'Man of the Mountains'. Every now and then the New China News Agency reports that Chinese soldiers in Tibet have shot and eaten a snowman. In the wild country either side of the Cascade Mountains, which run down the Pacific Coast of America from Canada through Washington and Oregon, reports of sightings of Bigfoot or the sasquatch now run into hundreds.

In 1979, a British expedition which conquered a 14,840 foot (4,520m) peak in the Himalayas for the first time found distinct footprints in the Hinken Valley and heard 'scream-like calls'.

The lead climber, Squadron Leader John Edwards, said '. . . there is firm evidence of a strange creature in the Himalayas. One footprint we found was a really clear example and I think our pictures will prove to be the best taken yet. What is more, we heard this high-pitched scream and our Sherpas said it was a yeti.'

Although most zoologists scoff at the idea that there can exist, undiscovered, a manlike creature, a missing link in the evolutionary chain, it was that great zoologist, Charles Darwin, who provided the theoretical basis upon which many yeti hunters have built. Particularly in Russia, Darwin's theory of evolution has been taken to imply a 'missing link' and huge, uncharted mountains provide perfect cover for an animal shy of humanity. Fly from northern India to Nepal, Sikkim, Bhutan or over India's old North East Frontier, and range after range of inhospitable hill and mountain lies beneath, for the most part hardly inhabited.

Even in the Pacific northwest of North America, dense forests blanket the country along the Columbia river. Fifty miles can separate one small road from the next, and since the Second World War more than seventy aircraft have disappeared in the area without trace. Indeed, there is a macabre joke among people who know the area that, apart from the sasquatch or Bigfoot, another monster, which enjoys eating aircraft, lurks in the hills. But of all the 'missing ape men', it is the yeti, the Abominable Snowman, who is the most celebrated.

The Abominable Snowman

The Abominable Snowman, the yeti as the Sherpas call him, is the most venerable of all the mysterious ape men of the high country. He is tangled in a web of fantasy, religion, legend, chicanery and commercialism. He has been seen by supposedly reliable witnesses, his droppings have been analysed, his footprints recorded and examined in apparently unimpeachable circumstances. He was dismissed as a legend by expeditions in the late 1950s and 1960s but now the evidence for his existence seems to become stronger every year.

A traveller to Katmandu is embroiled, even before he arrives, in the yeti business. The Royal Nepalese Airlines' flight skims over the lower mountain ranges, the villages perched absurdly right on the peaks, seemingly in hourly danger of toppling into the ravines. Then, suddenly, the line of the great summits of the Himalayas comes into view, white and jagged, the rest of the earth blocked out by cloud. Shangri-La, the Lost Horizon, secret valleys, unknown tribes, the yeti – all seem plausible. But in the aircraft seat pocket is the menu for the airline's Yeti Service, and the new hotel for which you are bound, built by the World Bank, is called the Yak and Yeti. The yeti is a highly commercial legend, perhaps even Nepal's principal foreign currency earner.

The stories of the yeti, the great monster of the Himalayas, are legion among the Nepalese themselves and especially the Sherpas who live in the high mountains. At Thyangboche monastery in the shadow of Everest, the abbot talks quite matter-of-factly of the yetis that visit the monastery garden. Each year vivid descriptions of attacks by yetis are reported in Katmandu. One Sherpa girl, Lakhpa Domani, described an incident to a Peace Corps volunteer, William Weber, who was working in the area of Machherma village in the Everest region. The girl said she was sitting near a stream tending her yaks when she heard a noise and turned round to confront a huge apelike creature with large eyes and prominent cheekbones. It was covered in black and red–brown hair. It seized her and carried her to the water, but her screams seem to have disconcerted the creature and it dropped her. Then it attacked two of her yaks, killing one with blows, the other by seizing its horns and breaking its neck. The incident was reported to the local police and footprints were found. Weber says: 'What motive could there possibly have been for a hoax? My conclusion was that the girl was telling the truth.'

The actual evidence for the yeti falls into three main categories: footprints, eyewitnesses and physical evidence such as skulls and skins.

The footprints are certainly intriguing. Though prints had been reported by Westerners as far back as 1887, and then again by a British Army officer 21,000 feet (6,400m) up Everest in 1921, it is the photographs of them that present the main challenge. F S Smythe's were the first, taken at 16,500 feet (5,000m) in 1937. Eric Shipton's photographs – with an ice-axe carefully laid against the prints for scale – started serious enquiry. McNeely and Cronin from the 1972 American expedition found footprints clear and sharp enough for plaster casts to be taken. The following year, Lord Hunt found prints, and his 1978 pictures show huge footprints, fourteen inches (355mm) long and seven inches (177mm) wide.

Speaking at the Royal Geographical Society in London, Lord Hunt said:

> We were in a side valley below Everest. It was late in the evening and getting dark when my wife and myself came across the traces. They were very fresh indeed, and I will even say that they were certainly made that day. There was deep snow on a rather steep little slope and the creature was a heavy one, because he had broken through a hard crust on which we could walk without making an impression through the snow at all. The prints were oval, elongated. I put down an ice axe to measure. They were fourteen inches long and just about half as wide.

British mountaineer and surgeon, Michael Ward, was with Eric Shipton when the 1951 prints were photographed. 'We were about thirty or forty miles west of Everest,' he relates, 'and we crossed a large mountain range at about nineteen to twenty thousand feet and went into what is called a "blank" on the map. The map was absolutely white and there was no topographical detail at all.' On a glacier they came across some mountain goats and saw their tracks. Then suddenly there was another track.

> These were really well defined and quite different. We could see the toes of all the feet. The prints led off right down the glacier for several miles as far as I could see: My own feeling was the tracks had probably been made at night or earlier that day, because there was absolutely no blurring round the edges. In fact in some of the places you could see where this animal had crossed a small crevasse and you could actually see nail marks where he'd jumped from one side to the other. As you can see in the pictures, the tracks were much deeper than we were making. We'd have probably spent a great deal longer photographing them and describing them, but we were short of food and our main concern was to make our way out of this completely unexplored country where not even the Sherpas and Tibetans had ever been, and certainly no European.

Their concern was well founded, for Shipton and Ward had strayed into Tibet and were subsequently captured by armed Tibetan guards, only to be ransomed after protracted bargaining by their Sherpas for the princely sum of £1.

The sceptical view is that the footprints are those of other species distorted by the sun or snow conditions – perhaps the Tibetan blue bear, itself rare enough to be almost legendary, or a langur monkey, which is known to live at considerable heights. The snow leopard has also been named as the guilty party and one letter to the British magazine *Country Life* even suggested that it might be a bird – the Alpine chough – which had been observed to leave snowmanlike traces as it hopped across the snow.

However, the zoologist, W Tschernezky, of Queen Mary College, London, did a most exhaustive analysis of the Shipton footprints, using a reconstructed model and comparing it with gorilla, fossil man and human footprints. Noting the unusually large second toe and very short metatarsal bone, he concludes they are very unlike a bear or a langur monkey. 'All the evidence suggests,' he says, 'that the so-called snowman is a very huge, heavily built bipedal primate, most probably of a similar type to the fossil *Gigantopithecus*.' Such an assertion takes the yeti as near to being a living version of the 'missing link' as any reputable scientist would dare.

Of the people who have actually seen the tracks, the most convincing are probably those whose backgrounds do not lead them easily to espouse the yeti legend. Captain Emil Wick, Swiss pilot with Royal Nepalese Airlines, has an elegant house on the outskirts of Katmandu. Sitting in his garden at dusk over a bottle of beer he was forthright:

> My God, I tell you I had no interest at all in these damned yetis when I came to Nepal. I came here to fly close to the mountains with the tourists because I am a damned good flyer in these little planes, and to enjoy myself when I am not flying, just like I did in Bangkok and Indonesia and wherever. Then, one morning last year, I was flying some Japanese to Kangchenjunga when I saw these tracks at a terrific height. There were three of them, three separate tracks and it was obvious that they were made by a two-legged creature. They came up either side of a steep ridge, then they came together and went down to a lake which I had never seen before, perhaps for a drink. I know it was fresh snow and it wasn't later than half-past seven in the morning so the sun cannot have played tricks. I went round for two or three looks and you'll never believe me – there was a Japanese woman beside me with a camera and I begged her to take pictures. 'I will even give you the flight free,' I said. But she just said, 'Stop flying around for your own amusement. We pay you to go to Kangchenjunga. That's where we want to take our pictures.'

A Frenchman, the Abbé Bordet, of the Paris Geological Institute, followed three separate lots of tracks on a 1955 expedition. In his account for the *Bulletin* of the Musée National d'Histoire Naturelle, Paris, he says he followed one track for more than half a mile. At times, the impression was so clear he could make out the snow marking the separation of the toes. At one point, the creature had jumped off a little rock wall four or five foot (1–1.5m) high and its footprints had sunk six inches (150mm) or so into the snow. Father Bordet had his photographs examined by the two most senior mammalogists in France and they declared the tracks to be those of an unknown species.

Squadron Leader Lester Davies of the Ullswater Outward Bound School, in England, was also struck by the depth of the prints he filmed in 1955 on the RAF Himalaya Expedition.

They'd sunk in about five or six inches. With cine cameras and ruck-sack, I was weighing about twelve and a half stone, and only went in about one or one and a half inches. I thought, this thing is huge!

Men of unquestioned probity say they have actually seen the creature. Don Whillans is the dour and down-to-earth propri-etor of a Welsh guest house and indomitable hero of climbs on Everest and Kangchenjunga. He was on Annapurna in June 1970.

We were in the Annapurna sanctuary, as it is called, which is a ring of very high mountains. I was anxious to find a decent place to camp for the night and as we slowly came round a spur of the mountain, I heard what sounded like bird cries from behind me. I looked at the Sherpa and he said 'Yeti coming, Sahib.' So I whipped round and looked up the mountain and I saw two black crows flying away and a black shape drop behind the ridge. My first thoughts were, What do I do now, grab the ice-axe or what? Anyway, it didn't reappear so I said, 'Come on let's get the camp up.' The following day, we continued up the valley to complete this reconnaissance of the south face and I saw the tracks obviously left by the creature, the night before. These tracks were nearly eighteen inches [457mm] deep, the snow was very soft and they seemed to be roughly about the same size as my own foot, which sort of corresponded with what the Sherpas had said, that they were baby yeti. I suppose yetis, if such a thing exists, come in different sizes, the same as people.

Later on that evening, it was a very, very moonlit night and, for some reason, there had been a strong feeling as far as I was concerned that this creature was actually still around. So I stuck my head out of the tent. It was so moonlit that you could actually read. I watched for about a quarter of an hour and I was just beginning to think, Oh well, maybe whatever it is has gone, when I saw something move. When you do a lot of climbing, you get used to looking at moun-tains and looking for very small figures and very small alterations. And this creature, which looked to me in its movements apelike, sort of bounded along in a funny gait towards what obviously in a few weeks' time, when the snow had gone, would be a clump of trees. It appeared to be pulling some of the branches. Anyway I watched for about twenty minutes. I got the binoculars out and all I could make out was a black apelike shape. Then, quite suddenly, it was almost as if it realized it was being watched, it shot across the whole slope of the mountain. It must have travelled half a mile before it disappeared into the shadow by some rocks. What was really strange to me was the behaviour of the Sherpas. If it had been a bear – they're very familiar with bears – they would have said, 'Oh, it's a barlu', as I believe they call it, and that would have been the end of it. But they were very subdued for a couple of days and if I ever tried to mention the subject or was looking at the tracks through the binoculars during the day I would hear them passing comments to one another.

Now whether it was a langur monkey, as has been said, I don't know. It might have been an extremely thin bear, just come out from the winter. But it didn't seem like that to me. And the actual tracks that I saw had very peculiar indentations between the actual footprint, which didn't strike me until about twelve months later when I was looking at a picture of a gorilla in a normal animal book. That could very well be the knuckle marks of this creature, between the actual footprints.

In 1975, a Polish trekker, Janusz Tomaszczuk, claimed to have had a terrifying encounter. He had been hiking in the Everest area and had sprained his knee. As he limped back to a nearby settlement, he saw a figure approaching him. When Tomaszczuk shouted for help, the figure came nearer. It was then that he saw that the 'man' he had asked for help was an apelike creature over six foot (1.8m) tall with arms down to its knees. His screams drove it away.

Such stories are accepted as normal by the Sherpas. In 1978 there were more reported attacks by yetis, particularly in Sikkim, where the Forestry Department sent out a series of fruitless expeditions in pursuit. The most serious attempt to resolve the enigma of the yeti was sponsored by the American *World Book Encyclopedia*. An expedition set out in 1960, led by Desmond Doig and Sir Edmund Hillary, the first man (along with Sherpa Tenzing) to stand on the summit of Mount Everest. They stayed ten months, through a fierce winter, in the region where most of the yeti sightings had been reported. The expedition was lavishly equipped with trip-wire cameras, and time-lapse and infra-red photography. There was worldwide excitement when Hillary persuaded the villagers of Khumjung to lend their legendary yeti scalp for six weeks for scientific examination. This scalp, along with two others and a couple of skins (which were later identified as blue bear) were alleged to be the only remnants of the yeti in existence.

Hillary and Doig set off in the autumn with the guardian of the scalp, Khunjo Chumbi, on a worldwide tour that took them to Honolulu, Chicago, Paris and even Buckingham Palace. At every stop Chumbi imitated for the television crews the high-pitched howl that the yeti is supposed to make. Meanwhile, posses of experts examined the scalp.

Like latter-day Phileas Foggs, Hillary and Doig had to return to Khumjung within forty-two days otherwise, by agreement, the land and property of their Sherpas would have been forfeit. They arrived on the last day, dropping out of the sky in a helicopter with the scalp safe in its box, but sadly convinced that the scalp was almost certainly made from the hide of a serow goat. The expedition had no better luck with its cameras and hideouts and Hillary turned to the problems of a difficult climb of Mount Makalu.

In their accounts of the expedition, Hillary and Doig dismissed the yeti as the stuff of myth and legend. After all, they had exposed one of the scalps as false and devoted nearly a year, in the heart of the supposed yeti habitat, to as thorough a search as experience and technical virtuosity could devise.

Desmond Doig is wryly sceptical of the 1960 expedition and has since reversed his opinion, now believing that the yeti exists. 'After all, we may not have seen a yeti,' he says, 'but we didn't see a snow leopard either and we *know* they exist. In fact, we hardly saw any creatures at all. The expedition was too big and clumsy. Also, years afterwards, I think I solved the scalp mystery.' He tossed what appeared to be a perfect facsimile of the Khumjung scalp across the room. 'I was travelling near the Sikkim border when I met a tribesman wearing that thing and not much else. It turns out that they are made quite regularly around there to be worn as hats.' So the scalp may have been a genuine mistake – but even if it was a deliberate fake it does not mean that yetis do not exist.

It was Doig, too, who subsequently obtained from a monastery in Bhutan a magnificent blue-bear skin which was sold at Christie's in London in 1978 for £1200. The catalogue note said: 'It has been suggested that this very rare skin is that of the Yeti or Abominable Snowman.'

Doig, who speaks many of the area's languages, points out that the Sherpas talk of three different kinds of yeti. There is the dzu teh, which is large shaggy and attacks and eats cattle. This, he feels, is almost certainly the Tibetan blue bear, which has never been seen by a Westerner even though the first skin found its way to the Asiatic Society in London in 1853. To this day there are only half a dozen known blue-bear skins, a skull and some bones. 'I once met a Tibetan lady who told me there had been one in the Panchen Lama's zoo in Shigatse in Tibet,' Doig went on. 'She said it walked on two legs, was as big as a tall man and had a face like an ape or a bear. Unfortunately, it and the whole zoo were swept away in a flood.'

The second type of yeti is called the thelma by the Sherpas: 'a "little man" who runs along hooting and collecting sticks'. Doig says, 'I don't think there's much problem about that. It's almost certainly a gibbon, even though conventional zoology says that they are not found north of the Brahmaputra River in India.'

The third, the true snowman of the legend according to Doig, is the mih teh. It is savage, looks like an ape, is man-eating, covered with black or red hair, has the classic 'reversed toes' and prowls about at anything up to 20,000 feet (6,100m) or even higher.

> In 1961 we dismissed the mih teh as pure myth. I now think we were wrong. I've often shown Sherpas who claim to have seen the mih teh a sort of identity parade of different bears, humans, drawings of Neanderthal Man and *Gigantopithecus*, gorillas, chimps, gibbons, and the orang-utan. Invariably, though they have no knowledge whatsoever of the great apes, it is an ape they point to, usually an orang-utan. We know from fossils that the orang-utan once lived in northern India. Who knows? There are still immense jungles which could conceal whole tribes of yetis. Perhaps their rare excursions to the high slopes are, as Abbé Bordet suggested, in search of water. It can be very dry on the upper margins of the forest.

The yeti case rests on tales from the Sherpas, some Western eyewitnesses, but above all on the footprints of which there are now more than twenty reliable records, including the pictures brought back at Christmas 1979 by the Royal Air Force expedition. Doubters question where such a creature could find food at such altitudes. Believers quote the lynx, the woolly wolf, the ibex and the yak, which have all been seen at more than 18,000 feet (5,490m). But no one has come up with a convincing explanation for photographs like Shipton's and Lord Hunt's, which seem to show with such clarity the tracks of a creature much heavier than man, which walks for long distances on two legs, and leaves a footprint unlike any other known animal.

Bigfoot
Compared to the Himalayan yeti, the North American Bigfoot or sasquatch is almost insolent in the frequency of his reported appearances. A regular journal, *Bigfoot News*, for years was large with Bigfoot sightings, often by ordinary people who had no interest in publicity and no previous knowledge of the Bigfoot story. And, obligingly, Bigfoot occasionally leaves his tracks behind to lend some substance to the stories of witnesses.

A typical encounter took place in the Mount Hood National Forest in northern Oregon. Three loggers, Fermin Osborne, J C Rourke and Jack Cochran, were working in a clearing. On a July morning, Cochran was working the crane when he saw a manlike figure watching him. He got out of his cab to look. The figure was built massively, covered in dark hair and was walking upright. Fermin Osborne said:

> I didn't see it that time and apparently it just walked quickly away into the forest. But the next day I was with Rourke and we decided to take a break from work. We walked into the edge of the forest. All of a sudden, this great creature got up out of the undergrowth, right in front of us, not more than ten yards away. It was covered with dark hair, even over the head and face, and really heavily built. Rourke chased after it but he couldn't catch up with it. He just chucked a couple of stones at it. I've seen plenty of bears and it certainly wasn't a grizzly. More like a gorilla really.

Bigfoot put in an appearance for the law in the person of Sergeant Larry Gamache of the Yakima Sheriff's Department in Washington State. Sergeant Gamache was driving back from a fishing trip with his brother and sister-in-law, Kathy.

My brother was asleep in the back of the pick-up. Suddenly I saw what I thought was a man coming out of the timber on the shoulder of the road. Then I realized this was no man. It was naked and covered in long hair. I drove past slowly and then Kathy screamed. The creature had come over and peered in at her through the passenger window. She was terrified. And my brother slept through it all.

Over more than half a century, the sasquatch has made innumerable other personal appearances. In Canada in 1928, an Indian named Muchalat Harry told Father Anthony Terhaar that he had been kidnapped by a male Bigfoot and carried off to a 'camp' where there were twenty assorted Bigfeet, including wives and several curious young ones. They did him no harm and after a while, when their interest in him slackened, he escaped in his canoe. Father Terhaar met him when he arrived at Nootka on Vancouver Island clad only in his torn underwear. The experience had turned his hair pure white. In 1922 a miner called Fred Beck and some companions were working a claim on Mount St Helens, Washington, when they saw and shot at what seemed to be giant apes. One was hit, and for several nights after, the miners' cabin was bombarded with stones and lumps of rock until finally, unnerved, they packed up and left. In 1966 two young men out hunting coyotes, in Jackson Hole, Wyoming, shot a 'gorilla-like' figure which, when they ran up to it, turned out to be massive and hairy, with a bare face and huge hands and feet. The men thought they might have shot a man, a local freak, so they leaped in their car and fled back home to Iowa.

The incredulity and mirth that these tales arouse start to fade away under the sheer frequency and detail of the North American sightings, often reported by sensible people at the risk of considerable local derision. Glenn Thomas, a logger from Estacada, Oregon, was walking down a path at Tarzan Springs near the Round Mountain when he says he heard a noise.

I was screened by the trees, but through them I could see these three huge figures digging in a rock pile. They looked just like Bigfoot is supposed to: hairy, huge hands and very powerfully built. There was a big one with a female and a young one. They were lifting rocks out, the big male one, and digging down all of 6 or 7ft. Then the male reached down and took out a nest of rodents and ate them.

This story may answer one of the many questions surrounding Bigfoot: what does he eat? When investigators went to the area they found thirty or more holes with rocks, obviously moved during the digging, that weighed 250lb (114kg) or more, and there was an abundance of chucks and marmots. Marmots do hibernate in nests under rocks, and it was October when Glenn Thomas claimed to have seen his Bigfoot family.

A Californian wildlife writer and his wife were driving on the road from Paradise to Stirling City one night when they saw a manlike figure in their headlights: 6 foot or more tall, covered with black hair but with a white, hairless face. The head was small and came to a peak at the top. It did not run but shuffled away, seemingly with a limp. 'My husband specializes in writing for such publications as *Field and Stream* and *Sports Afield*,' wrote Mrs Robert L Behme. 'I mention this in the hope that you will believe we are reasonable, not given to hallucinations brought on by the novelty of a backwoods road at midnight.'

Six people, family and friends, were with Robert Bellamy when he saw a Bigfoot in the Tygh Valley, Oregon, and they all watched it for several minutes. The two Welch brothers, Canadian mining prospectors, saw a Bigfoot, then followed tracks on to a lake to find a substantial hole knocked in the ice and the snow swept back. A creature was seen by boatmen, wandering along the shore in British Columbia, apparently feeding off the oysters in the shallow water.

The most fascinating of all the sightings is the famous, brief and jumpy film of Bigfoot rollicking about in the forest, taken in 1967 by Roger Patterson at Bluff Creek, northern California. As the clearer of the frames show, the creature is most assuredly female with breasts and very prominent buttocks. In the film she lopes along with a jolly gait which usually produces fits of laughter in people who see the footage for the first time.

However, the film has many intriguing features. The exact site, beside a small road near Onion Mountain, was not only known, but other investigators were able to reach it soon afterwards and, like Patterson and his companion Bob Gimlin, take casts of the creature's footprints and measure its stride. Furthermore, as the positioning of trees and fallen logs shown in the film was unchanged, it is possible to make some reasonably accurate estimate of the creature's height.

The most careful analyses of the film have been made by Dr D W Grieve, Reader in Biomechanics at the Royal Free Hospital in London, and by a group of Russian scientists. By comparing film of humans at the same spot, Dr Grieve calculates that the creature is about six foot five inches (1.95m) high – tall indeed if it is a human in a suit, but possible. The shoulder and hip widths, however, are well beyond the human range and, assuming that they are not padded with polystyrene, suggest a weight of 280 pounds (127kg). The length of stride seems to be about forty-two inches (1.07m), which is very long for a man. Dr Grieve remarks that it would be very difficult to imitate the free striding and arm swinging seen in the film if it was in fact a man in a furry suit encumbered with shoulderpads and a corset of cotton wool. 'If it is a fake, it is a very clever one,' he says.

Three senior Russian scientists, Doctors Bayanov, Burtsev, and Donskoy, spent a long time examining the film in Moscow, and came to broadly similar conclusions to those of Dr Grieve. Donskoy said: 'We can evaluate the gait of the creature as a natural movement without any of the signs of artfulness that one would see in an imitation.' Bayanov and Burtsev noted that the creature has an apelike head and almost no neck and that the tracks show, here as elsewhere, that the creature walks with less weight on its heels than a normal man, has no foot arch and seems to walk with slightly bent legs. They suggested that the nearest analogy is with Java Man or *Pithecanthropus erectus*, the apelike creature which, unlike even early *Homo sapiens*, is classified as an animal not a man, but which is thought to stem from the same evolutionary root.

The doubts about the film centre on the fact that it is not known at what speed – twenty-four or sixteen frames per second – it was shot. The two speeds produce very different impressions when it is screened. Also the footprints found on the ground at Bluff Creek do not chime with the film. They are fourteen or fifteen inches (38–41cm) long and suggest a much taller creature than six foot five inches (1.95m) and one that should have a much longer stride.

As with the yeti, the most dispassionate evidence probably comes from the footprints. Trails with more than three thousand footprints have been followed over distances of several miles, hard work for any faker. Tracks have been found in the most remote spots where it would ordinarily be pointless to indulge in a hoax. The footprints have been subjected to minute examination at Washington State University, in the Soviet Union and in many institutions in Canada and the United States. A typical print is sixteen to eighteen inches (41–46cm) long and seven inches (18cm) or more wide. There is no sign of a foot arch as in man, except in prints that seem to come from young ones. There is a distinct double ball, unlike the single ball on a man's foot, which indicates an adaptation of the foot to take great weight. The depth of the footprint impressions and projections from the creature's reported height suggest a bulk of at least 300 pounds (136kg), and some estimates put it at 500 to 1,000 pounds (227–454kg).

Elaborate curves, ratios, formulae and projections, pages of calculations, graphs, diagrams, articles in learned journals like *Northwest Anthropological Research Notes*, have all been devoted to Bigfoot's feet. A glance at the pictures of the foot-prints confirms that they are not those of a bear, which is the usual explanation of the sceptic, as there is no sign of claws. Grover S Krantz, who has contributed a lot to the slide-rule assessment of the sasquatch prints, says: 'Even if none of the hundreds of sightings had ever occurred, we would still be forced to conclude that a giant bipedal primate does indeed inhabit the forests of the Pacific North West.'

It is Krantz who advises anyone who sees a sasquatch to shoot it, as the only final way of providing scientific proof. And he matches action to word by driving round in Bigfoot country with a high-powered rifle constantly at his side and special swivelling fog lamps on the side of his car for penetrating the gloom of the roadside forests.

Convincing though the stories are, however, this is also the country of the hoaxer and the huckster. There are certainly at least two entirely fake films, and fake footprints have been made with anything from remoulded wellington boots to specially carved wooden feet.

Alma or 'Wildmen'

The search for the alma, the Russian version of the yeti and the sasquatch, is undoubtedly on a more continuous and scientific basis than for either of its rival hominids. Many stories have filtered out of Siberia, the Russian steppes and the Caucasian mountains of sightings of manlike creatures. During the Second World War prisoners and refugees fleeing either the Germans or the Russians, or both, claimed to have seen the alma. Slavomir Rawicz, in his controversial book *The Long Walk* about a 4,000-mile escape from a Siberian labour camp into India, claimed to have met a male and female alma which blocked his route for two hours and forced a disastrous detour; and in the prosaic surroundings of the seaside resort of Blackpool in Lancashire, England, a Pole, Mr Wiktor Juszczyk, regales his family with the story of his meeting with the alma in the area of Sinkiang and Soviet Turkestan. He was escaping from a Soviet prison camp when he was captured by Chinese soldiers who told him they regularly put food out for an alma – a piece of fish and a large loaf of black bread. On the second night, according to Mr Juszczyk, it appeared.

> It loped through 2 feet of snow right up to the table. Then it sat on its haunches, grabbed the loaf and ate. He must have been 7 feet high. He had a broad nose and slanting eyes, small and staring. I have never seen such a powerful-looking creature: long body, short legs, his chest, shoulders and arms covered in red-brown hair, but his hands were just like human hands. He spent a couple of minutes eating the bread and part of the fish, gave a few animal grunts and then ambled off.

The alma seems to be quite distinct from the yeti, inhabiting areas of inaccessible mountains right across from the Caucasus in the west of Russia to the Altai and the Gobi Desert in Mongolia in the east. Furthermore all reports indicate a manlike creature, as opposed to the more apelike form of the yeti.

The Communist Wildmen

If there are unknown 'wildmen' still to be found on this earth, the odds are that they lurk protected not only by some of the remotest landscapes on our planet, but also by the severe and daunting frontiers of what were the two great Communist superpowers. Details are slowly emerging of the extraordinary proliferation of sightings and evidence now being collated by researchers in both the former Soviet Union and China.

In 1985, the *China Daily* reported that a 3ft 7in (1.1m) tall male wildman had been caught in the mountains of Hunan and was living in a flat in the city of Wuhan. The story was soon to be retracted. But, in its resolution, it was to provide a fascinating insight into the state of 'wildman' research in China. For the creature turned out to be a previously unknown type of monkey – the very animal that had been predicted by Chinese researcher Zhou Guoxing in his analysis of wildman evidence.

Zhou Guoxing, a staff member at the Peking Natural History Museum, and his colleague, Professor Wu Dingliang, Director of Anthropological Research at Shanghai's Fudan University, took part in the vast Chinese Academy of Sciences expedition in 1977 to the Shennongjia Mountains. For nearly a year, more than 100 people collected casts of footprints, pieces of hair, faeces and, most importantly, collated the many accounts of 'wildmen' from the local people. From this evidence Zhou and Professor Wu concluded that there were two creatures involved. The first – apparently about four feet (1.2m) high – was an unknown type of ape or monkey. The second – seven foot (2.1m) tall or more – was a large unknown species of primate, they thought.

Within five years the first part of their theory was to be proved right; evidence for the second part accumulates rapidly.

The vast arc of virtually uninhabited territory which runs from Afghanistan along the Russian–Chinese border, through Tien Shan and then down southern Mongolia for more than 2,000 miles, is remote to an almost unimaginable degree. Even the nomadic herdsmen make only occasional excursions into the high mountains. It can be 400 miles from one road to the next. Tibet, to the south, is, by comparison, heavily populated. Much of the area is still thick primeval forest rising up the Shaal Tau and the Altai Mountains.

It was in 1981 that Zhou first heard that there were relics of a wildman preserved in Zheijiang province. The next year he was able to make a trip to investigate. In the village of Zhuanxian he met a woman, Wang Congmei, a cowherd, who as a girl (back in May 1957) had encountered the creature. She said it had a head like a man and almost hairless skin. When it stood erect it was at least one metre (3ft 3in) tall. Walking, it went on all fours, rather like a panda. The creature had been killed by Wang's mother, Xu Fudi, and a party of villagers. The local schoolmaster, Zhou Shousong, had preserved the hands and feet.

Even in their shrivelled state, the hands and feet presented a haunting sight. Zhou had heard similar stories before. Road builders in Xishuang Banna had killed what they called a 'wild-woman' in 1961. It had walked upright, being four feet (1.2m) tall or more. They said its hands, ears, breasts and genitalia were similar to those of a female human.

Many witnesses in Yunan said that such wildmen still walked about. Zhou took careful measurements of the severed hands and feet of the Zhuanxian wildman – it had been very certainly male, Wang Congmei said. He also took plaster casts and samples of hair back to Peking. After careful analysis and consultation he concluded that the creature was neither a man nor an ape, but an unknown type of large monkey. Within a year his theory was to be justified when a large monkey was captured in the Huang Mountains, measuring nearly one metre (3ft 3in) high, with hands and feet like Wang Congmei's creature.

The fact that local people's accounts of the small 'wildman' had been so swiftly and precisely justified, despite much academic scepticism, encouraged Zhou to pursue his analysis of the large 'wildman' sightings. These presented an altogether more fearsome picture. There have been hundreds of reports, but two in particular seemed worthy of note because they came from scientists.

Back in 1940 a biologist, Wang Tselin, had been travelling in the Gansu area. He had seen a 'wildman' killed by local hunters.

He had no camera and no means of preserving or transporting the body, but his description is precise and extraordinary. The body was a female with very large breasts. It was seven foot (2.1m) tall and covered with grey-brown hair. Above all, Wang was struck by the primitive but human configuration of the face, which reminded him forcibly of the famous (and then newly discovered) Peking man.

Ten years later a geologist, Fan Jingquan, was out with a group of local guides in the forest near Baoji in Shangsi Province. They came across two wildmen – apparently mother and son. The description was similar. Fan was struck by how tall they were. Even the child seemed nearly five foot (1.5m) tall.

In 1977 there was another spate of reports of wildmen in the mountains of Tabai in Qinling. Villagers who had encountered the creatures reported that they were six and half foot (2m) tall, walked upright, and were covered with hair. They left huge footprints.

Zhou and Professor Wu Dingliang remain convinced that there is an unknown large species living in the Chinese–Mongolian border area. Zhou concludes: 'I am of the opinion that it is quite possibly a descendant of *Gigantopithecus* which was thriving in the mainland of China in the middle and later Pleistocene period.' He points out that the panda and the orang-utan are survivors of the fauna of the Pleistocene which managed to remain in middle and western China – the panda right up to the present day. 'It is not impossible that *Gigantopithecus*, as the dominant member of this Pleistocene fauna, could also have changed its original habits and characteristics and survived to the present.'

Some anthropologists have even made a connection between *Gigantopithecus* and the famous Ice Man exhibited by showman Frank Hansen in the Minnesota area in 1968. This apelike corpse, frozen in a block of ice, was denounced by some as a rubber fake concocted in the environs of Hollywood. But Dr Bernard Heuvelmans, the 'father' of cryptozoology, who examined it over three days, was convinced it was genuine – certainly a hominoid, perhaps *Gigantopithecus*.

Russian and English anthropologists, notably Boris Porchnev and Myra Shackley, have proposed the most daring hypothesis for the 'wildmen' of Mongolia and the Altai mountains. They suggest that there may be surviving groups of Neanderthal man, who supposedly died out 30,000 years ago.

Myra Shackley, a Leicester University lecturer, made a 2,000-mile expedition to Outer Mongolia in 1979. In 1983 she published her review of the expedition. She had found a number of Neanderthal tool kits in open-air sites on the river terraces in the Altai Mountains. They included scrapers, rough chopping tools, and small flakes which had been used, then resharpened. They were made from jasper, agate and chalcedony, rocks much favoured by Neanderthals.

Myra Shackley estimated the Mongolian sites to be less than 20,000 years old. 'They may indeed be even more recent,' she says, 'since many of the tools are fresh and surprisingly unworn if they have been resting on the surface for that length of time.' She reports:

> My first line of approach was to show examples of Neanderthal tools to the people and ask whether they had seen anything like them. I obtained the same answer from a number of widely separated groups. All agreed that the tools had been used by people 'who used to live in this area before us' and who now 'live in the mountains'. The name given to these people never varied; the locals called them either the people of Tuud or, when asked to elaborate, gave them the name Almas or one of its local variations.

Shackley was convinced by the stories of the people she met. 'For me there is no question of whether the wildmen exist – I find the evidence compelling – but only of how they should be classified.'

Across the border in the Soviet Union, almost annual expeditions were taking place, concentrating particularly on the Pamir Mountains, in pursuit of the continuing reports of Almas. A member of the 1981 group, Vadim Makarov, found one of the biggest footprints ever discovered. The plaster cast shows a four-toed foot measuring over nineteen inches (50cm). There were several distant sightings on this expedition, but none so vivid as the one made the previous year by an eighteen-year-old student, Nina Grineva.

She had set up camp near a sandy riverbank where she had earlier noticed footprints. She was awoken one night by the sound of stones being knocked together. 'Sixty feet away stood a very hairy person about seven feet high. His figure was massive, almost square. He stooped and had a very short neck. His arms hung loosely. I was not scared and began slowly to advance towards him.' Nina had a toy rubber bird in her hand which she squeaked to attract the creature's attention.

> It was this that spoiled our contact. He made a sharp turn and quickly went down the slope to the river and disappeared beyond the steep bank. I noted the softness and grace of his walk, though he moved very fast. It was not a human walk, but as of an animal, as of a panther. Despite boulders and other obstacles, he moved quickly, softly and even gracefully. He must have a perfect sense of balance, and, to him, a steep and uneven slope is like a paved road to us.

The case for continuing research and exploration is championed by Dimitri Bayanov at the Darwin Museum, who points out that wildmen are prevalent in Russian and Mongol folklore and mythology. 'We say that if relic hominoids were not reflected in folklore and mythology, then their reality could truly be called into question. Of course the reality of relic hominoids cannot be supported by recourse to folklore alone. But the folklore is a valuable reinforcement of the other evidence we have.'

In 1983, Bayanov led an expedition to Tajikstan. He visited the site near Lake Pairon where two women, Geliona Siforova and Dima Sizov, had reported seeing a female wildman sitting on a boulder ten yards (9m) from their tent. It surveyed them for a long time, making munching sounds. They did not dare to approach it, and in the morning there were no traces of footprints or hairs.

Bayanov also visited the area of Sary Khosor and talked with Forest Service workers, who said they often had reports of wildmen. Two years previously, a shepherd had driven his sheep back down from the mountains two months early because he had seen a big black 'gul' or wildman near his pasture. It had frightened his dogs and he had not dared to stay. Another Tajik had told the officers of an encounter five years earlier with 'a giant hairy man, very broad in the shoulders, with the face like that of an ape'.

The Forest Service takes these reports seriously enough to prohibit its employees from spending the night alone in the mountains, for fear of these wildmen.

Bayanov had no personal encounter with wildmen, but he concluded his 1982 expedition report by saying:

> The abundant signs I witnessed of local fauna, particularly omnivores such as bears and wild pigs, indicate enough food resources for the presumably omnivorous hominoids the year round. The ninety-three percent of the Tajik Republic's territory taken up by mountains is virtually devoid of permanent human population, so the latter poses no special danger to wild hominoids. The long and continuing record of purported hominoid sightings, supported by these new accounts, leads me to the conclusion that such creatures do exist there.

The search for the yeti, the sasquatch and the alma, has stretched around the world. But they remain elusive. Like Sir Edmund Hillary, most people dismiss them as legends, part of the endless panoply of ghosts, monsters and giants that have always peopled the human imagination. Naturalists are, in the main, confident that the earth has few great secrets to surrender. But the mountain gorilla was dismissed as fantasy until it was finally captured at the turn of the century; the panda was first shown to people in the West only when it was delivered to Chicago Zoo in the 1930s; the orang-utan, closest of all to the mythical version of man's ancestors, had to be captured to be believed in the West.

The sceptics have written off many of the eyewitnesses. But can they all be hoaxers, fools, visionaries? If they are not seeing an unknown creature, what are they seeing? In North America, and even in the Himalayas, it might be a bear, but so many reports of sightings come from people who are experienced forest and mountain men who would be expected to recognize a bear or any other such familiar animal. And why do the descriptions tally so well, even those from people who have never heard of the alma or the Bigfoot? Why do the Sherpas of Nepal insistently identify an apelike creature?

Through all the uncertainties comes the evidence of the foot-prints. None of the theories seems to explain them, either in the Himalayas or in America, or in the former Soviet Union where according to Professor Khalkov they are very similar to those of Neanderthal Man. Hoaxers may operate in the Pacific North West but would they go 20,000 feet up the slopes of Everest and Kangchenjunga or venture into the wildest part of the Pamirs? Yeti, alma, Bigfoot – whatever its name, something seems to be there.

ARTHUR C CLARKE COMMENTS:

Personally, I would take reports of contemporary apemen more seriously if there were not so many of them, and in such heavily populated places. But if 'Bigfoot' does exist, I would like to propose an open season for shooting those people who want to shoot him – even in the name of science.

Although there is nothing impossible in the idea that some of our remote ancestors might have survived down to quite recent times, the sad fate of the Tasmanian and other aborigines suggests that it is rather unlikely. The Tasmanians were members of our own species; and where are they now?

Most zoologists are willing to admit that large creatures still remain undiscovered in the sea. But on land? Impossible, of course . . . but read on, starting with this delightful letter from Dr Dalrymple, which takes me instantly back to Saunders of the River:

Dear Professor Clarke,

We have been watching with great keenness your TV Programme The Mysterious World, *and I feel that the following might be of interest to you:*

In 1935, I was Medical Officer on the River Gambia in West Africa. One night, I was awakened by much noise, by the locals. The next morning, I discovered the excitement had been caused by the appearance of what they called the 'Nikenanka'. This animal was described as 'having the face of a horse, a neck like a giraffe, a body like a crocodile, a long tail, and being about thirty foot long'.

I asked the Head Men to let me know next time this animal was seen. It was said to appear only from time to time, on moonlight nights, from the mangrove swamps where it lived, submerged in mud.

Several months passed, and, one evening, I was told of the reappearance of the animal. However, the swarms of mosquitoes, off the swamp, were such that I turned back without seeing the 'Nikenanka'.

As M O Rivers, I regularly visited the various stations and had occasion to call on the Manager of one of the trading Companies. During lunch, we heard a great disturbance in the nearby local market. We went out to investigate and discovered one of the manager's servants waving the educational magazine called Animals of the World. *The excited crowd was shouting that the White Man had photographed the Nikenanka: it was, in fact, a photograph of a concrete dinosaur, in one of the New York parks. They all recognized this as the animal they had seen in the swamps, on moonlight nights.*

Later on, I was on board ship, travelling back to Nigeria, and a Marine Department Officer told me that, when checking the traffic lanes in the Niger Delta, his attention had been drawn by his crew to a large 'sea serpent'. He fired his gun but was out of range. The creature, however, must have heard the report, as it reared up, turned its head, and made swiftly for a mangrove swamp island. The sun was setting, and it was too dark to be absolutely certain, but he thought the animal was between thirty to forty feet long, similar to a dinosaur, as it heaved out of the water and disappeared into the mangrove swamp.

This is, I am afraid, all I can tell you, but, as the Gambia River is about 200 miles long and the mangrove swamps, on either side, vary from fifty to 100 feet wide, it represents a large expanse of, then, unexplored ground, and I always felt there was the possibility that some animals, long thought to be extinct, might be surviving there.

Some years later, I was stationed in the British Cameroons. I became very friendly with the Fon (Chief) of N'Saw. Later, I was accepted into the two most powerful Ju-Ju societies, known as the N'Fu Ba and N'Fu Gam. It was then, that I was told of the existence of 'Kabaranko', said to be a human, living down a well, and existing on human excreta. He was only let out for the funerals of very important chiefs. I saw him once at such a funeral. He was said to be endowed with superhuman strength and I watched (and photographed) him pick up a ram and tear it in two. I believe he also picked up a big car and threw it over a cliff, but I did not see this.

What he was I do not know, but he looked like a short human figure, covered in long black hair. He was greatly feared and, when brought out, he was controlled with ropes attached to his feet, one man walking in front and one at the back, in the same way farmers guide dangerous bulls. If he happened to escape, the natives whistled loudly, as a warning to everybody to keep out of 'Kabaranko's' way. The only way to recapture him was to hold a pregnant woman in front of him, when he would fall, unconscious, on the ground.

I never found out who or what he was.

Hoping the above will be of some interest to you.

Yours sincerely,

(THOMAS HARDIE DALRYMPLE)

Retired Medical Officer

West African Medical Service

DINOSAURS

Dr Dalrymple's letter is a most evocative contribution to one of the longest-running sagas in cryptozoology – the search for dinosaurs in Africa.

The daunting, but beguiling, geography of Africa has always tempted the imagination. Dr Dalrymple describes the great stretches of mangrove swamp along the Gambia River, but there are vast stretches of swamp throughout Central Africa which remain far more remote and unexplored. The great Likouala swamps in the Congo stretch to more than 50,000 square miles. Roads are none, tracks are few, and travel is mainly by river. This area has always been the focus of speculation about the existence of huge and strange creatures unknown to science.

Immediately after the First World War Captain Lester Stevens, MC, was heading for these swamps when he was photographed, somewhat inappropriately attired and, as the *Daily Mail* caption reported, 'accompanied by his ex-German war dog Laddie, before leaving Waterloo Station for Africa to search for the Brontosaurus'. Captain Stevens was encouraged by the prospect of a $1m reward offered by the Smithsonian Institution in

Washington, and by reports that two Belgian travellers, Gapele and Lepage, had recently seen the monster in the Congo.

Captain Stevens, though armed with a Winchester repeater, a Smith and Wesson revolver, a shotgun and a Mannlicher rifle, was sadly never to claim the reward. But his successors have returned, inspired by continuing reports that a great animal exists – and was even captured and killed within the last generation by the local pygmies at Lake Tele in the heart of the Likouala swamps.

Texan explorer James H Powell, with Professor Roy Mackal of the University of Chicago, gathered the most intriguing accounts of the beast – *mokele-mbembe*, as it is known – on their expedition to the Congo in 1980. Powell had already been in the area twice before, but on this occasion the pair were able to track down a number of informants able to tell them of the killing, some twenty years earlier. Powell had a simple way of establishing with his informants exactly what animal he was seeking. He carried cards showing known animals from Central Africa, animals from other regions which would be unknown in that area, and drawings of various types of dinosaur. He would gather, by showing the cards, the local names for gorillas, okapi, etc.; check that their observations were genuine by showing, say, a bear which they could not identify; then he would show his dinosaur drawings. A number of his informants unhesitatingly identified the dinosaur as *mokele-mbembe*.

The most vivid description of the killing of *mokele-mbembe* was given to Powell and Mackal by Lateka Pascal, a fisherman who works a regular stretch of water on Lake Tele. He had heard of the incident as a child. *Mokele-mbembe* had entered Lake Tele via one of the waterways which drain the swamps into Lake Tele on the western side. The pygmies had blocked off this water-way by constructing a barrage of stakes and tree trunks. When *mokele-mbembe* tried to return, it was trapped by the barricade and killed with spears. According to Pascal, the pygmies cut the animal up and ate it. Everyone who ate the flesh died.

Powell and Mackal gathered together at Epena a number of people who had seen *mokele-mbembe* in recent times. One, Madongo Nicholas, described the creature – thirty foot (9m) long or more – rising out of the water on the Minjoubou River just ahead of his boat. It had a long neck about as thick as a man's leg, the head slightly larger in diameter, and a long, pinkish-coloured back. On top of its head the creature had something which looked like a chicken's comb. Another man, Omoe Daniel, described the eight foot wide (2.5m) trail left by some animal for about 100 yards as it had apparently dragged itself through the undergrowth from a pool across to the main stream of the Likouala Aux Herbes River. Another witness had seen a strange creature only half a mile or so upstream from Epena, where Powell and Mackal had convened their meeting. He identified it from a copy of *Animals of Yesterday*, which Powell was carrying, as a brontosaurus.

All those present agreed that *mokele-mbembe* lives in deep and narrow parts of the rivers, has the distinctive chicken's comb on its head – and, above all, is a dangerous animal to have seen!

The political exigencies of the People's Republic of the Congo – Africa's first Marxist state – prevented Powell and Mackal from remaining. Their visas ran out.

Mackal led another expedition the following year, but with nothing more substantial to show for another gruelling venture through mud, swamp, jungle and river. He was, however, accompanied by a professional Congolese biologist, Marcelin Agnagna, who, two years later, was to provide the latest dramatic twist in the story of the swamp dinosaur.

The 1981 expedition, which included some rigorous scientists, such as Richard Greenwell and Justin Wilkinson (both from the University of Arizona), had come to respect Agnagna's professional competence. So when, in 1983, he reported sighting *mokele-mbembe* himself, he was treated as an extremely reliable witness. Sadly, he proved to be a much less reliable cameraman.

Agnagna and a team of seven had reached Lake Tele on 1 May 1983. Agnagna himself was filming some monkeys at around 2.30 pm when there was a sudden shout. One of the local helpers called him down to the lake shore. About 300 yards away across the lake he saw an animal. It had a long back, perhaps fifteen foot (4.5m) overall, a long neck sticking out of the water and shining black in the sun, with a small head. He could see the eyes, but no other distinguishing features.

Agnagna had his movie camera in his hand, and he started to wade into the lake shallows until he was about 200 feet (60m) from the animal. All the time he was filming. Then the animal, which had been slowly casting its head and neck from side to side, slowly submerged. The observers had had as much as a quarter of an hour to watch the creature, but no film emerged. As so often happens in the annals of cryptozoology, the pictures failed to come out. Agnagna had left his camera on a macro setting – another instance of the malign force which strikes photographers so unvaryingly when truly sensational events occur.

However, Agnagna was certain enough of his sighting. 'The animal we saw was *mokele-mbembe*. It was quite alive and it is known to many of the inhabitants of the Likouala. I saw the animal. *Mokele-mbembe* is a species of sauropod living in the Likouala swamps and rivers.'

TIGERS OUT OF TIME

According to scientists, the Tasmanian tiger, or thylacine, has not existed on the Australian mainland for at least 3,000 years. The creature seems to have been unknown to the Aboriginals, and was not seen by any of the early settlers. It hung on only in Tasmania, where the question of its survival is a separate and intriguing mystery, since the last known tiger died in Hobart Zoo in 1936.

Therefore, Kevin Cameron's photographs (see photo section) of one digging at the roots of a tree seem to defy belief. The striped rump and thick tail can be seen clearly. Undoubtedly there were once thylacines on mainland Australia and, indeed, stories of their survival were finally corroborated in 1966 when David Lowry found the skin of a thylacine in a cave on the Mundrabilia cattle station in Western Australia. It was lying among the bones of other animals, including other thylacines, bats, snakes, rabbits, kangaroos, wombats and a Tasmanian devil. These bones were dated as thousands of years old. The thylacine, by contrast, was only partly decayed. Lowry said:

The animal lay on its right side, with its head raised off the ground. The skin and hair were largely intact on the exposed surfaces and the characteristic dark bars were clearly visible. The soft tissue had decomposed. However the tongue and left eyeball were clearly recognizable. The tail was some twelve inches away from the rest of the body, probably moved there by rats.

Many zoologists found it difficult to believe that the corpse could have lain in such conditions in this state of preservation for thousands of years. The first crack in the wall of certainty had appeared. It then emerged that there were people who claimed to have seen mainland tigers, especially in South and Western Australia around the area of the Nullarbor Plain and in the bush that runs away to the south-west tip of the continent. Dr S J Paramanov, a scientist working at Warrego in New South Wales, saw what he believes was a Tasmanian tiger in 1949. A party of five people travelling across the Nullarbor on horseback saw a thylacine, they say, early one morning in May 1976. Mr Huon Johnston said he clearly saw the stripes and that his group was close enough to distinguish the bull terrier-like head.

Ian Officer of Benger, Western Australia, reports that there have been numerous sightings in recent times, including twenty-two reported in one year. One witness, Mr Buckingham, said that he had a very clear view of a dog-like animal, grey-brown, with very marked either dark brown or black transverse stripes running across the rump, and a thin tail.

But it is the 1985 photographs, taken in February by Kevin Cameron of Girrawheen in Western Australia, that provide the most challenging evidence – something far more concrete than anything that has turned up in fifty years of searching in Tasmania itself. Sceptics have asked why Cameron did not get a picture of the animal bounding away; why he did not shoot it, as he clearly had a rifle; why the animal seems to be in exactly the same position in the two photographs; and there have been critical analyses from a technical photographic point of view.

Cameron offers no comment. He is of aboriginal descent and an experienced bushman who works with a pair of highly trained dogs. Until recently he was illiterate. He seems hardly equipped to perpetrate a major deceit. And the photographs themselves are beguiling. They have a lack of artifice, and the position of the animal seems full of naturalness and energy.

Athol Douglas, until recently Senior Experimental Officer at the Western Australian Museum in Perth, is convinced that the animal is a thylacine. Dr Ronald Strahan of the Australian Museum, and formerly Director of Sydney's Taronga Park Zoo, regards the pictures as authentic and says that the animal could not be anything but a thylacine. Kevin Cameron also possesses casts which show the distinctive pattern of the Tasmanian tiger: five toes on the forefeet and only four on the hind.

Meanwhile, in the rough terrain of the centre and north of Tasmania itself, expeditions continue to try to prove that the animal survives. It is hard to credit that a wolf-like creature the size of an alsatian, so distinctively coloured, which carries its young about in a pouch and is not notably afraid of humans, could have evaded its pursuers for fifty years. Most of the tigers were wiped out in the last years of the nineteenth century by bounty hunters protecting sheep. The last known killing of a wild thylacine was in 1930. London Zoo's last specimen died in 1931, and the last of all at Hobart in 1936. Since then, and particularly in recent years, there have been numerous recorded sightings – at least 100 of them of sufficient clarity and detail to be accounted as reliable.

The distinguished zoologist Eric Guiler has been involved in many forays to try to locate the thylacine. He has placed electronic surveillance equipment and night cameras at likely spots, but without success. His interest has been sustained by the apparent authenticity of so many reported sightings. In the early 1950s he managed to interview a number of old men who had been tiger bounty hunters. One of them, H. Pearce, described seeing a female and three pups in the late 1940s – with the clear implication that he had wiped them out, as he had so many in the past. The old shepherds were unrepentant.

Another incident near the area known as the Walls of Jerusalem was described by a cattle drover. His three dogs were involved in a scuffle in the bush near his cabin. Only two came back. Next day he found the third dog dead, with its heart eaten out. He took his horse and two dogs to a nearby gully. The dogs ran under the horse and then a tiger appeared on a nearby rock.

Guiler lists dozens of modern sightings, often backed up by more than one witness or by other evidence. In 1960, by the Manuka River (near the spot where a sighting had been reported), he himself heard the strange yapping hunting noise that the thylacines made. In June 1976 there was a sighting on the Pieman River, and nearby a fresh wallaby kill. In 1981 at Mount Eliza there were quite clear tracks of the distinctive five toes followed by four toes. Since the 1960s there has been a whole clutch of sightings at Woolnorth, which was one of the most profitable areas for the bounty hunters of the last century.

Almost annually now, well-equipped expeditions set off to try to obtain final proof that the Tasmanian tiger managed to survive the depredations of less ecologically minded generations of Tasmanians. Yet so far the nearest thing to evidence comes from Kevin Cameron's photographs, by all accounts taken far away on the Australian mainland, 2,000 or 3,000 years out of time.

STRANGE ANIMALS ON THE LOOSE

There is no doubt that there are strange animals loose in Britain. There are wallabies in Derbyshire, feral porcupines in Devon, beavers and racoons, and probably some Arctic foxes. Many animals were released when the 1976 British Animal Act introduced much stricter controls on the keeping of large and dangerous animals. Animal societies believe that at least two black leopards were turned loose at that time. And who would have been believed if they had reported seeing a fully-grown bear on a Hebridean island? Yet Hercules the bear, famous for his television commercials, lived quite happily for two weeks on Benbecula in 1980 after escaping from his owner.

Evidence does turn up. Ted Noble, a farmer at Cannick near Loch Ness in the Scottish Highlands, repeatedly, over several months, saw his sheep savaged by what looked like a panther or leopard. His neighbour, Jessie Chisholm, had seen the animal only yards away when her hens suddenly started to clamour. By the hen run was a black cat, bigger than a labrador dog, with a thick tail longer than its body. Then a visitor to Mr Noble's farm brought in the carcass of a lamb: he said he had seen it dropped by a large cat as it jumped over a deer-proof forestry fence. The head of the lamb had been almost severed and there were deep puncture wounds on both sides of the chest.

Mr Noble and his sister-in-law saw the animal several times, once even stalking one of his Shetland ponies. Finally, spurred by local derision, he constructed a trap. The bait was a sheep's head hung at the back of a disguised cage. One October morning in 1980 Mr Noble found the trap sprung. Inside was a full-grown female puma. Mr Noble's losses diminished and the puma went to the Highland Wildlife Park at Kincraig, where she lived happily for another four years. Ever since, there has been the strongest suspicion of a hoax. The puma turned out to be well fed to the point of obesity and positively friendly to humans. Yet who was hoaxing who? And where did the puma come from?

Sightings of puma-like animals have continued in the Highlands, as have rapacious killings of sheep and deer. At Dallas in Moray three very large black cats were shot which appear to be a large mutation of the Scottish wildcat. And in February 1985 another expert witness saw a strange animal in the Highlands. Mr Jimmy Milne is gamekeeper and ghillie on the Wester Elchies estate at Aberlour. Early one morning he saw an animal around 2½ feet (75cm) tall in a field on the estate. 'It was a massive beast with a black coat,' said Mr Milne. 'I've been a gamekeeper here for forty years and I have never seen an animal like it before.'

There are vast areas with neither roads nor tracks in the Scottish Highlands, and some exotic and unexpected sights – eagles that have been trained to hawk against deer by local gamekeepers, sea eagles and polecats illicitly introduced to ancient habitats where they had long been extinct. If there is a place where a wild leopard might subsist, then it is in the great wild tracts and glens to the north and west of the Caledonian Canal.

Least likely site would be the Hackney marshes in the East

End of London, yet here, just after Christmas 1980, the police were occupied for three days hunting a wild bear. The story had all the marks of a hoax, reported as it was by a ten-year-old boy, Elliot Sanderson, and his two twelve-year-old friends, Darren Willoughby and Thomas Murray. They said they had seen it claw at trees before it made off. But the story had had a macabre prelude. Only three weeks earlier, the bodies of two bears had been found floating in the nearby River Lea. They were skinned and headless. But they were bears all the same, and had presumably been alive and in the area not long before. There were what looked like claw marks on the trees. Then there were the footprints. Yeti-watchers know how difficult it is to draw conclusions from footprints in the snow. They melt and grow larger in the sun. However, they are also hard to fake. The Hackney bear left very distinct bear-like footprints – four-clawed and meandering across the marshes. Mounted police, dog-handlers, police with rifles, all scoured the East End of London for three days before calling the hunt off.

But the animal which has surely absorbed more of the British policeman's time than any other is the puma which has appeared now for more than twenty years in the back gardens, suburban roads, parks and woods of Surrey – or so many hundreds of people believe.

Policemen themselves have been among the most assertive witnesses. Back in 1963, in the early days of the puma, an animal (in this case described as a cheetah) was seen by Mr David Back. It apparently jumped right over the bonnet of a pursuing police patrol car, thus precipitating a search, fruitless, like so many that were to follow, by 126 policemen, thirty soldiers and assorted officials.

Just over the Surrey border in Hampshire, Police Constable Anthony Thomas was on patrol in Queen Elizabeth Park, Farnborough, when he had his encounter with the beast in June 1973.

> It was in the early hours of the morning, but the light was good. It stood about ten yards away from me. It was three or four times the size of a cat with a long tail and pointed ears. It definitely was not a dog or a fox. There were other officers in the park with me so I radioed for help. P.C. Martin King came to my assistance, but he

came up from behind the animal. As he came through the under-growth the animal fled, but he did get a look at it. I never believed all the stories about the Surrey puma before, but I certainly believe them now.

The puma was already established in the Farnborough habitat. Mrs Heather Barber had seen it cross her path when she was cycling from the town's Queensmead shopping centre. Bricklayer John Bonnor had seen it walk from behind a pile of empty crates at the nearby Royal Aircraft Establishment in 1971. There were other sightings that year in Canterbury Road and Harbour Close.

As it hangs out amongst some of the most expensive real estate in Britain, the Surrey puma has naturally had some distinguished witnesses. Maurice Gibb of the Bee Gees pop group saw it at his home in Esher in January 1985. He said, 'We were sitting around watching television, when the guard dogs suddenly tensed. I let them out and they were halfway across the lawn when they stopped dead and this huge shape sprang across the driveway and disappeared.' Mr Gibb had the large pug marks examined by experts from nearby Chessington Zoo. Their verdict was 'puma'.

Lord Chelmsford's daughter, Philippa Thesiger, came across the creature at Hazelbridge Court, near Godalming, and waved a walking stick at it to chase it away.

Mrs Christabel Arnold of Crondall, near Farnham, claims:

> I think I have been closer to this animal than anyone. I saw it face to face in Redlands Lane. I froze and we just looked at each other, then it spat all the time. It had marks like a cheetah on its face and was greyish browny beige with spots and stripes. Its back was deep red brown and massive at the back legs. It had a beautiful striped red brown and beigy white tipped tail. It had yellow slanted eyes, wire-like whiskers and tufted ears.

Mrs Arnold's neighbouring farmers also saw signs of the cat. Mr Leonard Hobbs of Marsh Farm glimpsed it once in his car headlights and often heard strange screams at night. Mr Edward Blanks found the remains of a 90-lb (40-kilo) calf which had been dragged across three fields, and then a heifer was found badly clawed.

The puma reports have waxed and waned over the years, and the animal's territory has spread over much of commuter-belt England. Mostly they refer to a black, panther-like creature, but Mrs Arnold, after her face-to-face encounter, spent some time looking at big cats in zoos, circuses or wherever they could be found, and was quite sure her animal couldn't be a puma. Her best guess was a lynx.

Again, neither hide nor hair nor convincing photograph has appeared in more than twenty years. Yet 1,000 people have surely seen something outside their normal experience. Something has been making a gory mess of a lot of livestock.

Author Di Francis, who has amassed a great deal of eyewitness evidence of sightings, believes there is a large unknown breed of British wildcat at large which has never been captured or classified, no doubt because of supernatural wiliness. The very variety of the descriptions (black and cat-like, striped, spotted, red-eyed, yellow-eyed, dog-like, tawny, huge-footed, lion-like) suggests that many different animals are involved. Pumas and lions do escape or are set free; domestic cats can grow to a daunting size, and they do go wild; any visitor to the annual Lambourn lurcher show in Berkshire knows that the mongrel and cross dogs do come out in the most fearsome dimensions and colours. But it is hard to associate any of these phenomena with the skull-crushing, sheep-stealing beast which has confronted more than 1,000 of our fellow citizens with sufficient clarity and certainty to warrant an official report to the constabulary.

Throughout Britain now the observers are out, the cameras ready and the traps set in the hope that the next animal that takes the bait will prove to be a genuinely wild big cat and not just a tubby puma that doesn't eat raw meat and likes being stroked.

THE SILENCE
OF THE PAST

THE CRYSTAL SKULLS

There are, in fact, two mysterious life-size crystal skulls. One of
them belongs to the British Museum. Surprisingly for a museum
in which the details of each exhibit are authoritatively displayed
to the public, the label on the crystal skull's case is vague.
As to the date, it says merely that the skull is 'possibly of Aztec
origin – the colonial period at the earliest'. The truth is that
even this attribution is guesswork by the museum's experts,
because there are almost no facts known about the skull's
history. The museum bought it from Tiffany's, the New York
jewellers, for the sum of £120 in 1898. No one at the Museum
of Mankind knows where Tiffany's got it from, although
it is said that it may have been part of the booty amassed in
Mexico by a mysterious soldier of fortune during the nineteenth
century.

The other skull belongs to a woman, Anna Mitchell-Hedges,
and the story of how she came by it is exotic and confused.
Anna's father was F A ('Mike') Mitchell-Hedges, a British adven-
turer who roamed the Americas during the early years of the
twentieth century, gambling with millionaires, riding the range
as a cowboy and fighting with Pancho Villa during the Mexican
Revolution. On one of his trips, Mitchell-Hedges met up with a
group of men in a hotel in Port Colborne, Ontario. With them
was a small orphan named Anna le Guillon whom he adopted
and who later took his name.

It was Anna who discovered the crystal skull. In 1927, Mitchell-Hedges was excavating the great Mayan city of Lubaantum in British Honduras. Mitchell-Hedges had discovered the city a few years earlier, during a search for the lost civilization of Atlantis which he believed to be in the area. On her seventeenth birthday, Anna noticed something beneath an ancient altar; it was the top half of the crystal skull. Three months later, just a few feet away, she found its detachable lower jaw, which had become separated from the rest of the head.

According to Miss Mitchell-Hedges, her father gave the skull to the Mayans who lived in the area. 'They prayed to it,' she says, 'and told father it was their god used for healing or to will death.'

When the Mitchell-Hedges' expedition party left the ancient city later in 1927, 'the Mayan people gave my father the skull as a parting gift because he had been so good to them, bringing them medicines and clothing'.

Almost from the moment of its discovery, however, the crystal skull has been a cause of controversy. Not only are its origins obscure, but the exact circumstances of its finding have never fully been revealed. For this reason, although there was no doubt that Anna Mitchell-Hedges had found it under the altar at Lubaantum, questions were raised about the events surrounding the find. How was it, asked some commentators, that one of the largest gemstones in the world had turned up so suddenly in the midst of excavations, and how was it that Anna failed to find the skull's lower jaw until several months had gone by? Furthermore, why would neither Mitchell-Hedges himself, nor other excavators at Lubaantum, give further details of the discovery? Inevitably, the vagueness of the story led some people to speculate that the skull might not have come from the Mayan city at all, and that it had been 'planted' by the altar so that Anna would be sure to find it. Since the day of the find was her seventeenth birthday, and she had apparently been depressed after a bout of malaria, perhaps, the argument ran, her father had planned the 'discovery' to cheer her up. He could have acquired it on his travels in Mexico.

Certainly the great explorer's own public attitude to the skull appears uncharacteristic at first sight. In his autobiography, *Danger My Ally*, published in 1954, five years before his death, he devotes only a few lines to it, and they are far from explicit. Writing of a trip to Africa in 1948, he says:

> We took with us also the sinister Skull of Doom of which much has been written. How it came into my possession I have reason for not revealing.
>
> The Skull of Doom is made of pure rock crystal and according to scientists must have taken 150 years, generation after generation working all the days of their lives, patiently rubbing down with sand an immense block of rock crystal until the perfect skull emerged ... It is at least 3,600 years old and according to legend was used by the high priest of the Maya when performing esoteric rites. It is said that when he willed death with the help of the skull, death invariably followed. It has been described as the embodiment of all evil.

Anna Mitchell-Hedges says any idea that the skull was 'planted' under the altar is 'nonsense' and that her father would not have spent many thousands of pounds on an expedition so that he could bury a crystal skull. On Mitchell-Hedges' reluctance to discuss the skull and the story of its discovery, she points out that her father allocated the account of the various finds and incidents at Lubaantum to different members of his team and was scrupulous in observing their right to give the facts first. He had decided that his daughter should tell the story of the crystal skull. However, she is still not ready to give her full version of the events that began amid the ruins of Lubaantum on her seventeenth birthday.

Anna Mitchell-Hedges has, however, shed some light on one much-discussed episode in the history of the skull she now owns. On 15 September 1943, it came up for auction in the famous salerooms of Sotheby's in London. It was listed as lot 54, and had been sent for sale, not by Mitchell-Hedges, but by a London art dealer, Sydney Burney. It had apparently come into Burney's possession as security for a loan made to Mitchell-Hedges. The files of the British Museum reveal that the museum tried to buy the skull at the sale, no doubt wishing to be able to display the world's only two life-size crystal skulls side by side. A terse pencilled note by H J Braunholtz, a member of the British Museum staff, records what happened when they bid for it through an art dealer. 'Bid at Sotheby's sale, lot 54, 15 x 43 up to £340 (Fairfax). Bought in by Burney. Sold subsequently by Mr Burney to Mr Mitchell-Hedges for £400.' This episode adds confusion to an already perplexing tale; the skull had obviously failed to meet Burney's asking price and had been withdrawn, but what does Braunholtz mean when he says, 'Sold subsequently by Mr Burney to Mr Mitchell-Hedges for £400'? Miss Mitchell-Hedges says the skull was placed with Mr Burney as collateral for a loan and redeemed by her father as soon as he saw it was for sale.

From that time onwards, the story becomes a little clearer. The skull remained in Mitchell-Hedges' possession until he died in 1959. Since then Anna Mitchell-Hedges, who has lived in both Britain and Canada, has kept the skull at home, occasionally lending it to exhibitions or researchers.

And, although she says that she will, in time, reveal the full circumstances of the skull's discovery, Anna Mitchell-Hedges is unable to shed any light on the central question of when the skull was made and scientific analysis of both crystal skulls has also failed to provide an answer. The most notable examination of the skulls took place in 1936, when Sydney Burney, who had the Mitchell-Hedges skull in his possession at the time, agreed to lend it to scientists at the British Museum.

The two skulls were compared in detail by the distinguished anthropologist Dr G M Morant, and his report was published in *Man*, the journal of the Royal Anthropological Institute of Great Britain and Ireland, Morant's report began by noting that while the skulls were similar in many anatomical details, the most significant difference between them was that the British Museum skull was in one piece, while the other skull's lower jaw was detached. Furthermore, the Mitchell-Hedges skull (or Burney skull, as Morant calls it) was far more lifelike and finely detailed than its counterpart. Morant, however, was most struck by the similarities he found between the two skulls. For a start, he decided that their general shape indicated that they had been modelled on a woman's skull. By superimposing tracings taken from photographs, he noted that the outlines of the lower jaws, teethlines and nasal openings matched almost exactly, and, although there were a few differences, he opined that it was 'impossible to avoid the conclusion that the crystal skulls are not of independent origin'. He added: 'In the writer's opinion it is safe to conclude that they are representations of the same human skull, though one may have been copied from the other.' Surprisingly, Dr Morant went on to claim that the more finely wrought Mitchell-Hedges skull may have been the earlier version, because it would have been unusual if a craftsman, copying from the cruder British Museum skull, would have been inclined or able to add anatomical details.

Morant's comparison, in fact, settled nothing. Other authorities immediately challenged his claim that one skull was a copy of the other, and none of them really tackled the crucial question of their date and origin, beyond mentioning that the museum skull, with its round eye sockets and 'merely indicated' teeth, was characteristic of ancient Mexican art. The Mitchell-Hedges version, on the other hand, had 'the character almost of an anatomical study in a scientific age'.

There can be little prospect of a definitive answer to the question of whether the crystal skulls are ancient or modern, because there is no scientific technique for dating crystal. Even deciding which country the skulls originate from its fraught with problems, not least because smaller ones are known to have been made in fifteenth-century Italy as well as in South America. French experts have, however, agreed on the date of a smaller crystal skull in the Musée de l'Homme, Paris. They believe it was made by the Aztecs in the fourteenth or fifteenth century, and that it may have been an ornament on a sceptre carried by an Aztec priest. The French argue that the Aztecs were obsessed with death and that it played an important part in their spiritual life. One typical fifteenth-century Aztec poem goes:

Where would we not go to find death?
For that desire, our heart bleeds.

Moreover, to the Aztecs, crystal was a favourite material because of its transparency and its 'ability' to ward off poisonous snakes and to help people foretell the future. To clinch the argument, the French also say that they have found traces of copper tools like those used by the Aztecs on the skull's surface.

When the British Museum laboratory examined the Museum of Mankind skull, however, they found no helpful clues as to its workmanship, although on one tooth there was the vaguest indication that a powered cutter may have been used. While the British experts, therefore, remained puzzled by the origins of the Museum of Mankind skull, Anna Mitchell-Hedges is in no doubt at all that the one she found is Mayan, like the city in which she found it.

And there, for want of any further evidence, the story of the crystal skulls must rest, except to say that it would be sad if their mysterious past were to obscure an appreciation of their beauty. The Mitchell-Hedges skull, particularly, has an awesome power. Its prismatic eyes and movable jaw make it easy for anyone to imagine it as an object designed to strike terror into the hearts of primitive people. Perhaps it was lit from below, and, shining in the darkness of a temple, uttered prophecies through its crystal mouth. Even if it is relatively modern, as a work of art it is as unforgettable as it is terrible in its beauty.

THE 'GIANT BALLS' OF COSTA RICA

Las Bolas Grandes – the Giant Balls of Costa Rica – present a rather different problem. Their place of origin is not in doubt, as it is certain that they come from the Diquís Delta in Costa Rica – but they are, none the less, some of the strangest objects ever discovered by archaeologists.

They came to light, literally, in the 1930s when the United Fruit Company began to clear the thick jungle of the Diquís Delta for banana plantations. As workmen hacked and burned their way through the forests, they came across dozens of stone balls, many of them perfect spheres. They ranged in size from a few inches to eight feet (2.4m) in diameter: the smallest are the size of tennis balls, weighing only a few pounds, the largest weigh 16 tons or more.

When American archaeologists began to study them in the 1940s, they were astonished. One of the archaeologists was Dr Samuel Lothrop of the Peabody Museum, Harvard University. Lothrop had run into one of the perennial problems of archaeology in Latin America: bandits. They threatened the safety of his team in an area in which he had planned to excavate, and he had to find something else to do. He decided to go to Palmar Sur, a farming community of the Diquís Delta, and it was on his way to a guest house there that he saw giant stone balls decorating a park and the lawns of private houses. It was, he wrote later, 'a fantastic sight'.

Like any archaeologist when faced with previously unknown artefacts, Dr Lothrop hoped to be able to answer the questions: who made them, how, why and when? He soon found that there were no easy answers. It was impossible even to find out how many of them there were in the jungle, because a number of them had already been removed to people's gardens or had been broken apart by the local inhabitants who believed they contained treasure. Others had been damaged by fire in the clearing of the jungle. There were certainly hundreds, probably thousands, and Lothrop learned of groups of them numbering up to forty-five. They were clearly man-made, because the granite, from which most of them were fashioned, did not occur naturally in the area where they were found. The strangest thing of all was that many of them were almost perfectly spherical. The larger ones, in particular, were so smooth and round that it was almost impossible to believe that they had been fashioned without some kind of mechanical aid, and Lothrop concluded that whoever carved the Giant Balls must first have made templates.

The giant stone spheres must have been of great importance to their sculptors, as their manufacture clearly demanded prodigious labour. There were no quarries in the Palmar area and Lothrop surmised that the stone must have been brought from the mountains many miles away. A few of the balls he came across were made of stone possibly from the mouth of the Diquís River – a journey of at least thirty miles (48km) by river to the place where they were found. To carve a sphere eight feet (2.4m) in diameter, the ancient masons would have had to start with at least a nine foot (2.75m) cube of rock, and whole teams of people would have had to turn it as it was rubbed smooth with other stones. Then they, or others, would have had to drag the completed balls to the mountain ledges or the far banks of rivers where they were found.

Finding clues to their meaning is almost impossible, as they suggest no clear patterns of human behaviour. Some small ones were found in graves, larger ones in long lines, straight or curved, and sometimes arranged in triangles. The usual device of looking for pottery beneath the artefacts did not help either, because although many of the broken pieces found were sixteenth-century, there were shards dating from other centuries.

Today, the Giant Balls of Costa Rica are still a mystery, although many of them adorn the gardens and business quarter of the country's capital San José. Archaeologists marvel at the ingenuity of the people who fashioned and transported them, for they are difficult to move even with modern machinery. The archaeologists are satisfied they know how they were cut: probably, people first found a block of stone that looked as if it could easily be turned into a sphere; then they ground it down with an abrasive of sand and water, pressing the sand onto the surface of the stone with another rock. But they can only guess why they were made. They are not mentioned in the early histories of Costa Rica written by the first Spanish settlers. Dr Luis Diego Gomez, Director of the Museo Nacional, Costa Rica, favours the idea that they represent the sun, moon or the whole solar system; others theorize that they may be grave markers, that they were aligned on heavenly bodies, or that their makers saw them as the physical embodiment of perfection. One local archaeologist sums up the problem: 'If anyone knows about it, we do – and we know nothing.'

The controversies surrounding the Giant Balls have not always been academic. In the late 1970s, two of the largest ever found turned up near Palmar and were sold to two men from San José who tried to move them to the capital. But Dr Gomez and the Museo Nacional decided they must be preserved, and sued on the grounds that their sale amounted to the desecration of the national heritage. The trucks carrying the Giant Balls were turned back on their way to the city and the precious national treasures were dumped by the airstrip at Palmar to await the court's decision. As the long legal wrangle went on, Gomez formulated a plan to display them if he won. Although his plan entailed knocking down the elaborate Spanish portico of the museum to roll them into the building, it was readily agreed to, because, whatever their significance when they were made, the Giant Balls of Costa Rica still have the power to intrigue and fascinate.

THE VITRIFIED FORTS OF SCOTLAND

High on a hill in the Scottish Highlands is a riddle which, like the crystal skulls, leaves experts struggling to find an explanation to fit the curious facts they have amassed.

Even from many miles away, the summit of the 1,850 ft (560m) Tap O'Noth near the village of Rhynie in northeastern Scotland looks oddly flattened; but its truly extraordinary nature is revealed only after an arduous climb to the top. Here, there is a high oval rampart of stones which once formed the defences of an ancient fort, built during the British Iron Age. It is a spectacular place, commanding views over a vast area of Aberdeenshire, but the strange thing about it is that the walls are made, not of dry stones, but of melted rocks. There are still vast blocks of them in position: what were once individual stones are now black and cindery, fused together by heat that must have been so intense that molten rivers of rock once ran down them. Now, cold once more, the walls are made of a material so hard and glassy that archaeologists call it 'vitrified'.

To find one vitrified fort would be strange enough, but there are at least sixty of them in central and northeastern Scotland: one of them, Dunnideer, is only a few miles from Tap O'Noth and clearly visible from its walls. Some of the forts are vast, like Tap O'Noth, built on thousands of square yards of headland or hilltop, others are tiny enclosures. All of them, to a greater or lesser degree, still have walls of melted rock. Nor is it a purely

Scottish phenomenon: vitrified forts have been found in England, France and Germany.

It is understating the case to say that archaeologists have not known what to make of vitrified forts since they began to study them about two hundred years ago. The harder they have looked, theorized and argued, the more intractable the problem has seemed to become: no one can explain to everyone's satisfaction how or why the forts' walls have been melted.

As usual, there are many theories. One, favoured in the eighteenth century, is that the hills on which vitrified forts are found were originally volcanoes, and that the people who settled there used stones thrown up by eruptions to build their settlements; another theory advanced maintains that the rocks were melted by the ray guns of that group so dedicated to the hoodwinking of modern archaeologists, the ancient astronauts. One rather more mundane notion is that melted rock was used as a kind of glue to bind loose stones together, but even this has been dismissed as impracticable by people who have taken the idea seriously enough to consider it: enormous crucibles would have been needed to prepare the 'cement', and no trace of them, or of the blast furnaces that would have been necessary to heat them, has ever been found.

The theories favoured by archaeologists depend on the assumption that the walls of the fort were made of stones laced with timber, and that there was a hollow in the middle filled with rubble – the wood acting as a stabilizing factor like the 'through-stones' used by drystone-wallers to hold the two faces of their walls together. Excavation has certainly revealed that this type of construction existed at forts at Abernethy near Perth and Dun Lagaidh in Ross and Cromarty. Moreover, no less an authority on forts than Julius Caesar described a wood and stone defensive wall called a *murus Gallicus* in his account of his Gallic Wars.

But with vitrified forts nothing is easy, and the people who have studied them are not even able to agree on the details of their construction. For example, no one can decide how much wood was used: some archaeologists claim there were beams running along the wall; others that joists only ran across it; yet

others that there was a combination of the two. There may also
have been vertical posts on the outside of the walls. No one has
even been able to say for certain whether hard- or softwood was
used. The remains of vitrified forts are distorted and have usually
collapsed, so it is hardly surprising that the archaeologists have
no clear answer even to this basic question as they pick their
way through the ruins.

Whatever the details, they do, however, agree that vitrification results from the burning of timber-laxed stone walls, and
the real controversy is over why the vitrification was produced;
was it part of the building process – perhaps to make the walls
stronger or to insulate them – or did it come about by chance,
in the destruction of the forts by fire?

The idea that the fort builders deliberately melted the rock
walls of their settlements was advanced by some of the first
Scottish antiquarians when they came across the phenomenon
two hundred years ago. Their theory was that fires had been lit,
and an inflammable material added, to produce walls strong
enough to resist the dampness of the local climate or the invading
armies of the enemy. It is a curious notion, and there are many
objections to it, not least that there is no evidence that such a
technique, if it was used, did strengthen the walls; rather the
opposite, in fact, because in many cases firing seems to have
caused the walls to collapse. Moreover, it could hardly have
proved to have been an effective building method, as the walls
of many of the forts are only partially vitrified. A Scottish archaeologist, Helen Nisbet, who has excavated vitrified forts, has also
provided another telling argument against the idea that vitrification was deliberately engineered. In a thorough analysis of
rock types used, she reveals that most of the forts were built of
stone easily available at the chosen site, and that, even when
stones were brought from a distance, they do not seem to have
been chosen for their property of vitrification.

Yet scientists who have studied the problem are reluctant to
allow the archaeologists to abandon the idea that the walls were
somehow designed to produce vitrification. One team of chemists
from the Natural History Museum in London stated their view
quite bluntly after studying material from several vitrified forts:

'Considering the high temperatures which have to be produced, and the fact that possibly sixty or so vitrified forts are to be seen in a limited geographical area of Scotland, we do not believe that this type of structure is the result of accidental fires. Careful planning and construction were needed.' Another team of chemists did not go as far as that but, after subjecting rock samples from eleven forts to a rigorous chemical analysis, stated that the temperatures needed to produce the vitrification were so intense – up to 1,100°C – that they could not have been produced by setting fire to a simple *murus Gallicus*. 'Rather,' these researchers added, 'there must have been a careful design of the wall and a contained burning process.'

The argument that the forts became vitrified because they were accidentally destroyed by fire is just as imperfect and contradictory. Significantly, perhaps, there is more than one theory on how they came to be burned. One is that the walls were ignited by sparks from domestic fires, signalling beacons or foundries. This idea, however, has been generally discounted, not least because there are so many vitrified forts that chance destruction of this kind seems improbable, unless their inhabitants were habitually and astonishingly negligent in their fire precautions.

The other main theory is that vitrification came about almost accidentally when the forts were destroyed by invaders, and the fact that there are clear signs that many of the forts were occupied for some time before being set on fire supports this. In two famous experiments in the 1930s, the great archaeologist Gordon Childe and his colleague Wallace Thorneycroft showed that forts could have been set on fire by invaders piling brushwood against the walls, and, more importantly, that the fires started in this manner could generate enough heat for the stones to vitrify.

In March 1934, a model *murus Gallicus*, 12 ft (3.66m) long, 6 ft (1.8m) wide and 6 ft (1.8m) high, was built for them at Plean Colliery in Stirlingshire. They used old fireclay bricks for the faces, pit props as timber, and filled the cavity between the walls with small cubes of basalt rubble. Finally, they covered the top with turf. Then, they piled about four tons of scrap timber and brushwood against the walls and set fire to them. Despite a snowstorm the wood caught fire, and, three hours later, the wall began to collapse. This exposed the inner core which, fanned by a strong wind, grew hotter and hotter.

When Childe and Thorneycroft went through the remains of the wall the next day, they found that they had successfully reproduced the kind of vitrification they had seen in ancient forts. And they did it again in June 1937, when they fired another wall actually on the site of a vitrified fort at Rahoy in Argyllshire, using the rocks found there.

But the experiments do not by any means resolve the questions posed by the vitrified forts not least because Childe seems to have used a larger proportion of wood to stone than many experts believe made up the original structures. It is hard, for example, to understand why people should have built defences that invaders could destroy with fire, when great ramparts of solid stone would have survived unscathed. It is also difficult to see why people should have persisted with the design for a thousand years or more, and in so many places in a relatively small area, if they were so susceptible to the firebrand. There is not even a clear answer to the question of who set the walls on fire: if it was the work of invaders, could the defenders of the forts not easily have put the flames out, for as Childe's experiments showed it took some time for the brushwood to ignite the main structure? And there is always the lingering doubt, raised by the chemists, that the walls must have been specially designed to allow the inner cores to reach great heat and vitrify, suggesting that the fort builders of ancient Scotland may have known something about building which we today do not.

THE NANJING BELT

The most puzzling archaeological mystery of ancient China came to light in the true tradition of buried treasure when a workman's spade broke through the roof of a long-forgotten tomb.

It was 1 December 1952. The Jingyi Middle School of Yixing City in the Jiang-su Province of China was building a sports field. The first task was to level the ground, for the school authorities had chosen a patch of land dominated by an oblong hillock.

Another feature of the site, four curiously shaped mounds, complicated the work. That day, a labourer's shout brought everything to a halt. His spade had penetrated a thin layer of earth and rubble and a hole had appeared, releasing a rush of musty air. Peering into the darkness, the work gang could dimly make out a chamber stacked with dusty objects.

They called the police, who climbed down through the opening and soon announced that the workers had made a major archaeological find. The place was obviously a tomb. After taking into safekeeping a motley collection of grave goods, including five pieces of porcelain, eleven of pottery, some scraps of gold, two pottery stands and 'four gold articles', the police sealed the chamber and the Huadong Historical Relics Working Team was summoned to conduct a full-scale excavation.

The dig revealed that there were in fact two tombs, both built in an unusual style. Each had chambers with an arched roof constructed of wedge-shaped bricks, topped with a square slab. More bricks, laid in a herringbone pattern, covered the floor. The roof was adorned with carvings: circles, tigers or the faces of animals. Conveniently, the 'Number 1 tomb' contained an inscription which enabled the archaeologists to date their find precisely. On one side it read: '20th September of the seventh year of Yuankang the late general Zhou . . .'; on the other, the tomb builders had left their official titles and signatures: 'Yicao Zhu Xuan, jianggongli Yang Chun, workman Young Pu made.' This, then, was the burial-place of a nobleman called Zhou Chu.

Zhou could be traced in the historical records. A renowned military man and scholar, he had lived during the Jin Dynasty (AD265–420), and had died fighting the Tibetans in 297. There could be no doubt whatsoever about the dates, and this made one discovery all the more astonishing. Encircling what had once been the waist of a rotted skeleton found in the 'Number 1 tomb' were about twenty pieces of metal, obviously the remains of a belt. 'The factor worth noting,' wrote archaeologist Luo Zong-chen with what proved to be breathtaking understatement, 'is the chemical composition of these ornaments.' For analysis of one fragment by the Chemistry Department of nearby Nanjing

University revealed that it was composed almost entirely of aluminium. Now, although aluminium is widely used in modern life, it was not isolated in the West until the early years of the nineteenth century, and a generation later was still so rare that it was a showpiece of the 1855 Paris Exposition. The production of aluminium requires something thought to have been quite unknown in ancient China: electricity. The discovery of the belt therefore raised a question which fascinated archaeologists, metallurgists and chemists both inside China and far beyond its boundaries: did the Chinese beat European scientists to the isolation of aluminium by a cool 1,500 years?

While it would be going too far to say that archaeologists have become used to pondering such problems – their working lives are usually devoted to the painstaking accumulation of more prosaic evidence of the daily lives of ancient peoples – a few objects like the Nanjing belt have presented them with an irresistible and potentially unsettling challenge. Did the scientists, artists and builders of the past know secrets that their successors have taken centuries to rediscover? Should our ideas about the level of technology achieved by the ancients be drastically revised?

How then did the experts set about finding the answer to the puzzle of the Nanjing belt? As so often happens, they first fell to arguing. In China itself the pages of the academic journals were full of the controversy. In the magazine *Koagu*, one expert, Shen Shi-ying of the North Eastern Engineering College, reported that he had carried out several methods of analysis on a small broken piece of the belt which he had obtained from the Nanjing Museum. 'But,' he announced, 'the results of these various analyses all pointed to these alloys being silver-based rather than aluminium-based.' Another piece gave similar results, but yet another fragment, originally sent to a different analyst, really did seem to contain aluminium. Yet Shen Shi-ying remained sceptical and concluded: 'It is impossible to tell from its structure whether it was made in ancient times. At the same time, it was unlike the product of a 1960s factory.' He suggested that the aluminium might have been made at the beginning of this century, but added cautiously, 'This is only a supposition, and to know definitely, all round research in depth is called for.'

Stung by Shen's reservations, and particularly by his suggestion that the piece of metal which analysis *had* proved to be aluminium had been introduced into the tomb at a much later date, perhaps by grave-robbers (who had undoubtedly broken into the tomb at some time in the past), one of the original excavators, Luo Zong-chen, published a riposte. The belt pieces, he wrote, were certainly of the Jin period, for most of them 'were underneath the accumulated earth, showing that they had never been disturbed'. Luo also attacked Shen's assertion that most of the fragments found had turned out to be silver. Four pieces, he conceded, had indeed been shown to be silver, but four others *were* made of aluminium.

The Cultural Revolution of the 1960s, which so disrupted Chinese academic life, brought the controversy to an abrupt end with nothing resolved, but by then the story was out. One of the many experts in the West who learned of the Nanjing belt was Dr Joseph Needham of Cambridge University, author of the monumental *Science and Civilisation in China*, and perhaps the greatest authority of all. He was intrigued and did not entirely dismiss the idea that the ancient Chinese had somehow found a way to isolate aluminium. 'For the present it would be unwise to rule out the possibility,' he wrote in 1974.

One group of Western scientists, however, did not stop at simply expressing interest in the Nanjing belt. In 1980, inspired by Joseph Needham, Dr Anthony R Butler and his colleagues, Dr Christopher Glidewell and Sharee E Pritchard, of the Chemistry Department of the University of St Andrews decided to continue the search for the truth, begun a quarter of a century earlier in China. In 1986 their report was published, and was eagerly consulted by scientists and lay people whose curiosity had been whetted by the Chinese controversy. Its title, 'Aluminium Objects from a Jin Dynasty Tomb – Can They Be Authentic?' held out the promise that the three investigators had found an answer to the mystery.

They began by acknowledging that modern research into Chinese science and technology has revealed many previously unsuspected scientific and technological achievements, some astonishingly advanced. 'Consequently we believe that no report of a medieval Chinese chemical achievement, however remarkable, should be rejected without adequate modern re-assessment.' Even so, they judged that the production of aluminium in the Jin Dynasty, an age without electricity, 'would have been truly remarkable'. The St Andrews researchers then went on to pose questions which many had asked but none had proved able to answer: 'How reliable are the chemical analyses? What metallurgical techniques were available at that date? Is it possible to prepare an aluminium alloy by any of them? If an aluminium alloy was prepared, was it by design or by accident?'

Their discussion of the archaeological evidence did not detain them for long. They argued that standards of excavation are high in China – the painstaking manner in which the first emperor's terracotta army has been uncovered and preserved at Xian is one of the most recent examples – and concluded that 'there can be little doubt that the aluminium artefacts were found in the tomb'. They also gave short shrift to a suggestion that the belt had somehow been 'planted' by grave-robbers:

> It is difficult to see why they should have left the silver objects in place and have carefully inserted pieces of aluminium for the confusion of future excavators. A tomb-robber is scarcely likely to have had scraps of kitchen utensils about his person and to have discarded them accidentally. It would also need a miraculous breeze to replace the dust.

Butler and his colleagues devoted most of their paper to the central question: Did the Chinese of the Jin Dynasty have the know-how to produce aluminium? While the modern method of isolation uses electricity, aluminium has been produced in furnaces, though these need to be extremely hot. The Chinese certainly had furnaces capable of producing high temperatures, perhaps as great as 1,500°C, but, the St Andrews team concluded, these would have been capable of making metal containing only very small amounts of aluminium. And there was no method available to Jin Dynasty metallurgists which would have enabled them to manufacture aluminium of the purity of the metal found in Zhou Chu's tomb.

So what is the answer? How can it be that pieces of almost pure aluminium should turn up in an ancient tomb? With a touch of the theatrical, the Scottish researchers saved their theory for the last paragraph of their report:

> We are led to suggest, for want of something better, that the aluminium was introduced as an academic prank by a participant who was probably greatly embarrassed when he realized the consequences of his actions. Fortunately for scholars in the West, the Chinese themselves were the first to doubt the authenticity of the claims. It is perhaps a mark of our regard for the enduring genius of the Chinese people that the claims were taken seriously for so long.

The St Andrews paper seemed to have settled the argument. Hoaxes, of course, are nothing new in archaeology, and the story of the Nanjing belt was duly dubbed 'the Chinese Piltdown' after the most celebrated hoax of modern times, in which a weird amalgam of a human cranium and an orang-utan's jawbone, unearthed in the south of England in 1912, was successfully passed off for some forty years as the skull of an important 'missing link' in the evolutionary chain.

Yet in 1985 the *Bulletin of the Chinese Academy of Geological Sciences* reported a discovery which revived the possibility that aluminium had been available in China at the time of General Zhou's burial. Geologists from the Shenyang Institute of Geology announced that they had found grains of 'native aluminium' in Guizhou Province. 'Native aluminium' is extremely rare, indeed only a handful of claims for its discovery have ever been made. According to the Chinese geologists, their specimens contained 'some copper and sulphur, also chromium and iron' and were harder than pure aluminium, but they were satisfied that they had been found 'in a situation where contamination by men was eliminated'.

The report brought this comment from Dr Anthony R Butler of the St Andrews team:

> I think the evidence for the presence of native aluminium is good but the manner of its production is obscure. The grain size indicates that it could not possibly have been used to make the Nanjing belt. For

native aluminium to have been used for that, an even rarer geological process, giving lumps of aluminium rather than grains, would be necessary. While this is a possibility, made more possible by the discovery of grains of native aluminium, it remains a remote hypothesis. However, a general rule is never to underestimate the Chinese. After all, they did invent the compass, printing and gunpowder.

THE BAGHDAD BATTERY

In Baghdad, Iraqi archaeologists are glad to discuss what they believe to be proof that their ancestors could make electricity a full 1,800 years before Galvani produced enough current to make the famous frogs' legs twitch.

The story begins in 1936 when a consignment of finds from a settlement which had once been occupied by the Parthians was sent to the Iraq Museum laboratory. At the time, Wilhelm König, a German, was in charge. He wrote later:

> Something rather peculiar was found, and, after it had passed through several hands, it was brought to me. A vase-like vessel of light yellow clay, whose neck had been removed, contained a copper cylinder which was held firmly by asphalt. The vase was about 15cm high; the sheet-copper cylindrical tube with bottom had a diameter of 26mm and was 9cm long. In it, held by a kind of stopper of asphalt, was a completely oxidized iron rod, the top of which projected about 1cm above the stopper and was covered by a yellowish-grey, fully oxidized thin coating of a metal which looked like lead. The bottom end of the iron rod did not extend right to the bottom of the cylinder, on which was a layer of asphalt about 3mm deep. The question as to what this might be received the most surprising answer. After all the parts had been brought together and then examined in their separate parts, it became evident that it could only have been an electrical element. It was only necessary to add an acid or an alkaline liquid to complete the element.

It seemed to be a battery. Yet it had been found in the ruins of a Parthian village, and the Parthians had lived in the area between 248BC and AD226. König was claiming that they had electricity, and that Volta and Galvani, who up to that time had been credited with the invention of the first batteries, had merely introduced them to the West.

Despite suggestions that König misinterpreted the find and that it is the remains of a scroll that was stored in a pottery container, or of a relatively modern battery dropped perhaps by telegraph engineers in the late nineteenth or early twentieth centuries, another German has provided dramatic support for König's theory. He is Dr Arne Eggebrecht, an Egyptologist from Hildesheim in West Germany, and he first came across the battery when a touring exhibition of treasures from ancient Iraq went on show at the museum where he works. Of all the exhibits – the lofty marble statue of an ancient king, the hexagonal cuneiform tablets and the finely worked vases – it was the apparently humble group of the copper cylinder, iron rod and pot that most intrigued him. Like König he says: 'If you take all these things together, they can only mean an electric cell or battery to a scientist.'

Since the first realization, Eggebrecht has tested the theory many times with a battery made with exact replicas of the pieces. For the alkaline liquid called for by König, he uses juice freshly pressed from grapes bought at a local fruit shop. As soon as the liquid is poured into the copper cylinder, a voltmeter connected to the battery registers half a volt of electricity. Eggebrecht's is no idle curiosity: he believes the existence of such a battery may help solve a mystery that archaeologists have so far been unable to explain. The museums of the world are full of gilded objects, and, in many cases, the method used to gild them is obvious: sometimes gold leaf was pressed round them or even glued on. But such techniques do not seem to have been used in every case. For example, Eggebrecht has a small statue of the Egyptian god Osiris made in about 400BC. It is made of solid silver topped with a layer of gold which he believes is far too thin and smooth to have been applied by the crude techniques of beating or gluing. Could batteries, he wonders, have been used to electroplate it? It was a question which, with the replica battery to hand, could easily be answered. By immersing a silver statuette in a gold-cyanide solution, and running an electric current through it from the Baghdad Battery, he was able to produce a finely gilded object in little more than a couple of hours. Having done this several times, a disconcerting thought struck him: perhaps many of the treasures that the museums of the world display in their collections as being made of gold are, in fact, made of silver with a thin veneer of gold, and he hopes that, in the light of his finding, many museums will begin the unwelcome task of re-examining their treasures to make sure that all that glistens in the display cases really is gold. In the case of the Baghdad Battery, therefore, the suggestion that an ancient civilization may have possessed electricity may prove to be a mixed blessing.

THE PERUVIAN STONE WALLS

While on a visit to central Peru in 1979, Professor Jean-Pierre Protzen, Chairman of the Department of Architecture at the University of California at Berkeley, became fascinated by the ruins of buildings constructed by the ninth emperor of the Incas. The huge blocks of stone, some weighing well over 100 tons, were put together in a most remarkable way: each block fitted together so tightly that it was impossible in many cases even to slide a knife-blade into the joints. What was the secret of the Inca stonemasonry? Professor Protzen assumed that when he returned to Berkeley he would be able to find out from a book in the university library. But there was no book, and no one seemed to know the answer.

In 1982 the professor set out for Peru once more, determined to crack the mystery. First he examined the spectacular Inca walls at Cuzco, Saqsaywaman and Ollantaytambo. Then he visited the quarries from which the stones had been cut, marvelling in passing at the slides down which the blocks were transported from the rockface. One slide, at Kachiqhata, had 'an awesome 40-degree slope with a 250-metre vertical drop'. At another quarry Protzen found 250 large stones which, he realized, were 'examples of all the stages of production, from raw stone to finely dressed blocks'. Scattered amongst them were stones which had obviously come from outside the quarry, probably from the banks of the Vilcanota River nearby. These, he decided, were hammers with which the blocks had been worked.

He identified three types: the heaviest probably shaped the stones immediately after they had been cut from the main rockface; the medium-sized ones could have been used for dressing the blocks; and the edges would have been fashioned with the smallest hammers.

The time for theorizing was over. The professor chose a likely looking block and set to. With just six blows of a nine pound (4kg) stone hammer, he shaped a rough block, and then, with another hammer, pounded one of its faces until it was smooth. To protect it from the impact of heavy blows to the next face, he used one of the smallest stones to draft the edges before turning the block over. Ninety minutes later, three sides were dressed. A comparison of the test block with those worked by the Incas confirmed that Professor Protzen's hypothesis was plausible.

Now it was time to tackle the heart of the mystery. How had the Inca stonemasons managed to make the blocks fit together so tightly? The examination of ruined walls provided the clues. Joints – usually concave depressions – were cut in the lower blocks so that the upper course could fit into them precisely. The sides of each block were slotted together in the same way. Once again, Professor Protzen tried the technique himself. He took the block he had already dressed and placed it on top of another. Then he traced the outline of the upper stone upon the lower, removed the top block, and pounded away until he had hollowed out a depression for the top one to fit into. Before long, both stones were tightly locked together.

The enigmas of Inca stonemasonry had yielded to an enquiring mind and an energetic arm.

ARTHUR C CLARKE COMMENTS:

I am happy to see a solution to the mystery of the 'ancient' Chinese aluminium belt, which has worried me for years. Technologically, such an artefact would be almost as anomalous as a medieval transistor radio. Of course, the solution may not be right, but it is highly plausible – and one possible solution is infinitely better than none.

The origin – and method of manufacture – of the stone 'Giant Balls' of Costa Rica is still an archaeological enigma. Surprisingly, it turns out that nature can make almost perfect spheres of stone. Hundreds of specimens of up to eleven feet (3m) in diameter have been found in Mexico. They appear to be of volcanic origin, and were formed some forty million years ago when a torrent of incandescent ash cooled and crystallized. Although many of these natural spheres are almost geometrically perfect, they lack the finish of the man-made ones – though James Randi has suggested that they may have inspired their production. And, one might add, greatly assisted it: any sensible sculptor starts with a piece of rock as near as possible to the shape he's aiming at.

I am indebted to my old friend Colin Ross for information about much smaller spheres (the 'Moerake Boulders') which occur in New Zealand. These are concretions, i.e. masses that have 'grown' from the surrounding rock by chemical precipitation over immense periods of time. Some are up to six foot (2m) in diameter, and range from perfect spheres to 'highly irregular and fantastic shapes'.

Natural spheres can also be produced when rocks are trapped in holes on the beds of rivers, and strong currents continually turn them over and over. I am grateful to Rubert Siemerling for this information; he tells me that farmers in the Alps used this method to make stone cannon balls, so the process must be fairly swift.

Never underrate Mother Nature. In this case, she has come up with several solutions to a problem which at first sight seems insoluble.

MONSTERS
OF THE DEEP

Our planet, no doubt, should be called not Earth but Sea. And nothing is more certain than that the three-quarters of its surface that is covered with water still holds many surprises for Man.

The terrors of the deep are genuine enough. In 1985 a large shark was killed in the Gulf of Thailand. In its stomach were the skulls of two men, 'adults of Caucasian origin'. The same year, sharks, unusually, started taking surfers off the coast of California. The theory emerged that people wearing black wet suits look like seals, one of the sharks' food sources. In 1986 in Kiribati – once the Gilbert Islands – local fishermen watched in horror as a creature with tentacles grabbed first one and then another of their colleagues and dragged them down to die in the depths.

Recent years have seen some of the mysteries of the deep resolved, others rendered all the more intriguing. Some fears have been allayed. The sea snake, with the deadliest venom in the world, seems to reserve its lethal powers for fellow marine creatures and hardly ever attacks man. Other horrors have been reinforced – not least sharks.

The incident in Kiribati added another makeweight to the balance of evidence which now suggests that there may indeed be truly giant octopuses lurking in the vast biosphere of the sea. There is room enough. Not only does the sea cover nearly three-quarters of the earth's surface, but its great depths mean that there is perhaps 300 times as much living space than is to be found on the plateaus of earth's dry land. Reminders of our ignorance are regularly delivered.

THE DOMAIN OF
THE MEGAMOUTH SHARK

In 1984 the fishing vessel *Helga* netted a megamouth shark off Catalina Island, California – only the second member ever seen of what is now established as an entirely new species. It now floats in a tank of ethanol at the Los Angeles Museum of Natural History – a fifteen-foot-long (4.5m) symbol of how little we know of the sea. And the marine biologists regularly outline the huge area of darkness in which they operate. Biologist Malcolm Clarke, studying sperm whales, found in their stomachs not only huge quantities of squid – up to 30,000 squid jaws in one whale's gut – but species rarely or never caught in the plethora of nets and devices which the scientists use to prospect the sea. Yet the weight of these unknown creatures eaten by whales each year, he calculated, exceeds that of the entire human race put together. The squid, some of them very large to judge by their beaks, must exist in their millions, yet many species rarely fall into the hands of man.

GIANT SQUID

Several times in the last century, at intervals of thirty years, twenty or thirty foot (6 or 9m) specimens of squid, probably relative midgets, have foundered ashore in Newfoundland. They seem to be deceived by periodic changes in the cold Labrador current and decoyed into the shallows and away from the North Atlantic deeps. Their aggressive armoury is awe-inspiring: first the tentacles, which grab the prey; then the arms with sucker discs acting like vacuum pads on the victim's flesh; inside them, rows of claws dig in for a firmer hold. Then, as the prey is drawn in, it is cut by a beak, powerful enough to sever heavy wire. This beak, like a nightmare version of a parrot's but with the top closing over the bottom, tears chunks from the victim, before tiny teeth, further down in the mouth, finally shred the meat. It is thought that the squid prey even on the big sperm whales and the whales on them.

What is known is that squids have a strong attraction for the colour red. Off the shores of Newfoundland, the squid fishermen often eschew bait and merely hang red-painted metal or spark plugs near the hooks. These suffice to catch the squid. There are ghoulish stories of what happened to torpedoed men in the area during the war as they floated in their bright-red lifejackets.

In the nineteenth century, the British writer, F T Bullen, aboard the whaleship *Cachelot*, described a titanic encounter between a whale and the kraken (the Norse name by which the whalers knew the squid) bursting out of the water. The whale was in the toils of the kraken, but with part of the squid's body already in the whale's mouth. They then disappeared below.

In the death agony, a harpooned sperm whale vomits up the contents of the stomach often thousands of squids, large and small. Bullen describes pieces of tentacles as thick as a man's body floating past his harpoon boat. Huge sucker marks found on the bodies of sperm whales seem to bear witness to these struggles in the deep, suggesting vast creatures far bigger than the twenty-one foot (6.5m) squid that drifted ashore in Trinity Bay, Newfoundland in 1965.

It was just a year after this that the US Navy had yet another of its encounters with the mysteries of the deep. The research vessel *San Pablo* was 120 miles (200km) off Cape Bonavista, Newfoundland, on a normal oceanographic trawl in clear daylight. Suddenly a sperm whale hurled itself out of the water ahead of the ship, entangled in the tentacles of a giant squid. The scene was repeated, and the officers and men had time to go to their cameras as well as to their binoculars. The *San Pablo* was hamstrung with paid-out cable and could not move closer, so the photographs are not too enlightening; however, the men of the *San Pablo* were oceanographic experts and they all agreed that the whale was at least sixty foot (18m) long, yet the squid seemed to match it.

THE GIANT OCTOPUS

In 1984 a weird series of incidents off the coast of Bermuda gave a hint that the lair of the giant octopus may have been found. It has been clear that this creature is not merely a chimera ever since the day in 1896 when an enormous carcass was washed up on the beach at St Augustine in Florida. The main part of the body weighed around seven tons and was eighteen foot (5.5m) long by ten feet (3m) across. A local naturalist, Dr De Witt Webb, measured two of the tentacles, though he thought they were only stumps, at twenty-three and thirty-two feet (7 and 10m). His view then was that he was dealing with an octopus of daunting proportions – perhaps 200 foot (60m) across. His photographs leave no room to doubt the bulk of the animal, but what has sustained modern confidence in the veracity of his attribution was the happy coincidence that a piece of the animal's flesh was preserved in the Smithsonian Institute in Washington, DC. This meant that in 1963 Dr Joseph Gennaro could make a histological analysis. He concluded that the tissue was not from a squid or a whale and was probably from an octopus.

But the mystery remains: could such gigantic creatures really exist when the largest octopus otherwise known to man is a mere twenty-three feet (7m)?

In the summer of 1984 a Bermuda trawler owner, John P Ingham, was working on what he hoped would be a profitable theory. He thought that very large – and commercially attractive – shrimps and crabs might be found, if he could only get traps down to 1,000 fathoms or so – more than 6,000 feet (1,800m) – off the Bermuda shelf. The theory was working: he had brought up half a pound (500-gm) shrimps, and crabs two feet (60cm) across. Ingham now proceeded to construct really strong traps built of ¼- and ⅜-in iron rods, braced with two-inch (5-cm) tree staves. They measured between six and eight feet (1.8 and 2.4m) square by four feet (1.2m) deep. The traps were lowered and raised by winch from John Ingham's fifty-foot (15-m) boat, *Trilogy*.

By the beginning of September, Ingham had already had a couple of worrying incidents. First he lost a trap after a sudden strain on the line. There was nothing obvious to explain it. Then, a few days later, on 3 September, the crew were hauling up a new pot and had reached about 300 fathoms when they felt the line being pulled out. There was a series of jerks, and once again the line parted. On 19 September 1984, Mr Ingham had a trap set at 480 fathoms – around 2,800 feet (850m) down. This time, even with the full force of the winch, they could not break the pot clear of the bottom at all. *Trilogy* is equipped with a sophisticated type of sonar known as a chromascope, and Skipper Ingham went inside to use it. He set the 'scope on what is known as 'split bottom mode'. There, clearly outlined on the ocean floor, was a pyramid-like shape, measurable on the chromascope as fully fifty feet (15m) high: something was surrounding their trap. Ingham and his crew decided not to force the issue this time. They would settle down and wait, with the rope snubbed as tight as possible on the winch. After about twenty minutes, Ingham suddenly had the eerie feeling that the boat was starting to move – that it was being towed.

Again he went inside to check his array of navigation instruments. The positions given by the Loran are extremely precise. The instrument confirmed his view. The boat was moving steadily south at a speed of about 1 knot. After about 500 yards, whatever was towing the *Trilogy* decided to change direction and turned inshore. A short distance further on it abruptly turned again. By now Ingham was convinced that some creature had hold of his pot and was steadily advancing, trap, fifty-foot boat and all, towards some private destination. At one point Mr Ingham put his hand on the rope near the water line. 'I could distinctly feel thumps like something was walking and the vibrations were travelling up the rope.' The fifty-foot sonar lump, the peregrinations of the boat, the thumps, the previous lost traps – Ingham was now convinced that he was in the grip of some truly gigantic sea creature.

Suddenly the creature appeared to let go. The rope became slack and the crew had no trouble hauling up the trap. It was bent on one side and the top had been stoved in.

Neither cameras nor underwater scanners operated by scientists have accompanied Mr Ingham, but the circumstances point firmly to an octopus: a creature on the ocean floor with the power to retain a trap against a large ship's winch; an accumulation of bite-size shrimp and crab; the location off the Bermuda shelf. All lead inexorably to the idea of a large octopus. No other creature known or imagined could conceivably give such a show of strength in such circumstances. Perhaps the homeland of the great creature which was so mysteriously washed up almost a century ago in Florida has now at last been located.

SEA SERPENTS AND MONSTERS

With one possible Celtic and one Antipodean exception, neither hide nor hair, fluke nor fin, of a sea serpent has ever come into man's hands. Yet they have been seen by thousands of people, many experienced seamen, trained naturalists, and oceanographers among them. Sometimes hundreds of people at once have seen a sea serpent, but there are no acceptable photographs, no significant gap in the order of ocean life, to give credibility to the monster of the oceans. Yet so numerous, so precise, so detailed and sober, so similar are the witnesses' reports that it seems possible that at least one, and maybe three or four species of sea monster inhabit our seas. Monsters with humped backs, heads sticking many feet out of the water, often a mane and huge eyes, have been described since ancient times. There are vivid accounts from the Greeks, precise details from the old Scandinavian writers like Olaus Magnus, right through the medieval period, up to modern times. In 1848 there was a sensation when *The Times* reported that the captain of one of Her Majesty's frigates, the nineteen-gun *Daedalus*, had actually reported to Their Lordships of the Admiralty seeing a sea serpent on a passage from the East Indies. Captain Peter M'Quhae's dispatch said they had watched the monster quite close for twenty minutes. 'Had it been a man of my acquaintance I should easily have recognized the features with the naked eye. It did not deviate from its course to the southwest which it held at the pace of twelve to fifteen miles per hour, apparently on some determined purpose.' The swift speed, like the other details which

M'Quhae provided, were to become a staple of monster sightings: the large head of a snake, four feet (1.2m) out of the water 'which it never during the time it continued in sight of our glasses lowered below the surface of the water'; something like the mane of a horse washing about its back; and a dimension 'comparing it with what our main topsail yard would show in the water' of at least 60 ft (18m).

The great authority on sea serpents, Bernard Heuvelmans, has catalogued more than 500 sightings in the past 150 years, but inevitably it is the more modern reports in an era of sophisticated marine exploration that have the most fascination.

In 1959 two Scotsmen had a vivid sighting off the Isle of Soay. One was Tex Geddes, who had once crewed for Gavin Maxwell the naturalist, the other was a holidaying engineering inspector, James Gavin. They were out fishing for mackerel together in fine weather. They had already watched some killer whales and basking sharks when Gavin noticed a black shape a couple of miles away. Geddes described what followed:

> When the object appeared to be steaming towards us, we both stood up for a better view. I can't remember exactly how close it was when I heard the breathing, but I certainly could hear it before I could definitely have said that the object was alive. It was not making much speed, maybe three or four knots. I am afraid we both stared in amazement as the object came towards us, for this beast steaming slowly in our direction was like some hellish monster of prehistoric times.
>
> The head was definitely reptilian, about two and half foot high with large protruding eyes. There were no visible nasal organs but a large red gash of a mouth which seemed to cut the head in half and which appeared to have distinct lips. There was at least two feet of clear water behind the neck. I would say we saw eight to ten feet of back on the water line.

The animal perused the men and the dinghy at its leisure.

> The head appeared rather blunt and darker than the rest of the body which seemed to be scaly and the top of its back was surmounted by an immense saw-toothed ridge. It seemed to breathe through its mouth which opened and shut with great regularity, and once when it turned towards us I could see into its cavernous red maw. I saw no teeth.

But monsters are not confined to the North Atlantic. In 1943, Thomas Helm, an ex-US Marine, was out with his wife off the west coast of Florida when they saw a strange creature making straight for their boat.

> It was unmistakably some kind of animal, the head about the size of a basketball on a neck which reached nearly four feet out of the water. The entire head and neck were covered with wet fur which lay close to the body and glistened in the afternoon sunlight. When it was almost beside our boat the head turned and looked squarely at us. My first thought was that we were seeing some kind of giant otter or seal, but I was immediately impressed by the fact that this was not the face of an otter or seal. The head of this creature, with the exception that there was no evidence of ears, was that of a monstrous cat. The face was fur-covered and flat and the eyes were set in the front of the head. The colour of the wet fur was uniformly a rich chocolate brown. The well-defined eyes were round and about the size of a silver dollar and were glistening black. Where I judged the mouth should be, was a moustache of stiff black hairs with a downward curve on each side.

Helm, an experienced game fisherman, thought it might be some kind of sea elephant or some relative of the West Indian seal which was thought to be exterminated two hundred years ago, but he dismissed the idea. As he said, 'All the seal family have long pointed noses and eyes on the sides of the head. The creature my wife and I saw had eyes which were positioned near the front of the face like those of a cat.'

There have been well-attested strandings of monsters going back at least to the Stronsa Beast which was washed ashore on Orkney off Scotland in 1808.

Almost invariably, as with the Stronsa Beast, these turn out to be basking sharks. The dead basking shark decays in the most deceiving manner. First the jaws, which are attached by only a small piece of flesh, drop off leaving what looks like a small skull and thin serpentlike neck. Then, as only the upper half of the tail fin carries the spine, the lower half rots away leaving the lower fins which look like legs. Time after time this monster-like relic has been the cause of a sea serpent 'flap'.

But there is one case, unknown to most students, which does challenge the assertion that no sea monster has ever come ashore.

It all began in the summer of 1942 when Charles Rankin, a council officer at Gourock on the River Clyde in Scotland, was diverted from cares of war by complaints of an awful stench coming from the shore. He went down with his foreman to be confronted by a most unusual carcass. Rankin was in a dilemma. The nostrils and indeed the health of the folk of Gourock required protection, but at the same time here was something perhaps unknown to science. As Rankin now testily recalls, he rang the Royal Scottish Museum, but that body was dismissive. Next he thought of photographing it, but it was a restricted area, and the Royal Navy gave him a stiff warning when he asked for permission. So finally the Gourock monster was chopped up and buried in the grounds of the municipal incinerator.

But Rankin was, and is, a precise man and his description cannot lightly be dismissed. He is very clear about what he found:

> It was approximately twenty-seven to twenty-eight feet in length and five to six feet in depth at the broadest part. As it lay on its side the body appeared to be oval in section but the angle of the flippers in relation to the body suggested that the body section had been round in life. If so this would reduce the depth dimension to some extent. The head and neck, the body, and the tail were approximately equal in length, the neck and tail tapering gradually away from the body. There were no fins. The head was comparatively small, of a shape rather like that of a seal but the snout was much sharper and the top of the head flatter. The jaws came together one over the other and there appeared to be bumps over the eyes – say prominent eyebrows. There were large pointed teeth in each jaw. The eyes were comparatively large rather like those of a seal but more to the side of the head.
>
> The tail was rectangular in shape as it lay and it appeared to have been vertical in life. Showing through the thin skin there were parallel rows of 'bones' which had a gristly, glossy, opaque appearance. I had the impression that these 'bones' had opened out fan-wise under the thin membrane to form a very effective tail. The tail appeared to be equal in size above and below the centre line.
>
> 'At the front of the body there was a pair of 'L'-shaped flippers and at the back a similar pair, shorter but broader. Each terminated

in a 'bony' structure similar to the tail and no doubt was also capable of being opened out in the same way.

'The body had over it at fairly close intervals, pointing backwards, hard, bristly 'hairs'. These were set closer together towards the tail and at the back edges of the flippers. I pulled out one of these bristles from a flipper. It was about 6in long and was tapered and pointed at each end like a steel knitting needle and rather of the thickness of a needle of that size but slightly more flexible. I kept this bristle in the drawer of my office desk and some time later I found that it had dried up in the shape of a coiled spring.

The skin of the animal was smooth and when cut was found to be comparatively thin but tough. There appeared to be no bones other than a spinal column. The flesh was uniformly deep pink in colour, was blubbery and difficult to cut or chop. It did not bleed and it behaved like a thick table jelly under pressure. In what I took to be the stomach of the animal was found a small piece of knitted woollen material as from a cardigan and, stranger still, a small corner of what had been a woven cotton tablecloth – complete with tassels.

Against such exactness and circumstantial detail, it is hard to maintain that Mr Rankin's monster was a shark or any other known species.

It was thirty-five years later before another such intriguing find turned up.

In the South Pacific and off the coast of New Zealand the Japanese organize squid fishing on a considerable scale. Satellite pictures have shown the lights of the fishing fleet, brighter than any other light source on earth, including the illuminations of New York City. And it was in that area that the Japanese fishing boat *Zuiyo-maru*, in September 1977, hauled up an unwanted catch.

Five key photographs were taken of the decaying monster that they pulled aboard. Along with the measurements and the evidence of the assistant production manager of Taiyo Fisheries, Michihiko Yano, and crucial pieces of flesh from the fin, they represent an unsolved riddle. For the crew of the *Zuiyo-maru*, fearful that their rotting monster would contaminate their catch, threw it back overboard. The creature was thirty-three feet (10m) long, apparently devoid of a dorsal fin, and certainly baffled the experienced fishermen on board. The pictures, portions of flesh and descriptions that they brought back were to baffle Japan's best marine scientists too. Some still thought it was a basking shark, too far putrefied to be easily recognized. But Dr Fujio Yasuda of the Tokyo University of Fisheries, and one of the world's leading marine biologists, disagreed. He noted first: 'In no known species attaining a large size is the trunk so elongated.' The body plan of the animal, the location of its fins, he declared to be quite different from that of a shark. He concluded: 'We are not able to find any known living fish species which agree with the animal trawled off New Zealand. If it is a species of shark, it may represent a species unknown to science.'

Two other Japanese were of similar opinion. Obata and Tomoda of the Tokyo National Science Museum said: 'Whether the animal belongs to a group of sharks or whether it is a marine reptile, we do not know any genera or species that agree with it.'

It is, however, likely that some at least of the sea-monster sightings have an explanation which, though still extraordinary, falls within the bounds of conventional biology. After a report from a trawler in 1962, the Russians are now speculating that Steller's sea cow, the four-ton 'dodo' of the Arctic which was supposedly exterminated in the nineteenth century, may still survive in the Bering Sea. The huge creature, which lived off seaweed and went to sleep on its back, is also being sought by the English explorer Derek Hutchinson who is mounting expeditions to the Aleutian Islands off the coast of Alaska. Steller's sea cow, vast and walrus-like, would fit many a good monster identikit. Researchers in the far north received some unexpected encouragement in early 1980 when the Russians reported seeing the Greenland whale, thought to be on the verge of extinction, herding in large numbers near Cape Stoneheart. More than 150 were counted and N Doroshenko of the Pacific Scientific Research Institute of Fisheries and Oceanography, Vladivostok, said: 'Perhaps they know of a patch of open water in the winter ice, and have been able to keep out of sight by not migrating south in the autumn.'

The world of the elephant seal, manatee, and walrus, all known creatures, already offers marine apparitions to terrify and confuse any innocent who has never seen one before. The leathery sea turtle, greatest of the turtles, can be up to 10 feet (3m) long, and travels remarkably widely. The Soay beast certainly has a hint of the turtle about him.

But all these put together can hardly account for the hundreds and hundreds of first-hand, detailed reports by respectable individuals of many nationalities, who had nothing to gain but derision, and yet who have persisted in recording their sightings of the sea serpents.

Perhaps more than any of the contemporary mysteries which intrigue the modern imagination, we can be sure that the sea serpent will one day surrender a final proof of his existence.

ARTHUR C CLARKE COMMENTS:

A few years ago an oil company engineer told me a story about divers who couldn't go down to inspect an oil-rig because it was covered by an octopus! I could not discover exactly – or even approximately – what percentage of the rig was so ornamented. Of course, objects are magnified under water, and the first diver down probably did not stop to make accurate measurements.

As an inoperative rig costs a few hundred thousand dollars a day in lost revenue, the oil company, sadly but understandably, did not call for marine scientists to come and examine this splendid specimen whenever it was convenient. They shooed it away with carefully calibrated underwater explosions – without, I hope, giving it a headache.

Some new light has also been thrown on the giant squid (genus Architeuthis*). These creatures of the deep apparently cannot survive long in warm waters because their blood will not transport oxygen efficiently at more than 10°C. So if you ever meet one on the surface in tropical waters (*vide *the chapter 'Squid' in* Moby Dick*), it is almost certainly dying. I would not suggest that even the most ardent conservationist attempt mouth-to-beak resuscitation.*

*

Whether or not life began in the ocean – and some scientists are now doubting this – there can be no question but that the largest, and most bizarre, of living creatures are to be found in the sea. No man in his right senses could have imagined the sperm whale, or the giant squid – or the hideous little dragons of the abyss. Compared to them, there is nothing particularly remarkable about the 'Great Sea Serpent' – except for its success in eluding us.

Probably it isn't a serpent – but a fish or even a mammal. Still more probably, it isn't an 'it' – but a 'them'.

In any event, the game of hide and seek cannot last much longer. The two most powerful nations on the planet are straining their resources to make the ocean 'transparent' – so that they can detect each other's nuclear submarines. One day their vast undersea sonar arrays and other secret devices will turn up some surprises for the biologists . . .

BLESSINGS
IN DISGUISE

In the Spring of 1974, it fell to a class of schoolchildren in Oakland, California, to witness a strange and disturbing manifestation. The bleeding wounds of Christ – the stigmata – appeared on one of their classmates.

For at least 700 years, since St Francis of Assisi first manifested these signs, there have been cases where devout Roman Catholics have apparently found their bodies beginning to shed blood, as depicted in the statues and icons of crucifixion to be found in almost every Catholic church, however small or poor. Invariably these people have found themselves propelled into the tempestuous waters of religious enthusiasm, hailed as saints, denounced as charlatans, the centre of healing cults, objects of pilgrimage, catalysts for flagellation. Some have been canonized, others exposed as frauds, or anathematized as heretics.

But Emery High School, Oakland, is as remote as can be from the feverish obsessions of European religion. The children are mainly black, their parents Baptists, their fathers longshoremen in the Oaklands docks, or bus drivers across the bay in San Francisco.

In Easter week 1974 the Revd Anthony Burrus was teaching the fifth grade – bright children whose families he knew well and who were keen to grab at education. It was mid-morning, and during a maths lesson, when the stigmata came in most dramatic fashion to twelve-year-old Cloretta Robertson, a chubby girl, always neatly dressed, with a round face and twin bobs in her hair.

Mr Burrus said, 'It just happened like she was shot with a machine-gun right across her forehead. Blood was flowing all down her face, all over her eyes. It was as though there was a crown of thorns around her head and she was just smiling and talking.' Anthony Burrus had no doubt that he was seeing the final stage in an extreme case of stigmata – even St Francis had not displayed the signs of bleeding from the head – and a case unique in that it was happening to a non-white, non-Catholic girl.

The first signs had in fact begun two weeks earlier. 'She started to bleed in her hands,' said Mr Burrus. 'She would open her hands and the blood was coming out like a natural oil well. We went into the Principal's office and it was shocking to him. He called Cloretta's mother and she took her away to the doctor.' Over the next few days, Mr Burrus was to become used to the appearance of the stigmata. 'Many times she would sit in class doing her work and, without warning, she would come to my desk and say, "Mr Burrus I'm bleeding and I have to go to the back room." We would just go into the back room and pray together. We would hold hands and when I opened mine they would be covered with her blood. Sometimes she would go round showing it to the children. It just paralysed them.'

The very first signs had begun two years before. And every year since, as Easter has approached, Cloretta Robertson has been struck by the stigmata, sometimes just in a hand, but sometimes in all the six places of the traditional wounds of Christ: the hands, the feet, the left side and on the forehead. She has been exposed to repeated medical examinations and tests. Cloretta's mother, on the very first occasion, took her to the local doctor who cleaned her up, could find no sign of a wound in her hand, and sent her home. When she bled again the same day, Mrs Robertson took her to the Kaiser Hospital in Oakland where she was seen by Dr Kaia. Again she was cleaned up, but her hand kept on producing blood. 'I think practically every doctor they could get to her came,' said Mrs Robertson, 'and all they could say was "This is strange, this is very strange."'

Cloretta was referred to Dr Loretta Early, paediatrician at the West Oakland Health Center. Cloretta was sitting in her office, drawing, when she felt her hand starting to bleed. She showed Dr Early two or three drops of blood in the palm of her left hand. The doctor then watched transfixed for three or four minutes as blood welled up from the centre of the palm and spread down the palm's creases. When she wiped the blood away there was no wound, only a pea-size bluish discoloration.

Dr Early conducted elaborate tests on Cloretta's blood and the blood from the stigmata, but could prove only that the two were identical. She summoned a psychiatrist from the University of California at Berkeley, Dr Joseph Lifschutz, but they could find no medical explanation for Cloretta's condition except psychogenic purpura, that is, psychologically induced bleeding. All they were certain of was the event itself, which by now had been witnessed by nurses, schoolteachers, hospital staff, numerous doctors and the children of Emery High School. It was two years before they published their theories, by which time Cloretta had become the centre of a wondering cult at the New Light Baptist Church on the corner of Grove and Parker Streets in Oakland, and had felt herself able to cure minor illnesses, to halt the asthma attacks of the pastor's son Mark, to touch her aunt Winifred's stiff neck and restore it, and to heal cut legs and hands. 'Our church,' Pastor Hester told his congregation, 'has been chosen for the most wonderful manifestation, which we must cherish and be worthy of. The wounds of Christ have shown themselves on our Cloretta.'

Today, and in film taken in 1974, it is very apparent that Cloretta had been a happy girl, plump, smiling, attractive, a little shy but enjoying the attention the stigmata have given her. The doctors confirm that the family is 'very close, warm, positive and apparently emotionally and physically healthy'. But Cloretta was deeply religious even at the age of ten – the Bible virtually her only reading, praying every night and sometimes feeling that she heard her prayers answered, spending all Sunday in church and singing with the choir. A week before the stigmata began, a television film about the crucifixion had left her with vivid dreams, and then she had read *Crossroads*, John Webster's highly-charged book about the crucifixion. It is not difficult to imagine its impact on an impressionable young girl. But, as Dr Lifschutz says: 'Millions of people have felt the traumatic shock of visualizing the nails being hammered into the body of

Christ. Why should this thing happen to Cloretta? And more puzzling still – how?'

It was in September 1968 that the most venerated stigmatist of modern times, Padre Pio, was laid to rest at San Giovanni Rotondo in southern Italy. He had bled constantly from the hands and feet for more than fifty years and the process to have him declared 'Blessed' is already under way – the first stage towards what seems to be imminent sainthood.

The legends surrounding Padre Pio are legion. He is supposed to have had the gift of prophecy, even telling the present Pope John Paul II that he would one day be Pontiff. He is credited with innumerable miracles of healing, on a scale even larger than Lourdes: a girl born with no irises in the pupils of her eyes to whom he gave sight, paralysed people walking, cancer victims cured. Even the accounts of his life, which carry the 'Nihil Obstat' of the official Roman Catholic censor, include tales of 'bilocation' when the Padre is believed to have been in two places at once – appearing to Italian soldiers in North Africa in the Second World War and standing beside the beds of sick women when he was known never to have left the cloister. But above all the wonder of the stigmata brought worshippers in their hundreds of thousands to San Giovanni Rotondo, waiting often days on end to have their confessions heard by the celebrated priest.

Padre Pio was born into a peasant family at Pietralcina near Benevento. He entered the Capuchin brotherhood, already in poor health when he was ordained, but still noted for the most rigorous fasting and prayer. The stigmata appeared on him at the chapel of San Giovanni Rotondo – then an isolated and primitive village – on 20 September 1918, three days after the Capuchins had celebrated the feast of the stigmata of St Francis.

Padre Pio was alone in the chapel, praying. Suddenly, outside, a piercing cry was heard. One of the monks, Father Leone, rushed in to find Padre Pio lying unconscious on the floor with blood pouring from five places – both hands, both feet and the left side. For the next fifty years, the wounds seemed never to close, never to become infected, never to stop bleeding.

The Capuchins and the Vatican acted swiftly. Photographs were taken. Dr Luigi Romanelli was despatched to examine

Padre Pio; his report was, in essence, the same as the many that followed over the years, from Dr Festa, Dr Bignami and others. On the back and front of the hands, there were scabs, almost an inch across: the wound appeared to go right through them. The scabs always bled a little at the edges, and from time to time they came off, so that the wound bled more profusely. Both feet were in a similar state. Around the edges of the stigmata the flesh, even when examined under a magnifying glass, showed clear, almost translucent, with no sign of damage or inflammation. The chest stigma, like an inverted cross three inches long, gave the priest more pain than the other wounds, bleeding much more freely; Padre Pio reckoned he lost up to a cupful of blood on some days.

Almost immediately, as news of the stigmata spread, Padre Pio became the centre of an intense and enduring adulation. The Capuchins themselves carefully guarded their brother: none of the blood-stained garments was ever thrown away, but stored in a special room in the monastery. The Vatican was extremely circumspect, and in an ordinance which lasted to the end of his life, forbade him to publish any writings or to travel away from the monastery. This last, however, merely ensured that an unending stream of pilgrims came to him, queueing at the confessional, covering the walls of the chapel with scribbled messages imploring help and intercession, arriving in their hundreds at 5am each day, wheeling the sick and the dying into the church in the hope of a blessing and to hear him say mass.

The daily offerings and contributions soon mounted so that a gigantic hospital could be built beside the monastery. A vast array of literature appeared. The official biographer, Father Charles Carty, reflected the atmosphere which surrounded the long, early morning Mass, often an hour and a half or more: 'During Mass many of those present are bathed in the wonderful scent that comes from the father. Why does Padre Pio's Mass last so long? We cannot tell what transpires in his soul, so burning with love for Christ that he wears imprinted on his body the sacred wounds. If he has been called to suffer for all, surely his sufferings must increase during the Holy Sacrifice of the Mass, especially in the moment when Our Lord mystically renews the bloody sacrifice of Calvary. Padre Pio seems to be transfigured with grief, and in certain moments of the Mass his face shows signs of suffering incredible pain, his eyes seem on the verge of tears, his lips move as though in colloquy with Our Lord, truly present on the altar from the Consecration to the Communion.'

In this atmosphere of intense piety and adulation it is not hard to imagine the extreme pressure on a man who even in his youth had been wont to punish his body with fasting and spiritual exercises, beyond the usual demands of his faith.

After the early years of the stigmata no medical examinations were published, but Padre Pio appeared daily with his hands bandaged and often covered with woollen mittens. Only in his final days, in the late summer of 1968, according to the Capuchins, did the stigmata diminish. Over the years they had changed from the quite small holes shown in the early photographs of his hands taken 'under obedience', to the extensive scabs and bloodstains shown in the later pictures.

Padre Pio was buried in the monastery where he had lived all the fifty years since his stigmata had arrived. In that time the primitive remote village had been transformed into one of the major centres of pilgrimage in Europe. More than 100,000 people attended his funeral; the procession took more than three hours to move the open casket a mile and a half from the church. 'I was reminded,' wrote one priest, 'of another procession I had often read about. In 1226 the body of St Francis was carried the mile and a half from Porziuncula to Assisi. He too was a stigmatist. Neither Assisi nor San Giovanni Rotondo was a town rich in material things, but both were honoured with a stigmatist, a holy man of God.' And, indeed, Padre Pio did follow a line of intriguing cases of stigmata.

More than 100 years ago, the Belgian Academy investigated the case of Louise Lateau who, in the course of ecstatic trances, was producing stigmata in her hands. The Academy arranged for the girl's hand to be encased in a glass globe, 'a tube from which was carefully attached round the arm and sealed so as to exclude the use of any sharp instrument'. The blood flow was, nevertheless, found to occur as before. By the time she died in 1883 she had revealed the stigmata 800 times.

Louise was a peasant girl prone to receiving visions of St Ursula and St Roch and other, obscurer, saints. During meditation and prayer she would suddenly be struck rigid or collapse into paroxysms; until, one Friday in April 1868, the stigmata appeared – on hands and feet and beneath her left breast. From then on the pattern was utterly regular. Each Tuesday burning sensations would appear at the stigmata points, culminating, on a Thursday evening, in shooting pains. Large blisters developed on Friday mornings, the blisters would burst and the blood flow. Louise would then be given the communion wafer. The routine after that was prayer, followed, as the clock chimed two, by a half-hour trance. Next, a session on her knees. Then, finally, she would lie face down on the floor, arms outstretched, for an hour and a half or more. Suddenly the ecstasy would seem to end and she would get to her feet. By Saturday the bloody areas would have disappeared, leaving patches of pinkness on the skin but the body otherwise unaffected, until Tuesday came round again.

For fifteen years, until her death, Louise Lateau was studied by medical men and scientists. Dr Gerald Molloy, the rector of University College, Dublin in Ireland, described a visit to the Lateau house, which had already become half-shrine and half-circus: 'There is no wound properly so-called, but the blood seemed to force its way through the unbroken skin. In a very short time sufficient blood had flowed to gratify the devotion of pilgrims who applied their handkerchiefs until all the blood had been wiped away. This process was repeated several times during the course of our visit.'

The pattern of the Friday blood flow and the Saturday or Sunday restoration was repeated in two of the other cases which followed Louise Lateau. Gemma Galgani, who died at the age of twenty-five in 1903, acquired the stigmata after being, it was said, miraculously cured of tuberculosis. She was also endowed, her parish priest at Camigliani in Italy reported, with clairvoyant powers and with a talent for seeing ghosts. Her wounds appeared promptly at eight o'clock on a Thursday evening without any apparent preparation. 'The violence of the pain made her keep her hands convulsively closed, but the wounds seemed to go right through her hands and feet and were covered by a swelling that at first looked like clotted blood, whereas it was found to be fleshy, hard and like the head of a nail.' By Sunday, the marks were gone. Gemma in due course, became St Gemma, without being too much molested by men of science, protected by 'reverential delicacy inspired by the ecstatic in her mysterious state'.

No such consideration was shown to Therese Neumann, the stigmatic from Konnersreuth in Bavaria. She died in 1962 after thirty-seven years of attention from mystics, physicians and journalists. Therese was born in 1898 and by the time she was 20 had become bedridden, blind and paralysed, apparently from hysteria after a fire at a neighbour's farm. When St Theresa of Lisieux was beatified in 1925, Therese Neumann was suddenly cured of her blindness and, after visions of the child-saint, seemed to lose all her old symptoms and got out of bed. By the end of 1926 bleeding had appeared.

The American dermatologist Joseph V Klauder described the scene as he found it: 'The ecstasy began every Thursday between eleven and twelve o'clock and lasted until Friday afternoon. Therese would awaken suddenly from sleep, partly sit up and remain motionless for a short period. She would become deadly pale, with eyelids half closed and hands stretched out; blood-tinged tears would run down her face and clot on her chin and neck. After five or ten minutes she would sink back into the pillows and appear exhausted. When asked questions she would describe in a low voice what she had seen. Apparently she would live the whole scene at Calvary, following Christ at each step. In the final hour when she would experience the Crucifixion, she would sit for the whole hour in a half-upright position with arms extended and eyes wide open and staring.' Therese had stigmata on hands, feet and brow but, as time went on, it was only the passion of Holy Week which could produce bleeding from all the places at once.

Fraud is always a possibility, and with stigmata, self-inflicted wounding cannot always be ruled out. Dr Martini, in 1938, saw Therese Neumann making 'strange and very intense movements with her arms and legs under cover of her bed clothes during the hours before bleeding appeared'. Even with Padre Pio sceptics thought the iodine he used to rub into his hands might have damaged them and prolonged the bleeding. Confronted with the stigmata, local clergymen are usually devoid of doubt. 'These are the wounds of Christ', says Cloretta Robertson's Pastor Hester in Oakland. The American Capuchin priest, John Schug, described Padre Pio's marks as 'The real and visible wounds of the Crucifixion'. He asserted that Padro Pio also had the mark of the scourges: 'Cleonice Morcaldi gave Padre Pio a white linen shirt. Three days later he gave it back to her for washing. She looked at it and gasped: "Madonna, it is one flagellation." It was splattered with blood from top to bottom, from front to back.'

However the blood appears, it seems clear that the marks do not accord with the actual wounds of the crucifixion. All the evidence today is that the Roman method of crucifixion was to tie the arms to the cross with ropes and to drive in the nails through the wrists. (If the body had been supported solely through nails in the hands, the weight would probably have torn right through the flesh.) The stigmata, therefore, accord rather with the wounds shown on church statuary and in Renaissance painting – Gemma Galgani's wounds seem to have appeared in exactly the same places as those shown on the crucifix in her parish church. The variety of parts of the chest in which wounds manifest themselves seems to reflect the indecision of artists on a matter on which the Gospels are silent – where exactly did the Roman soldier's spear thrust penetrate? St John merely said the spear 'pierced his side, and forthwith came there out blood and water'.

But it seems hard to doubt that stigmata do appear. An intense religious devotion allied to a traumatic childhood seems to be a common factor – although Cloretta Robertson appears to have come from a happy and normal home, and a Swedish girl, studied by Dr Magnus Huss, produced bleeding without any religious overtones. The girl, Maria K, was beaten up when she was twenty-three years old. Afterwards, every couple of weeks, she would produce bleeding from the head, the ear and eyelids. Supervised in the Seraphim Hospital in Stockholm, she continued to produce blood without any marking on the skin except for a pinkness and tenderness. Dr Huss eventually found that Maria could produce the bleeding at will, simply by picking a quarrel with some other patient in order to wind herself up to the necessary emotional pitch.

Oscar Ratnoff, Professor of Medicine in Cleveland, Ohio, reported in 1969 that he had seen blood oozing out of the hair follicles on a patient's thigh, over an area as big as a silver dollar, during a period of severe emotional distress. Careful examination afterwards showed no signs of any wound, self-induced or otherwise. As Professor Ratnoff says, 'To describe such things is not the same as to explain them,' but he and his team have documented more than sixty cases in which patients, almost invariably women with hysterical personalities and the most gruelling of private lives, have been able to produce bruises on their bodies without any external damage. The whole process often took only an hour or two, therefore the patient could be reliably observed. First, there would be a redness or puffiness, soon followed by a blue ring around the site or a bruise covering the spot. Some of the bruises were spectacularly large – up to six inches – and the process could go on for many years.

Tests by American researchers Frank Gardner and Louis Diamond suggested that these patients might be sensitive to some element in their own blood, what is known as autoerythrocyte sensitization. But Ratnoff was left with the strong conclusion that the bleeding and bruising under the skin in his patients was triggered by their emotions. 'Our patients had more than their share of the griefs of the living,' he said. Eight had alcoholic husbands, twelve were repeatedly beaten by their husbands and five had had similar treatment from their parents. Eight more related experiences 'in which they had been confronted with individuals with severe physical disabilities of the lower extremities'. They all showed 'a predilection for painful and humiliating experiences, and a proneness to accidents, injuries and surgery'. Hysterical and masochistic traits were dominant. The picture seems convincing: intense emotional drives can produce weals, bruises, even bleeding through the pores of the skin.

During the Second World War doctors and psychiatrists working with troops became acquainted with the extraordinarily severe effects of battle on the minds of even the toughest soldiers. Almost no one could last longer than thirty days in continuous combat without first becoming battle-happy – a stage in which they would become reckless and wildly expose themselves to danger – and then collapsing into the total lethargy of battle fatigue. Usually the result was nervous collapse, often requiring very long periods of recuperation, and psychiatric and drug treatment. But sometimes, the fear and panic of combat produced more dramatic physical effects.

One of the most desperate episodes of the war took place just before Christmas 1944 at Bastogne in Belgium. The Germans had broken through the Allied front in the Ardennes and were pushing with their panzers towards the Channel ports in what promised to be a dangerous thrust behind the invading forces. At Bastogne, units of the American Army found themselves the last barrier to the success of this German offensive; a bitter and relentless fight developed.

On the morning of 21 December one soldier, a circus artist in civilian life and a veteran of the North Africa campaign, was knocked over by a shell explosion. He had no external injury. But he was blind. Back at the base hospital neurological ward, it slowly became apparent that there was no physical cause for the blindness, so the surgeons decided instead to try psychiatric treatment under hypnosis. The technique was the fearsome process of abreaction, in which, sometimes helped by drugs, the patient is made to re-live his experiences with an intensity that drives him to the point of total collapse. One session sufficed to bring back the man's sight but in the course of conjuring up the vividness of the battle experience, the psychiatrist told the soldier that he had been struck on the hand by a shell fragment. After he was awakened from hypnosis the soldier complained of a burning sensation in his hand. About four hours later a substantial blister appeared which eventually sloughed off, leaving a raw wound that cleared up three days later. The doctors were fascinated and tried other tests on the unfortunate soldier: they found that they could raise cold sores around his mouth by suggestion under hypnosis; they made identical small cuts in the fingers on both his hands, telling him that the right hand would bleed but that the left hand would feel no pain and would not bleed. The left hand did not bleed.

Since those wartime days, it has become clear that the scars of the mind can be transmuted into lacerations on the body, often years after the events themselves took place.

Dr Albert Mason, a Harley Street doctor, told of a disturbing experience with a patient he called Mrs Stavely. She obviously had a considerable effect on him at first meeting: 'large soft violet eyes, delicately chiselled features, perfectly shaped lips and rounded chin. A gay little hat suited her fair hair perfectly, her dark brown costume was expertly tailored, quiet and expensive, a large python had provided skin for her neat shoes and handbag. Her figure was trim, and I imagine that her vital statistics would have been applauded by the connoisseurs.' She also had a bad back.

Mason concentrated on treating the back trouble by hypnosis; it duly disappeared, only to be followed by a skin rash. Mason banished the rash, only to find the appearance of fibrositis. Clearly, there was some deep-seated problem and Mason set about discovering it. Mrs Stavely had by now developed an inability to hold anything hard or metallic, even a knife or fork. Once she was in deep hypnosis, Mason gave her a 'jerk' hammer to hold and told her to recall the experiences which had made hard objects repellent to her. 'Then occurred one of the most extraordinary things I have ever seen since I began to study as a medical student.

'Mrs Stavely began to move as though she were uncomfortable; she began to rub her shoulders on the couch and soon she started to scratch them. And as I watched with fascination, an urticarial weal began to form on her neck and on the part of her chest which I could see above her dress. It was a fantastic sight. There was this beautiful woman lying on the couch holding my hammer, and as the minutes went by a long raised weal, white in the centre and with inflamed red edges, tailing off into a flare of angry scarlet appeared on her neck and chest.'

The cause of the eruption soon emerged. As Mason puts it: 'Her husband was one of those unfortunate creatures who can get sexual feeling only through dressing up in women's clothes. He also found it necessary to suffer pain, and he kept asking his wife to hit him with a stick. She, highly sensitive, had shrunk from such brutish lovemaking, but had finally agreed and suffered for it by taking the pain to herself in her mind.'

Cases of weals, even blisters, appearing without physical wounding or damage are at least comprehensible to conventional medical science, for there is a rare condition known as dermatographia which has some similarities: sufferers react to the slightest touch. Anyone can write their name on a victim's back using only a feather. Even in normal people there is rapid reaction to quite light touch: run a pencil down the arm, and immediately a white line appears as the blood vessels contract to minimize any blood loss. Then the line turns bright red as the blood rushes back. Next a ridge shows up where histamine has leaked to start the healing process. The result is a striking weal, even from such a small 'injury'.

It is conceivable that a vividly imagined wound might initiate the same process and produce the still extraordinary sight of weals or blisters appearing without any physical cause. Dr Robert Moody reported in *The Lancet* a wartime case of an officer who in the past had been tied to his bed by the wrists to prevent him from sleepwalking. Years later, during his nightmares, he produced weals which bled.

Over the years the power of the human mind to produce physical changes in the body has produced some extraordinary, even comic, testimony. Thinking, it would seem, really can increase your sexual attributes.

Dr Richard D Willard of the University of Chicago in 1977 set about trying to increase the breast size of a number of women – by mind power. The women were hypnotized then treated to luscious images of full and rounded breasts, visions of ripe and fruitful bosoms, suckling from erect and fulsome nipples, pictures of Hollywood perfection. After twelve weeks Dr Willard reported to the American *Journal of Clinical Hypnosis*, that forty-six per cent had found it necessary to increase bra size, and all but fifteen per cent had noted a significant increase in their breast size. 'This report shows that through hypnosis and visual imagery the size of an organ can be affected and, specifically in this experiment, enlarged,' pronounced Dr Willard.

In 1960 another doctor had tried a similar treatment on a small-breasted girl. Two years later Dr Milton H Erickson was able to report breast development of 'one inch thick on one side and one and a half inches on the other side'. The other results he claimed for these experiments may perhaps have been more useful: the girl broke off her engagement to a forty-seven-year-old unemployed alcoholic and took up weekly reading of those encouraging passages in the Song of Solomon:

> O Prince's daughter, the joints of thy
> thighs are like jewels, the work of the
> hands of a cunning workman.

> Thy navel is like a round goblet which
> wanteth not liquor; thy belly is like an
> heap of wheat set about with lilies.

> Thy two breasts are like two young roes
> that are twins.

> Thy stature is like to a palm tree and thy
> breasts to clusters of grapes.

Engagement to a more suitable young man was soon reported.

However they are produced, the stigmata at least can be very profitable. In southern Spain, at Palmar de Troya near Seville, there is currently a rival Pope, calling himself Gregory the Eighteenth, otherwise Clemente Dominguez Gomez, an ex-insurance clerk.

Gomez claims that at six o'clock in the morning on 2 April 1971 Christ came down and touched him on the forehead with a crucifix that was dripping blood. Since then, Clemente Gomez has from time to time exhibited the chest wound and the crown of thorns wounds on his forehead. He also persuaded a real archbishop to ordain him, first as a priest and then as a bishop – thus allowing him to ordain hundreds of others, mostly appealing youths – and then get himself elected Pope. He has a large green plastic cathedral in a field in which twelve-hour Masses are conducted every night for the thousands of pilgrims who come to the site. He now owns an array of property in Seville and in Palmar de Troya. The Vatican has excommunicated Clemente Gomez, but the stigmata continue. So do the pilgrims. And so do the donations.

In the same year that Cloretta Robertson's wounds manifested themselves, another American girl, Lucy Rael from Questa, New Mexico, exhibited the signs of stigmata which launched her on a spectacular career of Pentecostal evangelism. Through Texas, California, and the states of the south and west Lucy packs in the crowds, with the special bonus that her daughter Angelica now shows signs of bleeding too.

A reporter from the *Atlanta Journal* wrote: 'When Sister Lucy lifted her blood-stained hands, the crowd went wild. Mrs Callie Taylor of Hartford Avenue said, "I touched her hands, there were holes there and blood was coming out. Her feet also had wounds." ' There is an air of revivalist showbiz surrounding Lucy Rael's stigmata, which seem to appear without warning at the emotional height of her crusade meetings. She has never been reported to have undergone detailed medical examinations in hospital, but a Texas doctor, Charles Melenyzer from the Lutheran Hospital in San Antonio, saw her during a service. 'I've never seen anything like it before and I'll remember it for a long time. The blood was more the texture of serum, but it congealed as normal blood does. There was no evidence of any puncture of the skin.' More than ten years on, Lucy Rael is still running a flourishing healing ministry, and still bleeding. As her posters say: 'See for yourself this miraculous sign of blood that was foretold by the prophet Joel and confirmed in the second chapter of Acts. Thousands have been amazed by this stigmata. The deaf hear, the blind see, the lame walk.'

There are other signs of holiness, as well as the bleeding wounds, claimed by stigmatics. Therese Neumann, Louise Lateau and others are also supposed to have gone for months or years without taking food or drink (one of Louise Lateau's investigators did find bread and fruit in a cupboard in her room) but such claims are notoriously easy to make and serious investigation is liable to end in tragedy, as happened in 1869 with the little Welsh girl, Sarah Jacobs.

Sarah lived in a remote one-storeyed farmhouse at Lletherneuadd in south Wales, but she became a national celebrity when the local vicar wrote to the papers claiming that she had 'not partaken of a single grain of food for sixteen months. She did, occasionally, swallow a few drops of water during the first few months of this period; but now she does not even do that.' Within weeks the local boys were greeting trains at the nearest station with placards proclaiming 'Fasting Girl' and offering to guide visitors to the bedside where they found 'a very pretty little girl of twelve reclining fancifully dressed, crowned with a wreath and decked in all sorts of gay ribbons, who smiled upon them and was very pleased to be admired'. Shillings and half-crowns were, it seems, not infrequently left behind in appreciation.

Sarah had already emerged from two weeks of day and night supervision by a local committee without them detecting any evidence of deceit or chicanery when she had the misfortune to be visited by Dr Robert Fowler, vice president of the distinguished English scientific body, the Hunterian Society. Dr Fowler wrote indignantly to *The Times* demanding an investigation. Sarah's parents raised no objection, and so a medical committee was set up with four nurses brought down from Guy's Hospital in London – one Welsh-speaking – to supervise the girl under strict instructions.

The result was sadly predictable. For four days Sarah was fine and cheerful. Then she went into a decline, with a racing pulse, sunken eyes and insomnia. The London *Daily News* did complain about the 'grotesque proceedings which are taking place at the bedside of a little girl in Wales' but the medical magazine *The Lancet* and most of the press seemed quite content. No one on the medical committee or among the nurses seems to have thought of trying to make Sarah eat, nor of abandoning the vigil, even when she was 'threatening to sink'. On the second Friday she seemed to lose the power of speech and at three in the afternoon she died.

There was a posthumous uproar. Five of the doctors on the committee were charged with killing the girl, but they were released by Carmarthen magistrates. The parents were not so lucky. Mr Justice Hannen sent them both down to hard labour. All the evidence suggests they had truly believed in Sarah's powers. A little girl's fantasies had exacted a terrible price.

ARTHUR C CLARKE COMMENTS:

For over 700 years, Roman Catholics have revered a tiny but growing band of people who appear to bleed with the wounds of Christ. They're called stigmatics and the wounds they show – 'stigmata' – mimic those of Christ on the cross: the bleeding hands and feet, the crown of thorns, the pierced side. Many stigmatics have attracted huge bands of followers. Some have become saints, others have been denounced as heretics, or proved to be frauds. Behind the religious phenomenon lies a fascinating medical mystery, which doctors are still trying to untangle.

You may be surprised to know that I have no difficulty in accepting this phenomenon. Have you considered what happens when your mind orders your body to do something? If by an act of will you can raise your finger – why not a blister?

CIRCLES AND
STANDING STONES

STONEHENGE AND AVEBURY

On a fine Midsummer morning dawn breaks slowly over
Salisbury Plain. For a full hour before sunrise, Stonehenge and
the barrows of the great prehistoric cemetery which surround it
stand out eerily in the first yellow-green light of the day.

In the shadow of the stones, the Druids, hooded and robed
in white, have begun their annual ritual of fire and water, cele-
brating the advent of the year's longest day. Inside the circle
itself are the lucky few with official passes: journalists, photographers and the villagers of nearby Amesbury. Outside, beyond
a protective barbed-wire fence, a small crowd has gathered.

The sight they have all come to see begins a few seconds after
5am, when the first rays of the sun appear over the long lip of
the horizon. It is the start of an event precisely planned by the
people who built Stonehenge almost 4,000 years ago. Only at
Midsummer can watchers in the centre of the circle see the sun
rise in line with the Heel Stone, forty yards (37m) outside the
ring.

As the first rays appear, the Druids' celebration reaches its
climax with the cry: 'Arise, Oh Sun! Let the darkness of night
fade before the beams of thy glorious light!'

But the drama of their ceremonies, so fitting to the time and
place, masks the authentic mystery of Stonehenge: for these
Druids have no true place here.

There is no doubt that Druids did exist in Britain before the
Roman Conquest. Julius Caesar described them as men of great
learning 'given to discussions of stars and their movements, the

size of the universe and of the earth'. Some of their activities were less refined, as their rituals included human sacrifices in which they would use 'figures of immense size whose limbs, woven out of twigs, they fill with living men and set on fire, and the men perish in a sheet of flame'. However, historians and archaeologists have found no hard evidence to link the Druids with stone circles and although very little is known about the Druids at all, what evidence there is in ancient texts suggests that they were at the height of their influence a thousand years after the completion of Stonehenge, when its original purpose may have long since been forgotten.

Modern Druids, arriving for the summer solstice ceremonies by car and luxury coach, owe their place at Stonehenge to the romantic theories of seventeenth- and eighteenth-century antiquarians like John Aubrey (1626–1697) and William Stukeley (1687–1765). They read Julius Caesar's description of the Druids, and, quite without evidence, associated them with the standing stones and stone circles they came across in the course of their travels through the British countryside. So today, visitors to these 'Druid Temples' imagine that they were built by the mysterious priests of the cruel and ancient Druid faith.

In fact, no one knows for certain who erected the stone circles or why, and the reason is simple: the builders had no writing. The architects of Stonehenge could therefore not leave behind them any documents or inscriptions to explain why they chose to build this extraordinary construction on Salisbury Plain; why they mixed local stones with others quarried more than 200 miles away in southwest Wales; why they demolished and rebuilt it several times in the course of a thousand years; or why they balanced great stones on top of each other in a style more suited to building in wood. Above all, they left no clues to the function of Stonehenge, and, therefore, to the reason why the circle is aligned to the sunrise at Midsummer.

Stonehenge is no isolated mystery, for it is just one of a thousand prehistoric stone circles scattered throughout the British Isles and northern France. They were built, archaeologists believe, between 3250 and 1500BC. The circles that remain have survived because they were built in what are now remote and sparsely inhabited regions: perhaps thousands of others have not stood the test of time and have been deliberately destroyed or absorbed into the landscape.

In almost every respect, stone circles present a puzzle to archaeologists. Firstly, their size varies enormously. Keel Cross in County Cork, for instance, is only nine feet (2.75m) in diameter, whereas Avebury in Wiltshire encompasses a whole village.

Avebury, alone, is an incredible undertaking. It covers twenty-eight and a half acres (11.5ha) and its original ditch was higher than a two-storey house. It is difficult to imagine just how hard it must have been for the builders to cut the chalk upland, using 'picks' made of discarded deer antlers.

To make the main circle, stones weighing as much as sixty tons were transported many miles, perhaps on wooden sledges secured by leather ropes. Before the sledge could move, hundreds of trees would have had to be cut down to give a clear path in what was then a heavily forested area. In 1938, when a small eight-ton stone was restored to its original position in the circle, it took twelve men five days using steel hawsers. The building of Avebury must therefore have been the work of many generations of people whose equipment was primitive and whose life was a short brutal fight for survival.

A look at the map raises more questions: there are no stone circles in southeast Britain – perhaps because these people preferred to build in wood, while in northeast Scotland there are often several circles in a very small area.

Baffling, too, is the style of their construction which varies from area to area. In the west of England, the circles are spacious and open, while sites in northeastern Scotland are smaller with an extraordinary arrangement of stones as their focal point: a mighty rock on its side flanked by two uprights.

Furthermore, archaeologists have found almost nothing to help them explain the purpose of the circles. Professor Richard Atkinson, of University College, Cardiff, who began digging at Stonehenge in the 1950s, says:

> You have to settle for the fact that there are large areas of the past that we cannot find out about. Stone circles are barren archaeological sites. There is almost nothing in them to suggest what went

on there, and absolutely nothing has ever been found which has enabled us to know with certainty what they were for.

The finds at Stonehenge bear out this view. There are antler picks used to dig the stone holes, mauls for dressing the stones, pieces of flint and axe, fragments of pottery from different periods, bone pins, and the occasional skeleton. But neither separately nor together do they tell us what went on there or what was in the minds of the people who placed or dropped them within the circle. This is all the more surprising since we know the site was used for about a thousand years. The only clue may lie in the very scarcity of finds: there is no trace of 'litter' that you would expect to find where there had been houses and settlements. 'It is as though the people who built the circles treated them like we treat church,' says Atkinson. 'They were clearly special places where you didn't drop litter.'

PREHISTORIC GEOMETRY

While archaeologists flounder, mathematicians and engineers have discovered an additional mystery. They say that many circles were deliberately designed to be anything but circular. This strange property was first pointed out by Professor Alexander Thom, a former Professor of Engineering at Oxford University, who has been surveying megalithic sites since the 1930s. From measurements made in circles all over the British Isles and northern France, Thom has found several types of design. Some, like Machrie Moor on the Isle of Arran in Scotland, are ellipses; others, like a circle surrounding a tomb at Clava Cairns near Inverness, are egg-shaped; while others like the spectacular Long Meg and Her Daughters in the English Lake District, are flattened rings. 'In fact, so many stone circles aren't circular that my father and I no longer refer to them as circles. We call them stone rings,' says Professor Thom's son and collaborator, Dr Archie Thom. If the Thoms are correct, their conclusions suggest that the people of prehistoric Britain worked out geometry for themselves a full 2,000 years before Pythagoras.

Although this is quite possible, Dr John Edwin Wood, who has spent many years studying the layouts of stone circles, believes that all that was required was not so much mathematical geometry as we know it, but a highly developed sense of shape. Castlerigg in Cumbria, for example, may have been laid out with a few lengths of rope and some pegs. The circle builders would have laid out a series of equilateral triangles. Then, in a series of movements in which one main line would have swung round some pegs and free of others, the designers would have been able to describe the arcs that create a flattened ring or an ellipse. It still leaves the question why should the circle builders have gone to such lengths to make circles that are not circular? Since the patterns are repeated, and about a third of all stone circles in Britain fall into one of the half dozen categories, the people must have deliberately decided to draw these shapes. Moreover, egg shapes, flattened rings and ellipses are late developments: the earlier the circle, the more likely it is to be truly circular, so there is ample evidence that ancient man had perfected the art of laying out accurate circles.

This raises yet more questions. What prompted the circle builders to make their layouts more and more complicated? How were they able to transmit their ideas throughout prehistoric Britain where in many places the forests were so dense that, it is said, a squirrel could run from Chelmsford to Anglesey without breaking cover once?

ASTRONOMICAL ALIGNMENTS

Nothing about stone circles is more mysterious or magical than the question of their astronomical alignments. The idea that some circles were aligned to the sun, moon or even the stars is not new. It certainly dates back to the eighteenth century when William Stukeley noted in his book on Stonehenge that the stones were aligned to the Midsummer sunrise. The simplest and most dramatic evidence that prehistoric man studied and exploited the movements of celestial bodies comes not from stone circles but from two magnificent chambered tombs – one in Ireland, the other on Mainland in Orkney.

*

Newgrange Tumulus is sited on the banks of the River Boyne, a few miles down narrow country lanes from the city of Drogheda in the Irish Republic. Since being restored, its great curving mound, faced with brilliant white quartz and inset with oval granite boulders, reveals it to have been one of the architectural wonders of ancient times. Although it is little known outside Ireland, Newgrange has a special significance: it was built in about 3250BC, about 500 years before the Pyramids of Egypt. It is therefore the oldest existing building in the world.

Five thousand years ago, the people who farmed in the lush pastures of the Boyne Valley hauled 200,000 tons of stone from the river bank a mile away and began to build Newgrange. At the foot of the mound, they set ninety-seven massive kerbstones and carved many of them with intricate patterns. Inside, with 450 slabs, they built a passage leading to a vaulted tomb, and placed a shallow basin of golden stone in each of its three side chambers.

Newgrange had been discovered by chance in 1699. In the 1960s, Prof Michael O'Kelly of University College, Cork, began excavating and restoring it.

As O'Kelly's team removed the grass and weeds from the mound, they came across a curious rectangular slit above the door. It was half-closed by a square block of crystallized quartz, apparently designed to work as a shutter. There were scratches on the quartz: clearly it had often been slid to and fro, providing a narrow entrance to the tomb above the main door, which was firmly sealed with a five-ton slab of stone.

But what was the slit for? It was too small and too far from the ground to be an entrance for people. Professor O'Kelly remembered a local tradition which said that the sun always shone into the tomb at Midsummer. Perhaps the 'roofbox', as it came to be known, was designed to admit the summer sun to the tomb without the entrance stone having to be moved. 'But it was quite obvious to us that it couldn't happen at Midsummer because of the position of the sun,' says O'Kelly. 'So if the sun was to shine in at all, the only possibility would be in Midwinter.'

In December 1967, Michael O'Kelly drove from his home in Cork to Newgrange. Before the sun came up he was at the tomb, ready to test his theory. 'I was there entirely alone. Not a soul stood even on the road below. When I came into the tomb I knew there was a possibility of seeing the sunrise because the sky had been clear during the morning.'

He was, however, quite unprepared for what followed. As the first rays of the sun appeared above the ridge on the far bank of the River Boyne, a bright shaft of orange light struck directly through the roofbox into the heart of the tomb.

I was literally astounded. The light began as a thin pencil and widened to a band of about 6in. There was so much light reflected from the floor that I could walk around inside without a lamp and avoid bumping off the stones. It was so bright I could see the roof 20ft above me.

I expected to hear a voice, or perhaps feel a cold hand resting on my shoulder, but there was silence. And then, after a few minutes, the shaft of light narrowed as the sun appeared to pass westward across the slit, and total darkness came once more.

The builders must have sat here on the hillside, perhaps for a number of years, at the winter solstice period, watching the point of sunrise moving southward along the horizon, eventually determining the point where it began to turn back again. Having established this, they could then have put a line of pegs into the ground and laid out the plan of the passage.

However, there was one more problem to resolve. The roofbox would have had to have been precisely aligned to the horizon and, as each of the stone slabs weighs about a ton, the position of the slit would have had to have been determined before the building began. Add to this the fact that the tomb was built on a hill, with the chamber entrance six feet (1.8m) above the entrance, and the achievement of the builders of Newgrange is all the more astounding.

On Mainland in the Orkney Isles, stands Maes Howe, another passage grave built about 2670BC, 600 years after Newgrange. Set at the edge of a loch, flanked by the gaunt stones of the Circle of Stenness on one side and by the raked Ring of Brodgar on the other, Maes Howe is probably the least visited of all the architectural wonders of the ancient world. A passage leads from its low entrance to a chamber sixteen feet (4.9m) high. The walls are built of dry stones, so tightly wedged together that it is impossible to push a knife blade between them.

Every year, on 21 December, members of old-established Orkney families call at the farm across the road for the key to Maes Howe, and are let into the tomb at three o'clock in the afternoon. They come to its dark chamber to watch not the dawn but the sunset.

At the winter solstice, when the sun sets over the Barnstone twenty-two yards (20.1m) away, its last rays light up the dark chamber of Maes Howe for the only time in the year. Just as at Newgrange, the sun can penetrate the chamber through an eighteen-inch (46cm) 'letter box' above the tomb's blocking slab. This also may explain another mystery of Maes Howe – a strange bend in the entrance passage, which could have been designed to admit the sun after the tomb had been extended.

It is thought that stone circles were built many years after chambered tombs like Newgrange, and may recall their shape. This theory is reinforced by the fact that Newgrange is surrounded by the beginnings of a circle, and Maes Howe by a low earth bank. Whole 'complexes' – consisting of a tomb and a circle for each family – like the Circle of Stenness and Maes Howe tomb in Orkney were built at the same time and this suggests that a tradition of incorporating astronomical alignments into engineering projects may have arisen among prehistoric people. Certainly, there are clear alignments at many stone circles. One of the most spectacular of all is at Long Meg and Her Daughters in Cumbria. Here, at Midwinter, the sun sets over Long Meg herself, a stone more than nine and a half feet (2.9m) high, standing outside the circle and, significantly, of a different geological type to her fifty-nine 'Daughters'.

Professor Alexander Thom puts forward the idea that prehistoric man had built the circles as astronomical indicators and that the alignments to the sun, moon or stars helped him to determine key dates in the year. One way of doing this was, Thom believes, to align stones with distinctive geographical features on the horizon.

A HOUSE OF THE DEAD

The problem is that theories based on astronomy cannot provide the whole answer to the mystery of the stone circles, because most circles do not have precise astronomical alignments. It is far more likely that alignments provide only *part* of the answer to the mystery of stone circles and that they were an important element in the ceremonies and religious ritual of ancient Britain.

Professor O'Kelly believes that this is what the builders of Newgrange intended when they aligned their tomb to the midwinter sunrise. He believes that the people whose bones were placed in the stone basins in the chamber had qualities especially valued in their society – perhaps they had the gift of prophecy or the 'evil eye' – and that Newgrange was designed as a temple for the spirits of the dead. As he waits in the tomb for the sun to rise on the shortest day of the year, O'Kelly is fond of speculating about the ceremonies which may have gone on there five thousand years ago.

> I think that the people who built Newgrange built not just a tomb but a house of the dead, a house in which the spirits of special people were going to live for a very long time. To ensure this, the builders took special precautions to make sure the tomb stayed completely dry, as it is to this day. Sand was brought from the shore near the mouth of the Boyne ten miles away, and packed into the joints of the great roof stones along with putty made from burnt soil. And to make absolutely sure that there would be no possibility of rainwater percolating through, they cut grooves in the roof slabs to channel it away. If the place was merely designed to get rid of dead bones, there would be no point in doing all this.

On the day of the solstice he envisages a group of people gathered in front of the tomb's decorated entrance stone in the pre-dawn darkness. He believes that as sunrise approached, someone climbed up to the roofbox and removed the blocks of quartz which temporarily closed it. What then went on is pure speculation. Perhaps the people made offerings to the spirits of the dead. (There is evidence of such a practice at a similar tomb in Denmark where the remains of 4,000 food vessels were found in front of the kerbstones.) Or perhaps they wished to ask the spirits of the dead for their help in the year to come.

If O'Kelly's interpretation of the magical phenomenon at Newgrange is on the right lines, it is tempting to imagine similar ceremonies in the circles, triggered off by celestial events.

ENERGY TRANSMITTERS

But there are stranger theories to explain the purpose of the circles. Stonehenge, for instance, has been imagined as an ancient racecourse, a bullring, a war memorial, the tomb of Boadicea, and a base for UFOs. While few people now take those ideas seriously, another theory has caused much excitement in recent years (though not among archaeologists). Its adherents believe that the stones of ancient circles may harness and transmit energy from the earth and sun, and that they were erected in places where this energy could be tapped. This, they say, would explain the ancient belief that the stones have magical powers of healing, a claim recorded by the twelfth-century historian, Geoffrey of Monmouth. Writing of Stonehenge, he says, '. . . in these stones there is a mystery and a healing against many ailments . . . for not a stone is there that is wanting in virtue or leechcraft.'

It is a fascinating idea, and in many ways just as reasonable as the vague legends of dancing virgins and human sacrifice. In 1979, one group of investigators, instigators of an experiment they call the Dragon Project, published some intriguing preliminary results of a study undertaken at the Rollright Stones – a circle of seventy-seven weather-beaten stones in the Oxfordshire countryside. The team, led by a scientist, reported that around dawn it had detected ultrasonic pulses emanating from the stones. They made the same experiment at more modern versions of standing stones such as concrete Ordnance Survey Trig Points and detected no such pulses.

So were stone circles ancient transmitters of energy, electrical spas for the sick and lame? It will sound preposterous to many people, and the burden of proof undoubtedly rests upon the advocates of 'earth energies' but scientists have seen stranger theories proved correct. However, the likelihood is that the true purpose of stone circles is less exotic. The few people who have made an intensive study of stone circles see them as centres of religion and celebration for the families and communities scattered throughout the deep forests of prehistoric Britain. 'You have to reckon with dancing in stone circles,' says Stuart Piggott the former professor of Archaeology at Edinburgh University and one of the leading authorities on stone circles. 'There are, after all, two basic kinds of dance – in a line or in a circle. Did they perhaps dance round the stones or along the avenues leading to the great circle of Avebury?'

At one related site a musical instrument was found: a whistle carved from a swan's leg bone. At a site in Wales, an archaeologist found that the surrounding earth had been impacted by constant marching or dancing. 'They may be enclosures for the gods,' says Piggott, 'and the scarcity of finds may be due to ritual cleaning or to the possibility that people rarely invaded the sacred territory within the stones.'

RELIGIOUS RITUALS

Dr Aubrey Burl, an archaeologist, has made the most comprehensive study ever of the evidence gleaned from past excavations of stone circles and of the theories advanced to explain them. As a result, he believes the circles were the churches, chapels and cathedrals of ancient times and is prepared to speculate on what went on in them.

To explain his theories he chose the rugged but romantic setting of a small circle set in a golden barley field at Castle Fraser near Aberdeen in North East Scotland. This circle, like the others in the area, has a feature which, until Burl began to study it, was unexplained: a stone on its side, lying to the southwest, flanked by two upright stones. Even today, the precision of the circle's ancient builders is breathtaking. A spirit-level placed on any of these recumbent stones, in any circle, shows it to be exactly level after four thousand years.

Dr Burl discovered that the moon seems to pause above the recumbent stone and hover between its two flankers at some point during its nightly journey. Burl believes that since this could not have helped to establish points in a calendar, it must have been designed to play an important part in rituals, just as the sun may have dominated rites at Newgrange and Maes Howe.

Burl speculates: 'It could have been the place where people thought the dead went to, or where the living came from. It could have been the giver or the taker of life. It could have been the place from which good harvests or spirits came.'

Support for the idea that these Scottish circles, at least, were laid out for moon rituals comes from a curious discovery made in some of them: hundreds of quartz pebbles, which Burl says may possibly have represented miniature moons and almost certainly reflected the moonlight.

From the discoveries made at places like Castle Fraser, Aubrey Burl can evoke the rituals which may have been practised there.

> These are places of dread. The people who built those circles were people who had very insecure lives. They had no knowledge of what caused a blizzard or drought or an epidemic. They saw their children dying; they saw their crops failing: not every year, but, when it did happen, they had no means of stopping it, because they had no understanding of it. Now, if you're in that sort of situation, you either take an attitude of *Che Sera, Sera* – what will be, will be – or else you try to do something about it.

What the circle builders tried to do, Burl believes, was to pray to the spirits of the dead to intercede for them. The recumbent stones may symbolize the entrance to a tomb – there is a magnificent carved stone which may have inspired them at the entrance to Newgrange – and the deposits of bone suggest rites of death. Indeed, at Loanhead of Daviot, another recumbent stone circle near Castle Fraser, five pounds of tiny bones were found: the pitiful remains of many different children. There are traces, too, of fires which could have been funeral pyres. The ceremonies may have reached their height when the moon stood over the recumbent stone, framed by the flankers, and every nineteen years, because of the strange way the moon moves in the sky, its orb would have been so low on the horizon that it would have seemed to have rolled along the top of the stone itself: a miraculous event indeed.

Although Burl's theories seem far more plausible than tales of ancient astronomical élites or mysterious sources of energy, there can be no final answer. After so many thousands of years, we can never know for certain anything about the people who left behind these mute stone testaments to their beliefs except that they were our ancestors, and that the stones are therefore part of our heritage and culture.

ARTHUR C CLARKE COMMENTS:

Only one thing can be stated with certainty about such structures as Stonehenge: the people who built them were much more intelligent than many who have written books about them.

It cannot be too firmly stressed that the ancient architects – our ancestors of only two hundred generations ago! – were men exactly like us. If they had been snatched up by a time traveller as infants, and carried forward to our age, they could have been astronauts or scientists or newspaper editors – or you, gentle reader ... There is no need to invoke any magical or mysterious powers, still less the intervention of any 'superior' beings, to explain their achievements.

What we cannot explain – and may never be able to – is: why did they do these things? Yet throughout history men have engaged on vast enterprises which were often meaningless to later generations. We can no longer recapture the mentality of those who built the great cathedrals, even though we have good written records of the Middle Ages and often know the very names of the master masons involved. How much more difficult, then, to understand the motives of men who had no way of sending their thoughts and beliefs into the future – except by the mute evidence of their labours?

It is only very recently that clear-headed archaeologists – as opposed to woolly-minded mystics – have accepted the view that 'primitive' men may have known much more about astronomy, geometry, and surveying than – well, the average city-dweller of today. Just how *much more is still in dispute, and likely to remain so until many more of these ancient circles have been investigated and measured.*

It is always very dangerous to say 'there are some things that can never *be known'. We can now measure the temperature of long-vanished seas, the strength and direction of the earth's magnetic field ten thousand years ago, and recapture much other information locked up in bones, clays, tree rings, and sedimentary rocks ... So perhaps some day we may be able to open up a window on the past, as H G Wells dreamed long ago in his short story 'The Grisly Folk':*

> *A day may come when these recovered memories may grow as vivid as if we in our own persons had been there and shared the thrill and the fear of those primordial days; a day may come when the great beasts of the past will leap to life again in our imaginations, when we shall walk again in vanished scenes, stretch painted limbs we thought were dust, and feel again the sunshine of a million years ago.*

MALEDICTIONS

Even today men and women are hexed to death – killed by fear and spells – not only in Dahomey and Haiti, the lands of voodoo, but in London and New York, Montreal and Oklahoma City.

The symbols and instruments of death are freely on sale. Call in at the Cracker Jack Store, 435 South Rampart Street, New Orleans, or down the road at 521 St Philip Street, and the black candles of death are only three dollars each. The system is to buy seven candles and burn them for seven minutes on seven days. Underneath must be a picture of the victim – or merely the name, on a scrap of paper. If the candles are turned upside down each day, the hexing is allegedly even swifter and more efficacious.

In the Harlem market in New York City, the stalls offer bats' blood and graveyard dust. In Brazzaville, in the Congo, there is a thriving export market in the potions and implements of killing, displayed in rows of competing stalls beside the butchers and the yam sellers. While a severed gorilla's hand is worth a king's ransom, the heads of tropical birds and dried corpses of bats are available by the kilo. Much of this is for domestic use, but agents send regular supplies to Paris and to Notting Hill in London.

Europeans have testified to the effectiveness of hexing ever since the age of exploration began and they came into contact with more primitive, or at least less rationalist, peoples. In 1587, Soares de Souza saw men from the Tupinambas Indians collapse and die when sentenced by the priests of the tribe. In New Zealand, one of the early settlers reported that a Maori woman died within the day when she was told she had eaten 'forbidden fruit' taken from a tabooed place. Another New Zealander reported in 1890: 'I have seen a strong young man die the same day he was tapued; the victims die under it, as though their strength ran out as water.'

In Australia, Dr Herbert Basedow saw a man 'boned' – a bone pointed at him as a sign of death.

> He stands aghast, with his eyes staring at the treacherous pointer, and with his hands lifted as though to ward off the fatal medium, which he imagines is pouring into his body. His cheeks blanch and his eyes become glassy, and the expression of his face becomes horribly distorted. He attempts to shriek but usually the sound chokes in his throat, and all that one might see is froth at his mouth. His body begins to tremble and the muscles twist involuntarily. He sways backwards and falls, and after a short time appears to be in a swoon, but soon after he writhes as if in mortal agony and, covering his face with his hands, begins to moan.
>
> After a while he becomes very composed and crawls to his wurley. From this time on he sickens and frets, refusing to eat and keeping aloof from the daily affairs of the tribe.

Death quickly follows.

The only escape seems to be to persuade the person who inflicted the 'boning' to withdraw its power. Dr S M Lambert of the Rockefeller Foundation was called to deal with Rob, a missionary's assistant in Queensland. He had been boned by Nebo, a famous aboriginal witch doctor. Dr Lambert could find no physical symptoms of fever and disease, yet it was plain that Rob was seriously ill. Dr Lambert went with the missionary to Nebo and threatened that he and his people would have all their food supplies cut off if the boning were not lifted. Nebo went with them to see Rob, merely leant over his bed and told him the boning was a mistake and, according to Dr Lambert, the very same evening Rob was restored to full physical strength and back at work.

The psychiatrist, Dr John C Barker, most diligent and indefatigable of researchers into 'voodoo death' in our own time, recorded an episode in Kenya. The head dresser at a medical centre discovered that one of his staff at an outlying station was delivering only half of every prescribed injection and selling the rest off privately. The man was disciplined but, soon after, the head dresser found himself bewitched.

He told the doctor that his strength was ebbing away. 'I did not feel there was much I could do at the time,' the doctor reported. 'Then one day the head dresser came to me with a little bundle of sticks and leaves. This he informed me was the witch doctor's spell and he said that if it were opened there would be found in it some object that at some time had been part of his body: hair, nail clippings or even a tooth extracted years before. The little bundle had been found over the entrance of his hut. Every time he passed under it the spell would exert its baneful influence.'

The doctor was a decisive man. He immediately summoned all the dressers from the outlying stations. Despite threats and cajolements he could make no impression. Sterner measures were required. 'I went to my dispensary and prepared a most revolting concoction of drugs, which had an evil appearance and smell, but was quite harmless. The assembled company were then told they must take the medicine; the innocent would not be harmed but the guilty one would be immediately struck dead. Only one man refused. I then told him I was going to make him take the medicine by force and that it would undoubtedly kill him. Thereupon he confessed. I gave him twenty-four hours to arrange for the witch doctor he had employed to remove the spell. He carried out my orders without delay. Thereupon the head dresser, who had manifestly grown weaker day by day, began to recover immediately and, as far as I know, is still alive to this day.'

Equally decisive was brainwashing expert Professor William Sargent. He had seen hexings, so when a woman came into St Thomas's Hospital in London, turned her face to the wall and announced she had been hexed, Sargent gave her two massive electric shocks. When she came to, he told her the shocks had conquered the hex. She believed him, and recovered. In recent times, though, it has become apparent that the Western medical sophistication, which saved Rob in North Queensland and the head dresser in Kenya, can often fail when confronted by the powers of death in Europe and America.

One day in January 1960, a man was brought into the Veterans Administration Hospital in Oklahoma City, Oklahoma. He was fifty-three years old and a successful businessman. Before the year was out he was dead, killed, doctors believed, by a curse laid upon him by his own mother.

The hospital is one of the best equipped in the whole of the United States, with a distinguished medical staff. At first they were perfectly convinced that they could cope with their patient. Mr X, as the official records describe him (thus protecting themselves from accusing a named person of causing a death), was brought in, semi-conscious, suffering from asthma. After two weeks he had recovered sufficiently to be allowed home.

It was six months before the Veterans' doctors saw their patient again – later research has revealed him to be Finis P Ernest, a nightclub proprietor – but during that time it appeared that he had been in and out of private hospitals six times. Though he was by now having fits and convulsions, they could find nothing organically wrong. Cardiac readings showed no sign of heart trouble. Again, after rest, he recovered and went, as it transpired, directly to his mother's home.

As the case report recounts: 'In a few hours he was wheezing again and in less than forty-eight hours he was re-admitted by ambulance in a near-terminal condition. Medical management aborted the attack, but the patient became extremely depressed and voiced feelings of utter futility and hopelessness.' Another recovery followed, then a further relapse after he had been allowed out to visit his mother. By now, the psychiatric doctors had tumbled to the connection and allowed him out only on condition that he did not visit his mother. He progressed well until the fateful evening of 23 August. At 5pm that day ne naa a long and cheerful interview with a doctor. Some time around 6pm he telephoned his mother. At 6.35pm he was found gasping for breath and semi-conscious. By 6.55pm he was dead.

Distressed and perplexed at his patient's death, one of the Oklahoma doctors, James L Mathis, determined to investigate further. He discovered that Ernest's father had died when the boy was in his early teens, leaving him effectively the 'man of the house', responsible also for four other brothers and sisters as well as the mother. Twice before the age of thirty he married against the wishes of his mother; twice there was a quick divorce. Then, at the age of thirty-one, in partnership with his mother, he opened a nightclub which proved to be very successful. At thirty-eight, he at last met a woman of whom his mother approved, a schoolteacher some years younger than himself, and Finis and Josephine were married. All went well for fifteen years until he received a handsome offer to sell the business and, with Josephine's support, decided to accept.

The wrath of his mother was immediate and overwhelming. 'Do this', she pronounced, 'and something dire will happen to you.' Though he had had excellent health for at least ten years, this man of fifty-three was, within two days, stricken with difficulties in breathing. He went ahead with the sale and in a final outburst his mother shouted repeatedly, 'Something will strike you, something will strike you.'

Dr Mathis reports: 'Numerous hospitalizations, asthmatic attacks three or four times per week, three convulsions and the apparent inability of the medical profession to help him dovetailed into Mr X's growing idea that mother was right again. The depression for which psychiatric consultation was sought was marked by his frequent protestations of the hopelessness of his condition. A hopeful sign appeared when he was able consciously to see some connection between the asthmatic attacks and contact with his mother. However he did not forget that mother had previously proved infallible; in fact he reminded me of this on the afternoon of his death.'

Dr Mathis then went on to investigate the circumstances of the final phone call. After talking with her mother-in-law, Josephine was able to give him the gist of it. Her husband had plucked up the nerve to tell his mother that he proposed to reinvest the money from the nightclub in a new venture in which she would have no part. Dr Mathis's account ends: 'His mother made no attempt to dissuade him but ended the conversation with a statement to the effect that, regardless of how he or the doctors felt, he should remember her warning and be prepared for her prediction of "dire results". Give or take a few minutes, Mr X was dead within the hour.'

Dr Mathis was left with no alternative but to label it, as he put it, a 'sophisticated version of voodoo death'.

If the sinister mother of Oklahoma City loomed like a character from the Brothers Grimm, not long afterwards some doctors from Johns Hopkins University in Baltimore felt they were facing another fearful fairytale, ending before their very eyes in the City Hospital. This time it was the wicked fairy attending a baby girl's birth, but without a good fairy to transmute death into gentle sleep.

The Baltimore patient was a black woman of twenty-two. She was overweight, breathless, clearly anxious, but otherwise, as far as every available test could show, perfectly healthy. Yet the medical staff had seen her go into a steady decline. Three days before her twenty-third birthday, the woman told her doctor the story of the day of her birth.

She came from a remote area of the Okefenokee Swamp in Georgia. There was only one midwife. On that day – a Friday the 13th – she had delivered three baby girls. The midwife told the mothers that the babies were hexed: the first would die before her sixteenth birthday, the second before her twenty-first and the last before her twenty-third. The first girl duly died in an accident the day before her sixteenth birthday. The second, fearful of the hex, was filled with relief when her twenty-first birthday arrived, and insisted on going out to celebrate. As she walked into a saloon, a stray bullet hit and killed her.

It was the third girl who now lay, in that August of 1966, convinced she was doomed, in front of Dr Gottlieb Friesinger and his colleagues. She developed a galloping pulse and heart irregularities. They tried an operation to ligate the veins, but the improvement was only temporary. The day before her twenty-third birthday, she started to sweat profusely; her breathing became wild. By nightfall she was dead. At the post-mortem no natural cause could be found. Only the hex.

A Dutch nursing-home matron was confronted with another bizarre case reported that same year. Two women arrived at the front door of the home with their mother one Friday afternoon, and insisted in the most vehement terms that the old woman should be admitted at once, as she was going to die the following Thursday. The mother was apparently in the best of health and merely stood there silently while her daughters argued. Finally, the matron gave way and let the mother stay. For the next few days she pottered about the home doing odd jobs and occasionally discussing her imminent demise. The nursing-home doctor pronounced her to be fully fit and, on the Thursday, she got up and took breakfast as usual. But then, in mid-morning, the matron was staggered to see the old woman's entire family – half a dozen in all – appear at the door, all in their Sunday best. They had taken a day off from work, one daughter from a launderette and the son against a specific threat from his boss that he would be fired.

The mother, who was about seventy years old, went to lie down. By half past one she had gone into a coma and the family gathered round her bedside singing psalms. The doctor, by now thoroughly alarmed, never left her patient's side. But by half past three she was dead. The death certificate read: 'Heart failure'.

The reasons for hex death are obscure, despite recorded medical evidence. Some victims weaken themselves by refusing food and drink. Also, extreme anxiety does seem to influence the so-called sympathetic nervous system; the blood pressure falls, plasma escapes from the body cells and a state of shock ensues. The heart beats faster and faster, finally collapsing into a state of constant contraction. On the other hand, some believe that the familiar image – 'he was rigid with shock' – may continue into a state of prolonged rigidity or catalepsy when the lungs are paralysed with fear and simply fail to supply the necessary oxygen. Again, the evidence about the Australian Aborigines would seem to suggest that, in their hopelessness, it is the parasympathetic nervous system of the victims which comes into play, slowing down breathing and heart rate until life expires, leaving, for the post-mortem knife, only a heart distended with blood – and no other clues.

The reactions from the victim in these cases are complex. First and foremost appears to be the absolute certainty of the power and immutability of the death prediction. And it is a certainty which seems to be able to transcend many years.

In 1965, three doctors from Labrador in Canada wrote to *The British Medical Journal* about a case of a mother of five children who had died suddenly after an apparently successful minor operation. She was one week short of her forty-third birthday. An hour after the operation, she collapsed with all the symptoms of shock, including low blood pressure. Oxygen, cortisone, the full array of indicated treatment, had no effect and she died the next day at five in the morning. On the morning of the operation she had told a nurse she was sure she was doing to die. Unaware of this, the doctors went ahead with the operation. At the post-mortem they found bleeding round the adrenal glands and elsewhere, but nothing to indicate why a perfectly healthy woman had succumbed. Only afterwards did the doctors discover that, thirty-eight years previously, when she was five years old, a fortune teller had informed her she would die before the age of forty-three.

Once the prophecy, the hex, the threat of death is known to a victim and the conviction of its power has lodged in the mind, it seems it can achieve its end in different ways – sometimes by a submissive and deadly abandonment of hope, sometimes by naked terror. For fear itself can kill.

Early in 1975, the people of Britain were for many weeks agog with speculation over the fate of a seventeen-year-old girl from Bridgnorth in the English Midlands. She had been kidnapped and a ransom demanded. Only when she was found, more than seven weeks later, was it realized that she had undergone perhaps the most horrific experience of unremitting terror known in modern times.

Lesley Whittle was the daughter of a wealthy man who had made his money in the road transport business. From time to time his name, tales of his expansive gestures and pictures of his family had appeared in the local newspapers. When he died, his substantial will received a lot of publicity. This attracted the attention of Donald Neilson, an ex-soldier who, quite coldly, was looking for a victim for a big kidnap coup. He selected

Lesley. For many weeks beforehand Neilson carefully scouted the area around Bridgnorth. It was an elaborate undertaking, for Neilson was a loner and there would be no assistants to give him away – or to share the takings.

Everything had, therefore, to be planned most carefully – the kidnapping itself, the getaway, the victim's hiding place, a means of securing her while he returned to normal life with his wife and daughter in a terraced house a hundred miles away, the delivery of the ransom demand, its collection and his own safe escape. But by 14 January 1975, everything was ready.

Neilson watched from his car as Lesley's mother went out to a dinner party. Lesley was alone in the house. She went to bed early. Shortly before midnight, she was awoken by a light shining in her face and a hand over her mouth. The man wore a navy blue woollen hood over his face. In his other hand was a sawn-off shotgun. It was a cold night and she was wearing a light nightdress. Neilson grabbed her and hurriedly took her out to his car. Lesley was dumped in the back seat, apparently with her hands, eyes and mouth taped. Neilson, the gun beside him, set off on the sixty-five-mile drive to his destination – a large area of heath and parkland at Kidsgrove in Staffordshire. He pulled Lesley out of the car and carried her across the heath to a small hillock. There, he dumped her on the ground beside a manhole which led into a new system of underground drains and floodworks, completed only two years before. He pulled back the cover and carried Lesley into the frightful catacomb that was to be her prison.

The shaft dropped straight down fifty feet to a roaring torrent full of winter floodwaters running away to the Brindley Canal. A fixed metal inspection ladder ran down the side with, about twelve feet from the surface, a small working platform. There was a wire noose attached to the ladder at exactly the right height to padlock round Lesley's neck. Then he told the girl her fate. If the ransom were not paid, she would be despatched into the raging tunnel of water below. If she moved, slipped, fainted and fell from the platform she would be hanged by the wire noose.

Neilson climbed back up the ladder and closed the manhole. By five o'clock that morning, he was back home and in bed in

Grangefield Avenue, Bradford, Yorkshire. Over the next days, Neilson, using tape recordings planted in telephone boxes, attempted to extract a £50,000 ransom from Lesley's brother, Ronald. Desperately, Ronald tried to meet the conditions of the kidnapper, but Neilson was never satisfied there wasn't a police trap. At least twice during that time he went back to the dark manhole where the girl still stood, inside a sleeping bag, in the dark and cold, the noose around her neck, the floodwater still tumbling past in the blackness twenty feet below.

It is not known how long she lived. But at some time – probably when Neilson returned one night – the unutterable terror finally overcame her. Though it was many weeks before the body was found, the post-mortem doctors were quite clear. Lesley had died, not of violence or exposure, but of 'vagal inhibition'.

Vagal inhibition is familiar to doctors who have seen 'voodoo death'. At first, the victims show all the symptoms of panic – adrenaline is pumped out, the heart rate accelerates, there are wild movements and sweating. But then, as the realization of the hopelessness of their situation takes over, there is a reverse reaction – what is known as a parasympathetic reaction – the heart slows, the breathing slows and there is a steady drop in blood pressure. Sometimes death comes quite quickly.

A research team at Johns Hopkins Medical School was able, during some other experiments, to produce a similar condition in rats. Taking the fierce, wild Norway rat which usually shows the utmost aggression and determination in escaping from difficult situations, they put it first in a tight grip from which it could not struggle loose and then released it into a glass jar full of warm water.

The team, under Curt P Richter, discovered that the wild rats seemed almost instantly to give up hope when they could see no possible means of escape. They died within minutes from the same 'vagal' death. But if they were once released from the grip or plucked from the water and returned, then they seemed to be immune to this particular kind of death: they knew that there was hope of rescue and no longer became susceptible to what the team call 'death from fear'.

The curse of the witch doctor – voodoo's dramatic ritual – strikes immediate terror. But it seems the fatal stroke can be laid on men and women by slower and more insidious means.

The Revd Donald Omand, the well-known Anglican 'Chaplain to the Circus', was handed a letter by an old lady, 'a true fairground queen, the head of five generations, ruling her children, grandchildren, great-grandchildren and great-great-grandchildren with what might be described as a velvet hand within an iron glove'. She asked Omand to keep the letter unopened until her death. Assuming it to be her will, he locked it away.

Some seven years later she died, and Omand was asked to conduct the funeral service. Afterwards the envelope was opened in the presence of the family. But it was not a will. Inside was a piece of paper folded seven times. On it was simply scrawled the day, the month and the year of her death.

This was not the first time the Revd Omand had encountered such a phenomenon. He had been sent for by the family of a circus owner who had died of a heart attack. They were in great distress because only a week before the man had summoned his sons and told them he had just a week to live. They had brought in a doctor who assured the man that his heart, blood pressure and all his vital functions were in perfect order. Yet he had died on the predicted day.

Omand was then shown a curious bundle of envelopes – thirteen in all – which had been found among the man's effects. Posted from different cities in Europe, but all in the same handwriting, they had arrived once a year on the same date. In each was an ordinary printed birthday card. But, on every card, the word 'birthday' was crossed out and the word 'deathday' written in. Then just a date and a man's signature. The date was always the same – the date on which the circus owner eventually died. It transpired that the man who had pursued his victim with such a patient vendetta had been a performer dismissed for drunkenness in the same year that the first deathcard was sent.

Some victims seem almost glad to embrace their fate. In Norway in 1934, a prediction and death resulted in a celebrated murder trial. The accused was an attractive Oslo woman called Mrs

Ingeborg Köbler. She was alleged to have drowned her father, an eminent judge, while they were swimming in the Oslo fjord at Hanko. Mrs Köbler had predicted the time, place and manner of her father's death while supposedly in a sleeping trance. As he was worth 60,000 kroner in accident insurance, sceptics felt this was too neat to be true and took out a bill of indictment.

Ingeborg Köbler, daughter of Judge Dahl, had started producing phenomena after her brother Ludvig drowned, followed five years later by another death – her brother Ragnar. She would begin with a sleeping trance, progressing to a waking trance. There were various 'wonders' performed: messages coming from Ludvig via a suspended pencil and planchette; Ludvig reading lines from Wordsworth's poetical works and other books selected by guests at the séances; Ingeborg writing letters from various dead people in their own handwriting – once indeed, two different letters at the same time, one with the right hand and the other with the left. But the fatal communication came via a number code the Dahls had been using: each letter of the alphabet was given a number, apparently unknown to Ingeborg.

Then, in her sleeping trance state, she would produce a string of numbers which, when decoded, gave a message from someone 'on the other side'. One day in 1934, Judge Dahl and his family took down the numbers which spelled out what was to be the manner of the judge's death. All the evidence is that the judge had become a passionate believer in his daughter's powers. Indeed, so much of the family's money and the judge's time had been spent supporting Ingeborg's work that the family had run into debt and the mother had gone so far as to purloin funds from her work as local community treasurer in Fredrikksstad. As she wrote in a later suicide note: 'My husband, the judge, felt it was his life work to bring this message to mankind. In doing so he took a great and unselfish task on his shoulders. But he was quite innocent of the great demands of daily living and did not realize that our family economy was threatened.'

From the evidence of two years' examination by the Norwegian police and judicial authorities, it seems indisputable that the judge, calmly and with total certainty, accepted his daughter's message about his death. Ingeborg had been in a supposed sleeping trance and the family never subsequently mentioned the subject.

On 8 August 1934, Judge Dahl and Ingeborg went for a walk along the beach at Hanko. Four months had passed since the prediction séance. The judge decided he would swim. Ingeborg declined. He took off his clothes, plunged into the sea and stayed swimming for a long time before suddenly being attacked by cramp. There were no witnesses, but Ingeborg said she then rushed into the sea, and succeeded in getting the drowning man back to the shore. She tried to revive him, failed and went for help; but, by the time she got back with others, he was dead.

It was only when the President of the Norwegian Society for Psychic Research, Professor Thorstein Wereide, revealed the story of the prediction at what he thought was a closed meeting that the newspapers got hold of the tale and started the rumpus which resulted in Ingeborg's arrest. She was held in prison for five months while the investigation proceeded. Finally, she was released on the grounds that she could not have known in her sleeping trance the content of the message about her father, nor had she been told later.

Whatever the truth about Ingeborg, it seems clear that Judge Dahl was a firm believer. Quite deliberately and calmly, under no immediate duress, on that warm summer's day at Hanko, he went out to meet what he believed to be his fate.

Since the 1970s, there have been a number of doctors' reports confirming such powers to induce death, whether self-inflicted, or through some outside agency like a fortune teller. Dr Francis Ellis, of Cheshire in England, described a pregnant woman with signs of heart disease who was in hospital and well-controlled as her partition time approached. Unfortunately during a bedside discussion the words 'heart failure' were mentioned. 'Although it was discounted at once by our tutor,' recalls Dr Ellis, 'I could see the look of terror remain on the patient's face for several seconds.' The same day, she collapsed and died.

A London doctor, Peter Young, said he had seen a number of similar cases. One concerned a man of thirty-seven who was terrified of having an operation for varicose veins and the operation was postponed twice. On the day when it was actually to take place, he collapsed and died. A post-mortem revealed no cause for the fatal heart attack. Another of Dr Young's patients was a market gardener who suffered a heart attack. 'He told me that after a full and satisfying life he now expected to die,' recounts Dr Young, 'and that he had left his will and a letter to his solicitor on the table at home. He was told that after a few weeks' rest he should be able to go home, but he contradicted this with a smile. His condition improved rapidly, but he never doubted his end was near. Three weeks after admission, he suddenly collapsed and died.' The man was a bachelor and deeply religious. Perhaps the prospects after death seemed more attractive than those if he lived on, deprived of the work he loved.

In the Western world there seems little doubt that fortune tellers are responsible for directing many people to their appointments in Samarra. Today they flourish as never before.

The St Leger horse-race meeting at Doncaster in Yorkshire is traditionally accompanied by one of the best fairs in England. The fastest hurdy-gurdies, the most ferocious dodgems and the latest rides are invariably gathered in September on the Town Moor. And each year there seem to be more fortune tellers in ever more luxurious *vardos* and wagons – in 1983 more than a dozen Genuine Gypsy Rose Lees 'as seen on television', their doorways papered with testimonials to their powers from the great and the famous. Standing affably at the top of their caravan steps, or peeking from behind gaily coloured curtains, they rarely lack for custom. They claim never to speak of death, even when it makes its ubiquitous appearance in the cards, the tea leaves, the palms or the crystal ball.

But there is no doubt some fortune tellers do call the design of death. Dr William Nixon of University College Hospital, London, had a patient of thirty-five, obviously under dreadful terror as the birth of her first child approached. 'I asked why she was so fearful,' said Dr Nixon. 'All her pent-up emotions exploded when she recounted that at the age of ten when walking on the South Downs between Worthing and Brighton she had met a gypsy who predicted that either she or her baby would die in childbirth.' On this occasion, both mother and baby survived, but Dr Nixon had already seen death ensue from such a warning. While he was working at the Tsan Yuk Maternity Hospital in Hong Kong, one of his patients, aged twenty-one, had a perfectly normal delivery but refused to suckle the baby or even speak. Eventually, on the sixth day, she spoke and said she was going to die. On her way into hospital she had gone into one of the fortune tellers' booths which cluster round Tsan Yuk and had been told that, on the sixth day after the birth, she would die. It happened as predicted, and, at the autopsy, nothing could be found to account for her death.

Dr John Barker bravely submitted himself, along with a gallant assistant whom he calls Mrs Noble, to a series of contemporary English fortune tellers, in order to discover what they did actually tell their customers.

They applied to a dozen varied practitioners, specializing in everything from tarot cards and psychometry to clairvoyance and astrology, operating mainly from London and the English south coast. Both Barker and 'Mrs Noble' were singularly impressed by some – though by no means all – of the fortune tellers. They both paid five guineas for a thirty-minute session with a gypsy-clairvoyant with a booth on a south-coast pier.

Barker wrote: 'She was remarkably and uncannily accurate. I gave her no information whatsoever. After practising psychiatry for eleven years I could not possibly have told her a fraction about herself to compare with her quite amazing knowledge about myself and my past life.' The gypsy used a crystal ball, holding Barker's hands wrapped around it. She got his occupation right, his literary work and salient features of his past life.

Mrs Noble emerged from another session with the gypsy and noted: 'Her accuracy was fantastic. She showed remarkable insight into my personal conditions, giving the date of my marriage correctly and the number and sex of my children.' In this instance, the gypsy predicted bereavement and not death. Indeed she predicted, alas wrongly, a long life for Dr Barker.

But many of the other fortune tellers in Barker's survey did predict death.

Another gypsy, described by Barker as 'a brusque elderly woman' immediately opened the session by telling him that he would die suddenly of a stroke when aged just over seventy. This was given added force for, 'she claimed I nearly died three and thirteen years ago, which was substantially correct since I had severe illnesses at both these times'.

Two others forecast that Barker would live a long life, and some flatly refused to predict a time of death. Both he and Mrs Noble were told that they would soon suffer bereavements. They were very impressed by how convincing some of the fortune tellers could be – a feeling reinforced by meeting other clients in the waiting rooms who had travelled the breadth of England for a consultation 'because we have heard she is so good'. Barker had personally treated two women who had been terrorized by the threats of gypsy palm-readers – one after refusing at first to pay to have her hand read, and the other because her short and broken life-line had been pointed out.

An Indian palm-reader told John Snell of Poole in England that he would die on his forty-fifth birthday. For twenty years he ignored the warning; he became a Guinness drinker and long-distance lorry driver. But in his forty-fourth year, he began to worry. He gave up drinking altogether. On his birthday in October 1982 he refused to leave the house. Two days later the local newspaper reported the death of John Snell of Poole on his forty-fifth birthday. But the palm-reader was wrong – there were two John Snells, living 100 yards apart – and the one whose palm was read is still alive.

' "Scared to death" is not an idle saying,' as Dr Ansel Fry wrote. 'A feeling of "I am afraid I am going to die" may actually result in death.' The extent of lethal voodoo, particularly in the United States, seems to be growing. The Haitian refugees who have congregated in Brooklyn and Miami seem to be responsible for some of the more lurid cases – a man's body found on a New York lot in 1980 burned, mutilated and surrounded by chicken

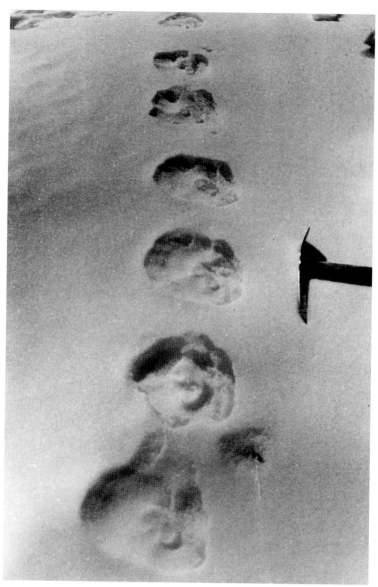

Footprints in the Himalayan Mountains, thought to be those of the Abominable Snowman

Dr and Mrs Lothrop, leaning against one of the 'giant balls' in Costa Rica

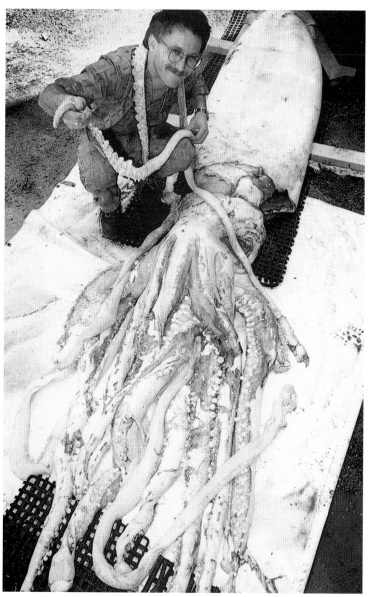

A giant squid (24 feet) found off the coast of New Zealand

The famous stone circle at Avebury, Wiltshire. It is the largest in England and older than Stonehenge.

Masterpiece and mystery: Pisac, Peru. How did builders manage to fit the stone blocks so tightly?

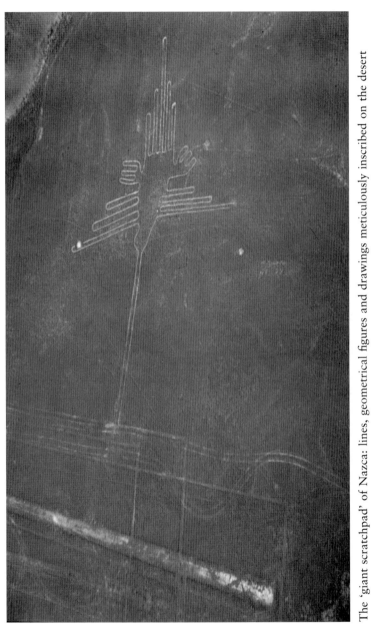

The 'giant scratchpad' of Nazca: lines, geometrical figures and drawings meticulously inscribed on the desert

The Cerne Giant in Abbas, Dorset, nicknamed 'The Rude Man'

Nagasaki after the atom bomb (1945)

Tunguska after the 1908 explosion

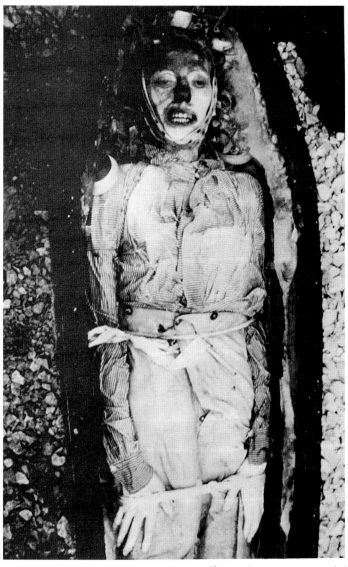

Lost in mysterious circumstances: Petty Officer John Torrington of the Franklin Expedition, 1845. The hands are immaculate, as though recently having scrubbed a deck, the eyes open and the teeth shining. Only the forehead and nose show the blackening of frost.

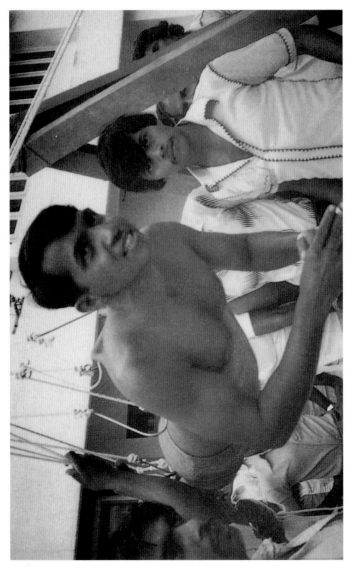

The happy hook-hanger. The secret lies in a positive mental attitude and the careful distribution of weight over several hooks.

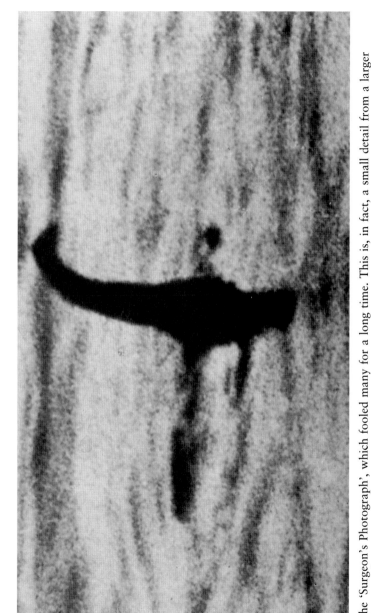

The 'Surgeon's Photograph', which fooled many for a long time. This is, in fact, a small detail from a larger photograph.

The Nanjing belt. The discovery of aluminium among the fragments suggested that the Chinese isolated the metal at least 1500 years before Western scientists.

Padre Pio reckoned he lost up to a cupful of blood on some days from his stigmata, or 'wounds of Christ'

A Bolivian witch doctor, selling her roots, herbs, potions and llama foetuses, believed to ward off evil spirits

Voodoo offerings, Brazil

One of the frogs said to have fallen onto Mrs Vida McWilliam's garden in Bedford during a shower of rain in June 1979

All that remained of Dr John Irving Bentley, Pennsylvania, 1966. Spontaneous human combustion?

feet, feathers and candles; a head found in a bag in Miami, together with wax, and chicken and turkey bones. But voodoo seems also to have an extensive hold all across the old South.

Professor Kenneth M Golden of Little Rock, Arkansas made an initial report on voodoo death in *The American Journal of Psychiatry* in 1977 and thus alerted his colleagues in Little Rock and also at St Louis, where he is visiting professor at Webster College. By 1982 he was able not only to report more than a dozen cases of hexing which had been brought to his attention – but also to suggest treatment for the hexed patients.

A black man had come to the University Hospital, bent double and in great pain, but showing no symptoms to normal examination including a brain scan. It emerged that the man's wife practised black magic; she suspected him of infidelity and had probably placed a hex on him. Furthermore, the woman's two previous husbands had both died for no apparent medical reason.

Of another patient involved in an eternal triangle Golden says: 'He was confused, agitated and almost delirious on the ward, necessitating bed restraint and large doses of chlorpromazine. All neurological findings, including a brain scan, proved normal. The patient died two weeks later of cardiac arrest. The autopsy provided no basis for the failure.' The man was only thirty-three years old. According to his wife, it was the 'other woman' who had hexed him: she was known to cast spells and heal people.

Golden's reports include a woman hexed and suffering uncontrollable spasms of her arms and legs after rejecting lesbian advances from a voodoo woman. A man of thirty-six became 'emaciated, dehydrated, disoriented, apprehensive, unshaven, his hair long and matted', after his wife had 'throwed at him' when he left her for another woman. This man was cured by being given a placebo – no drugs in it whatsoever – and being assured by the doctor in the strongest possible terms that it would work. Indeed, the treatment Dr Golden recommends to his fellow physicians is to all intents and purposes white counter-magic:

Use placebos and emphasize their potency as positively as you can.

Do not belittle local healers and spiritualists; offer hospital treatment as an alternative not a substitute.

Try hypnosis.

Do not disdain getting the patient to healers whom they think can counter spells, especially if they are unwilling to go on seeing a local doctor when they go home.

Golden himself had had great trouble with the lady suffering from the lesbian hex. He tried all his usual methods and succeeded in reducing the spasms in her arms and legs but, as the time came for her to be sent home, her fear reappeared. 'She still felt a powerful hex was upon her house,' says Golden, 'and that harm would befall her. I suggested she knit a small square that would protect her. She did so readily and was much relieved. She told me she would put it in her top dresser drawer with her panties as soon as she arrived in her house.'

At the time of writing, this most bizarre of prescriptions was still successfully working its wonders.

ARTHUR C CLARKE COMMENTS:

Like the reports of stigmata, these stories prove the extraordinary – even fatal – power the mind can have over the body. After listening to the doctors, I'm convinced that people can literally be scared to death.

Yet I don't believe that spells can work, unless the victim knows he's a target. What kills is not any occult power of the witch doctor, but the victim's own belief that he is doomed. This destructive influence of the mind over the body could become a power for good. Doctors have always known what a crucial role a patient's psychological state plays in the progress of his disease. So perhaps these dark tales of fear and death could lead to new techniques for harnessing the mind – not to kill, but to cure.

OUT OF THE BLUE

No book of mysteries should fail to acknowledge the work of Charles Fort, an American who devoted his life to collecting reports of bizarre happenings. Fort was born in the Bronx district of New York in August 1874 and for many years worked as a journalist with a notable lack of success. However, a small inheritance which came his way at the age of forty-two gave him the freedom to devote himself full time to the work for which he is now remembered.

For almost a quarter of a century, Fort sat in the New York Public Library or, when he was living in London, in the Reading Room of the British Museum, scouring scientific journals and newspapers for reports of anything that could not easily be explained or did not fit into accepted categories of knowledge. From this eye-straining labour and the almost indecipherable notes he made came four exotic books published between 1919 and 1932: *The Book of the Damned, New Lands, Lo!* and *Wild Talents*.

Near the beginning of *The Book of the Damned*, he proclaims his method: 'I have gone into the outer darkness of scientific and philosophical transactions and proceedings, ultra-respectable, but covered with the dust of disregard. I have descended into journalism. I have come back with the quasi-souls of lost data.'

Fort is true to his word; his books are bizarre catalogues of unexplained events which have become known in memory of their recorder as *Forteana*. Within the pages of *The Book of the Damned*, for example, he records falls from the sky of red dust, frogs, 'manna', jelly-like substances, grain, vegetable matter, carbonate of soda, nitric acid, limestone, salt, coke, cinders, snakes, ants, worms and cannon balls.

Today, more than sixty thousand of Fort's notes are preserved in the New York Public Library. They contain accounts of UFOs collected decades before the terms 'flying saucer' or 'UFO' were coined, like the 'splendidly illuminated aeroplane' which passed over the English village of Warmley in 1912, or the triangular shapes reported in the sky over Bermuda in 1885, a strange foretaste of this century's alleged discovery of a Bermuda triangle said to be fatal to ships and aircraft. There are phantom soldiers, luminous owls, mirages, 'new' stars and planets, extraordinary coincidences, and strange booming sounds.

Fort died in 1932, but his work is continued by dedicated followers throughout the world. Many of them publish magazines crammed with Forteana, gathered, according to Fort's method, from newspapers and scientific journals.

FROGS THAT FLY AND FISH THAT RAIN

In Marksville, Louisiana, they still remember the day J Numa Damiens burst into the offices of the local paper brandishing a fish. The date was 23 October 1947. J Numa had telephoned the office a few minutes before, and was incensed at the scepticism to his extraordinary tale shown by the hard-bitten small-town journalists on the *Weekly News*.

The fish, he claimed, had fallen from the sky. It was just one of hundreds which had rained down from out of the blue. They were all over Main Street, in the yard of the director of the Marksville Bank, in Mrs J W Joffrion's property next door, on rooftops everywhere. Three of the town's most eminent citizens had even been struck by cascading fish as they walked to work. The morning rush-hour had been thrown into chaos: cars and trucks were skidding on a carpet of slithery scales.

The journalists heard their visitor out as he waved the fish in front of their faces, crying, 'Here's one of 'em; take a look and then see if you think I'm talking through my hat.' It certainly sounded very strange, but surely fish couldn't really have rained from the sky. Not on peaceful little Marksville, Louisiana. With their deadline upon them, and no time to check the story, the journalists wrote a rather flippant account of J Numa Damiens' visit for that week's edition, and concluded it with this folksy appeal to their readers: 'Please, Sister and Brother, won't you come to our rescue and tell us what's ailing folks who say fish are raining from heaven on a clear sunshiny day!'

It turned out that the paper had been wrong to scoff. By the time it hit the news-stands, eyewitnesses to the fish-fall had come forward with their own amazing tales to tell. Thirty years later, many of them could vividly recall what happened.

Said Anthony Roy Jnr: 'As I left the house to go to school that morning, I went through the back of the house, and as I got near the garage I heard something fall on the tin roof of the garage and simultaneously something hit me on my head and on my shoulders, and when I looked down I saw they were fish.'

Mrs Eddie Gremillion was ill at the time: 'I was in bed, not feeling good, and I didn't get up early. But my maid came early and she was out in the yard. She ran in excited like anything, and she's a black maid but that day she was white with excitement, and she came and she told me, "Miss Lola, Miss Lola," she said, "it's raining fishes. It's raining fishes." '

Mrs Elmire Roy's maid also panicked: 'When the fish fell on the tin roof, my maid, whose name was Viola, ran outside with me, and she was so upset, and she kept saying, "Lord, Lord, it must be the end of the world." '

Sheriff 'Potch' Didier was another witness. He was driving through Marksville at the time. 'I saw the fish fall out of the sky,' he said. 'I kept driving. I was very amazed.' At one house, the yard was 'just absolutely covered with fish. And just about that time some other people started getting here and everybody was just amazed at the whole thing, and we just couldn't believe it, believe that the fish had just dropped out of the sky.'

Yet the Marksville fish-fall, astonishing as it was to the citizens of the town, is not unique. All kinds of weird showers have been reported over the centuries, notably of fish, blocks of ice and frogs.

In the past, many experts flatly rejected the claims of eyewitnesses. For example, in 1859 a sawyer called John Lewis from the Aberdare Valley in Wales told this story to the local vicar, the Reverend John Griffith:

> On Wednesday, February 9, I was getting out a piece of timber, for the purpose of setting it for the saw, when I was startled by something falling all over me – down my neck, on my head, and on my back. On putting my hand down my neck, I was surprised to find they were little fish. By this time I saw the whole ground covered with them. I took off my hat, the brim of which was full of them. They were jumping all about.

Lewis added that the fish had arrived in two showers, about ten minutes apart. He and his workmates gathered some of them up and sent a few to London Zoo, where they were put on display. Although they proved a popular attraction, not everyone was impressed. J E Gray of the British Museum told the *Zoological Magazine*: 'On reading the evidence it appears to me most probably to be only a practical joke of the mates of John Lewis, who seem to have thrown a pailful of water with the fish in it over him.' Edward Newman agreed: 'Dr Gray is without doubt correct in attributing the whole affair to some practical joker.'

There are certainly reasons to be wary of frog-falls. Just because the creatures suddenly appear in large numbers at the same time as a shower, it does not mean that they have actually come down with the rain. In many cases the rain has simply brought the frogs out from their usual hiding places to enjoy the water. One observer put it rather quaintly:

> The little creatures have doffed their tadpole tails and have wandered in their thousands far afield. During the day a crack in the ground, a dead leaf, or an empty snail shell affords them shelter, and during the night they travel in pursuit of small insects. Then comes the shower of rain. It fills the cracks in the ground, washes away the dead leaves, and chokes up the snail shell with mud-splashes. But what matter? The little frogs are all over the place, revelling in the longed-for moisture ...

During a torrential downpour in August 1986, Melvin Harris of Hadleigh, Essex, happened to be out walking in the streets near his home. Shortly after the rain started he noticed a few frogs and toads, an uncommon sight in the suburbs. Soon there were dozens of them hopping about. He is certain that none came from the sky, and indeed watched several actually creeping out of nooks and crannies.

Sudden frog migrations have also caused confusion. When thousands of the hopping creatures appeared in Towyn, North Wales, in 1947, many of the townspeople believed that they had fallen from the sky. Three days after the invasion had begun, desperate householders were still trying to clear them from their property. 'They're swarming like bees,' said one weary citizen. It turns out that frog migrations are common around Towyn, for the town is situated between two marshes. One eyewitness, Jack Roberts, pointed out that 1947 was a vintage year for frogs. There were plenty of tadpoles in the spring, and the summer was extremely wet.

Writer Francis Hitching discovered that a plague of frogs at Chalon-sur-Saône in France in 1922 was also almost certainly simply a mass-migration, although Charles Fort had decided that they must have fallen from the sky. In 1979 Hitching checked the story while passing through the French town and concluded, '... it seems clear that what had happened was a migratory plague of frogs crossing the roads. Observers remembered being unable to avoid squashing them as they bicycled. No one had seen them dropping from the sky.'

In the twentieth century, a few apparent 'rains' of fish were caused, as it turned out, by birds dropping their prey in flight. For example, in Australia at Forbes, New South Wales, fish – some of them weighing up to ½ lb – fell from the mouths of hundreds of passing pelicans on to astonished observers below, and in 1979 a golfer was struck on the head by an airborne red mullet dropped by a clumsy gull.

Yet such explanations do not account for every case. Many reliable eyewitnesses have actually described seeing fish and frogs fall when there has not been a bird in sight, let alone the large flock necessary to convey the shoals of airborne creatures that have landed on or around them.

In 1948, Mr Ian Patey, a former British Amateur Golf Champion, was playing a round on a course at Barton-on-Sea, near Bournemouth. His wife was about to play a shot:

Just before she hit it, a fish fell down on the ground in front of us. And then we looked up in the sky and suddenly there were hundreds of fish falling in an area of about a hundred yards. They were live, they were larger than whitebait, possibly smaller than a sardine. My reaction was one of complete surprise. After all, there wasn't a cloud in the sky.

During the Second World War, Joe Alpin was stationed with the Artists' Rifles at an English stately home, Alton Towers in Staffordshire. One evening he was driving through the deer park in an army truck:

The sky suddenly darkened – very very dark indeed, like a thunderstorm. And then the frogs came, millions of them, raining out of the sky, millions upon millions of frogs about half an inch long. They fell all over us, all over the grass, all over the cars, down the neck of our tunics, on our feet, hands, everywhere. It rained frogs for at least an hour and a quarter.

At Esh Winning in County Durham in 1887, Mr Edward Cook, realizing that a storm was approaching, took shelter with his horse and rolley cart beneath the gables of a house.

In a few minutes large drops of rain began to fall, and with them, to my astonishment, scores of small frogs (about the size of a man's thumbnail) jumping about in all directions; and, as there was no dam or grass near, I could not imagine wherever they came from, until the storm was over and I had mounted the waggon again. Then I found several of the little gentlemen on the rolley, and knew they must have come down with the rain, it being impossible for them to have leaped so high.

In 1960, Grace Wright reported a similar experience to a magazine:

More than 50 years ago, I was walking along a street in Hounslow with my husband and small son when a heavy storm broke. We first thought they were hailstones until we saw they were all tiny frogs and were jumping about. My son filled a sweet-box to take home. The brim of my husband's hat was full of frogs while the storm lasted. They were everywhere.

On 28 August 1977, thousands of tiny frogs – some apparently no larger than peas – poured down on to Canet-Plage near Perpignan, France. Eyewitnesses said they bounced off the bonnets of cars.

In October 1986, *The Journal of Meteorology* published this vivid eyewitness account. It came from J W Roberts of Kettering, Northamptonshire, who, in 1919, was working at a farm during the school holidays.

> I was walking between the stacks of hay and straw when there was a sudden rush of air. I looked up towards a disused quarry cutting and I saw a dark, almost black, cloud coming rushing towards me. It was a whirlwind. It picked up some of the loose straw lying about, and when it reached the buildings it seemed to stop, and the dark cloud suddenly fell down and I was smothered all over with small frogs – thousands of them about 1¼ to 1½ inches long. I think they must have come from a lake a mile away up the cutting. Oh boy, was I scared. I ran across the footbridge over the brook right close to our house, and my mother could hardly believe me, only I had small frogs in my shirt, etc.

From earliest times, the theory usually advanced to explain these weird falls has been that the frogs and fish are carried aloft by freak winds, tornadoes or waterspouts. The creatures fall back to earth when the wind weakens. Tornadoes and whirlwinds certainly do play extraordinary tricks. For example, when a tornado passed through the Brahmaputra district of India in March 1875, a dead cow was found up in the branches of a tree, about 30 feet from the ground. After a tornado had hit Oklahoma in 1905, the Associated Press reported that 'all the corpses in the track of the storm were found without shoes'; at Lansing, Michigan, in 1943, thirty chickens were found sitting in a row stripped entirely of their feathers; and on 30 May 1951 people clearing up after a tornado at Scottsbluff, Nebraska, found that a bean had been driven deep into an egg without cracking the shell. At St Louis in 1896 a whirlwind was reported to have lifted a carriage into the air. It was apparently then carried along for 100 yards before being allowed to float back to earth so gently that the coachman's hat remained firmly on his head! In *Tornadoes of the United States*, Snowden D Flora tells the remarkable tale of two Texans, known only as Al and Bill, who chanced to be at Al's home in Higgins, Texas, on 9 April 1947 when a tornado struck.

> Al, hearing the roar, stepped to the door and opened it to see what was happening. It was torn from his grasp and disappeared. He was carried away, over the tree tops. Bill went to the door to investigate the disappearance of his friend and found himself, also, sailing through the Texas atmosphere, but in a slightly different direction from the course his friend was taking. Both landed about two hundred feet from the house with only minor injuries. Al started back and found Bill uncomfortably wrapped in wire. He unwound his friend and both headed for Al's house, crawling because the wind was too strong to walk against. They reached the site of the house only to find that all the house except the floor had disappeared. The almost incredible part of the story is that Al's wife and two children were huddled on a divan, uninjured. The only other piece of furniture left on the floor was a lamp.

If the wind can lift two beefy Texans and an Indian cow into the air, fish and frogs must present no problem, and many fish- and frog-falls do turn out, on close investigation, to occur at times when unusual winds are recorded. This is certainly true in the case of the Marksville fish-fall. We know this because, by a remarkable coincidence, one of the first people to reach the fish-strewn streets of the town was a biologist working for the US Department of Wild Life and Fisheries. A D Bajkov and his wife had been having breakfast in a restaurant when a bemused waitress told them that fish were raining down outside. The Bajkovs rushed to the sidewalk, their food forgotten, and at once set about identifying the airborne shoal.

'They were freshwater fish native to local waters,' Bajkov later reported in a letter to the American journal, *Science*. He found large-mouth black bass, goggle-eyes, two species of sunfish, hickory shad, and several kinds of minnows. There were more shad than anything else. Bajkov collected a jar-full of prize specimens for distribution to museums. Like a good scientist, he also took careful note of the weather conditions.

> The actual falling of the fish occurred in somewhat short intervals, during foggy and comparatively calm weather. The velocity of the

wind on the ground did not exceed eight miles per hour. The New Orleans weather bureau had no report of any large tornado, or updrift, in the vicinity of Marksville at that time. However, James Nelson Gowanloch, chief biologist for the Louisiana Department of Wild Life and Fisheries, and I had noticed the presence of numerous small tornadoes, or 'devil dusters' the day before the 'rain of fish' in Marksville.

À more obvious connection between a fall and unusual weather conditions was noted in a letter sent to the *East Anglian Magazine* in 1958. The writer, H Bye, had overheard a conversation between an old farmhand and a group of workers. The farmhand was telling them 'that at West Row and Isleham, on the Cambridge/Suffolk border, when he was a young man, a waterspout was seen over the River Lark. Some hours afterwards there was a heavy thunderstorm and it rained frogs.'

A waterspout also blew up near the site of another English frog-fall in 1892, according to *Symons's Monthly Meteorological Magazine*:

'During the storm that raged with considerable fury in Birmingham on Wednesday morning, June 30, a shower of frogs fell in the suburb of Moseley. They were found scattered about several gardens. Almost white in colour, they had evidently been absorbed in a small waterspout that was driven over Birmingham by the tempest.'

In 1982 Michael W Rowe, writing in the *Journal of Meteorology*, revealed that he had discovered a graphic account of fish cascading from a waterspout. It occurs in a book called *The Excitement*, published in 1830. According to the story, some travellers were sailing through the Strait of Malacca in about 1760, when:

They were surrounded with waterspouts, one of which was very near, and they fired to disperse it. The roaring was tremendous, and presently a torrent of water poured on the ship, which brought down with it many fish and weeds; yet the water was perfectly fresh; a phenomenon singularly curious.

Fish have actually been seen inside or emerging from waterspouts and whirlwinds. E W Gudger of the American Museum of Natural History, an avid collector of reports of mysterious showers, was told by his friend, E A McIlhenny of Avery Island, Louisiana, of 'a small waterspout on a fresh-water distributary in the Mississippi delta, which broke just in front of his fishing boats and then filled boats with water and fishes'.

Michael Rowe also dug out this tiny paragraph from *The Times* of 23 January 1936: 'Violent whirlwinds accompanied a storm which broke over Florence on Monday, and among various objects which were seen spinning in the air were some big fish which had evidently been drawn from the River Arno.' Rowe collects reports of whirlwinds and often writes to local papers appealing for information. A letter in the *Manchester Evening News* brought this response from E Singleton, who reported seeing fish and frogs actually 'taking off' at Newton-le-Willows, Lancashire, in 1947:

> I saw flocks of birds suddenly appear from behind me. Looking back, the reason was obvious, for approaching rapidly was a whirlwind which was carrying all sorts of debris. I threw my two children to the floor and lay on top of them while the wind passed by about 30 yards away. It travelled directly over a huge pond which was locally known as Thompson's Pit. Half the water together with fish, frogs and weed was carried away and was found deposited on house tops half-a-mile away.

Sometimes, ponds, lakes and rivers are completely emptied of water by the wind. Snowden D Flora, in *Tornadoes of the United States*, notes an example: 'When the destructive tornado of 23 June 1944 passed over West Fork River, West Virginia, the water was actually sucked up and the river left dry, momentarily, at the place where the storm crossed it.'

Another collector of meteorological curiosities, Waldo L McAtee of the US Biological Survey, told the Biological Society of Washington of two similar 'lift-offs'. The first was at Christian-soe on the island of Bornholm, Denmark, where 'a waterspout emptied the harbor to such an extent that the greater part of the bottom was uncovered'. The other took place at a town in France. There had been a violent storm overnight: 'When morning dawned, the streets were found strewed with fish of various sizes. The mystery was soon solved, for a fish pond in the vicinity had been blown dry and only the large fish left behind.'

Yet even though freak winds are almost certainly the cause of these exotic rains of fish and frogs, the scientists have not yet found all the answers. For example, who could have blamed Major J Hedgepath, US Army (retired), for being totally baffled by a discovery he made while stationed on the island of Guam in September 1936? He told the readers of *Science*: 'I witnessed a brief rainfall of fish, one of the specimens of which was identified as the tench (*Tinca tinca*) which, to my knowledge, is common only to the fresh waters of Europe. The presence of this species at a locale so remote from its normal habitat is worthy of note.'

Indeed, it is. Guam is the largest of the Mariana Islands. It lies in the Western Pacific.

THE JELLY METEORS

What is gelatinous, smelly and said to fall from shooting stars? The answer is *Pwdre Ser* (Welsh for 'star rot'), a strange jelly-like substance which, eyewitnesses have reported, rains down from the sky.

In 1978, Mrs M Ephgrave of Cambridge told a television weatherman about a mysterious substance which had landed on her lawn during a heavy rainstorm: 'It glided down, [it was] about the size of a football and settled like a jelly.' Other reports from earlier times describe a 'round patch as broad as a bushel, which looked thick, slimy and black' seen on Dartmoor in 1638; a 'gelatinous mass of a greyish colour so viscid as to "tremble all over" when poked with a stick' that hit Koblenz in 1844; and a 'body of fetid jelly, 4 feet in diameter' found by villagers from Loweville, New York, in 1846.

So what is *Pwdre Ser*? Sadly, not 'star slime', the last vestige of a shooting star, despite Sir Walter Scott's assertion, 'Seek a fallen star and thou shalt only light on some foul jelly.' There are probably several more mundane explanations. Some examples – if the jelly was not actually seen falling – may be colonies of blue-green algae, known as *Nostoc commune*, a fungus called

Tremella mesenterica, or even leftovers from the innards of frogs and toads devoured by birds.

Few samples have been analysed by scientists. The Cambridge jelly, for example, apparently disappeared overnight, but more than two centuries earlier, in 1712, the Reverend John Morton of Emmanuel College, Cambridge, boiled some *Pwdre Ser* and found it contained fragments of animal bones and skin. He also added two valuable observations: that he had seen a wounded gull vomit a jelly-like substance which turned out to be a ball of half-digested earthworms; and that a friend, Sir William Craven, had watched a bittern do the same thing.

In 1980, Dr G T Meaden, Editor of the *Journal of Meteorology*, seized a rare opportunity and sent a small sample from a blob of colourless jelly found in the garden of Mr Philip Buller at Hemel Hempstead, Hertfordshire, for analysis. The scientist, Mr T J Turvey, had only about one dessertspoon (10ml) of the stuff to work on, but he was still able to isolate all kinds of material in it, including plant debris, freshwater algae, roundworms and bacteria. His conclusion: that it was material which a creature normally found near fresh water, such as a heron, might first have swallowed and then regurgitated.

These, then, are clues which point to a solution to the *Pwdre Ser* mystery. Yet the full answer must wait for the day when a scientist can both observe and catch a falling 'star slime'.

ARTHUR C CLARKE COMMENTS:

Objects have been falling from the sky for centuries and have involved an amazing range of materials – as well as living creatures, such as frogs and fish.

The most spectacular and perhaps well-attested of all falls, however, consist of ice, sometimes in masses far too large to be explained as abnormal hail formations. This is a genuine mystery – but now, at last, we have an answer, though it may not be the only one. It involves a distinguished visitor whom I am sure you will all remember. If you don't see the connection at first, please be patient . . .

This week before Christmas 1985, I made my first serious attempt to locate Halley's Comet. According to the Ephemeris in The Handbook *of the British Astronomical Association, it would be almost directly above Colombo soon after sunset; unfortunately, a rather misty sky was suffused with light from the waxing moon, so I had no great expectation of success. Another observational hazard was the glare of floodlights from the garden of my next-door neighbour, the Iraqi Ambassador. (His concern for security was understandable: a few days later the papers reported a shootout at his front gate with the local Iranians.)*

I fitted my 8-in Celestron with the lowest-power eyepiece available (× 50 – even lower would have been better to look for a faint but fairly large object) and set it up on the flat roof, lining up the polar axis by the tiles, whose orientation I'd determined years ago. Such a crude procedure was hardly good enough for astrophotography, but quite adequate for visual observations. When the clock drive is switched on, an object will stay in view for an hour or more before drifting out of the field.

Now I had to aim the telescope at the exact point in the depressingly luminous sky. Luckily, there were some convenient signposts available – the brilliant planet Jupiter, and the stars in Aquarius, particularly the brightest one, Alpha, which is almost exactly on the Equator. By a stroke of luck, so was the comet on the night of 20 December, so once I'd found Alpha Aquarius only a very slight north–south correction should be necessary.

The conditions were such that I couldn't locate the third magnitude star Alpha visually. No problem; first I got Jupiter in the centre of the field, and adjusted the telescope's right ascension and declination (the celestial equivalents of longitude and latitude) circles so that they agreed with the planet's tabulated position in The BAA Handbook. *Then I moved east and north along the two circles to RA 22 hours 05 minutes plus ½ degree – and there was Alpha in the low-powered finder telescope. It was nowhere near the middle of the field (after all, I'd only aligned the polar axis by eye) so I made another slight adjustment to compensate for the remaining error. Now I was sure* that I was in reasonable agreement with the celestial coordinate system, and was ready for the final step.

Very carefully, I slewed the telescope through the calculated arc – about ten degrees eastwards and a smidgen north. Then, holding my breath and covering my head with a black cloth like an old-time photographer, I peered into the eyepiece.

I didn't really expect to see anything. Quite apart from the poor seeing conditions, my field of vision was only half a degree across – about the size of the moon, which is much smaller than most people realize. (Try covering it with your thumbnail some night.) It was more than likely that the residual errors of adjustment had caused me to miss my target, which meant that I'd have to do some searching.

I could hardly believe my luck – there it was, shyly but unmistakably lurking at the edge of the field! A slight twist of the declination screw, and it was properly centred. Honesty compels me to admit that it was not a conspicuous object; just a bit fainter, and it wouldn't have been visible at all. But it was there, and that was the only thing that mattered.

My first glimpse of the most famous of comets, still heading for its once-in-a-human-lifetime appointment with the sun, has left an indelible photographic image in my memory. It appeared as a misty blob of light, a few times the size of the planet Jupiter as I'd seen it with the same magnification just minutes earlier. Although it grew brighter towards the centre, there was no nucleus – no star-like condensation of light at its core, as is shown by many comets. Nor was I able to see any trace of a tail, though that was not surprising. Halley was still a long way from the sun, and its witch's cauldron of volatile ices and organic chemicals had not yet come to the boil.

As I watched that ghostly apparition glimmering in the field of my telescope, I could not help thinking that a small fleet of spacecraft was on its way to meet the comet in less than three months' time. How amazed – and excited – Halley would have been by this rendezvous with the visitor that will always bear his name! And perhaps Giotto, the Vegas and the Planets, when their mountains of data were analysed – a process which could take years – would confirm that comets are indeed responsible *for those massive ice-falls from a cloudless sky which have intrigued man for centuries.*

Today, of course, many such events can be all too easily explained: lumps of ice up to twelve pounds (5.5 kg) in weight can accumulate on high-flying aircraft until shaken or blown off. Chemical analysis has sometimes revealed their origin; if, as in one report, there are 'traces of coffee, tea and detergent', there's no need to invoke comets (though perhaps that doesn't exclude UFOs). But we must look for another explanation in the case of the 20-ft (6-m)-diameter block that fell on an estate in Scotland. Maybe a Jumbo jet with serious plumbing problems could produce such a mini-iceberg; however, Boeing 747s were not very common at the time of the report – 1849. Comets, on the other hand, have been around longer than the earth itself; they are part of the debris left over from the construction of the solar system.

It has long been suspected that many, if not most comets consist largely of ice – or, to be more accurate, of ices. In ordinary life, the only variety we encounter is frozen water, but in the extremely cold regions far from the sun where comets spend most of their lives it comes in many other flavours. There's ammonia ice, methane ice, carbon dioxide ice (well-known in the refrigeration industry under the name 'dry ice') and still more exotic varieties. As a comet heads sunwards, most of these vaporize beyond the orbit of the earth; but frozen water can survive not only the increasing radiation but even – if the initial mass is large enough – the frictional heat caused by passage through the atmosphere.

It seems very likely that some ice-falls are of cosmic origin: they are associated with the sonic booms heard when vehicles re-enter the earth's atmosphere. It's a strange thought that the largest of all icebergs do not lie off the coast of Antarctica, but drift between the stars.

THE CHINESE SEALS

While Fort gleefully collected tales of objects that fell from the sky, he was also intrigued by things that have turned up in unexpected places on the ground. Strangest of all these is undoubtedly the collection of ancient Chinese porcelain seals found all over Ireland in the late eighteenth and nineteenth centuries. They were, as Fort puts it, 'not the things with big, wistful eyes that lie on ice, and that are taught to balance objects on their noses, but inscribed stamps, with which to make impressions'.

The seals are tiny, consisting of a cube measuring about 1⅛ in (28mm) surmounted by a figure of an animal, and are made of a type of hard porcelain known as *blanc de chine*. It is now known that such seals were made for Chinese scholars. Each seal bore an auspicious message, and the scholar, who would have owned twenty or thirty, would have sealed his letter with the one he deemed to be the most appropriate. They were common in the East, but what were they doing in Ireland? Especially as they were found at a time when there were no known direct trading links between China and Ireland. Moreover, such seals have never turned up in a similar manner elsewhere in the British Isles.

It was a Mr Joseph Huband Smith of Dublin who first brought the seals to the attention of his countrymen in a paper he read to the Royal Irish Academy in 1839.

He had an extraordinary story to tell. For several years, Chinese seals had come to light in obscure places in the towns and countryside of Ireland. The first seems to have been found in about 1780, when a turf cutter found one buried in a bog at Mountrath near Portlaoise in what was then called Queen's County. Another was discovered in about 1805 in a cave near Cork harbour; yet another by some men who were digging up the roots of an old pear tree in an orchard in County Down. Then there was the seal found at Clonliffe Parade near the Dublin Circular Road in 1816. A sixth seal was turned up by a plough in a field in County Tipperary, and two more, in the bed of the River Boyne in County Meath, and in Killead, County Down, respectively.

In the years that followed Huband Smith's revelations, the mystery of the Chinese seals stirred fierce passions among Irish antiquarians. None of them could agree where the seals came from, what the animal on top of them was, whether the inscription on the underside actually meant something in Chinese, or how it was that such exotic objects had seemingly been scattered years before in such unlikely places. Smith lost little time in informing the Academy of his own theory: 'It is therefore, at least, possible that they may have arrived hither from the East, along with the weapons, ornaments, and other articles of commerce, which were brought to these islands by the ships of the great merchant-princes of antiquity, the Phoenicians, to whom our ports and harbours were well known.'

In the 1840s, a man named Edmund Getty from Belfast decided to try to answer some of the questions about the seals. He consulted a naturalist who confirmed suspicions that the apelike animal on the top of them had been modelled to look like a Chinese monkey. He then decided to take impressions of all the seals that had so far turned up – there were now about twenty-six of them – to determine whether they bore an inscription in Chinese. This was quite an undertaking, but fortunately one of his friends was appointed to a job in Hong Kong, and he was able to ask two groups of Chinese scholars to attempt to translate them.

Such was the pace of communication between Ireland and the East in Victorian times, that two years went by before Getty received the answer to his question. It was that the seals were undoubtedly Chinese and that the type of script on them was in use in about 500BC, the time of Confucius. The scholars agreed on the meaning of many of the inscriptions; one seal, for example, bore the legend: 'A pure Heart', and another 'The Heart, though small, most generous'. Sometimes, however, the Chinese scholars disagreed with each other as to meaning. According to a group of scholars in Nanking, one seal's inscription read 'Some Friend', while Shanghai academics maintained that it meant 'Plum trees and Bamboos'.

Still, some progress had been made, and by 1853, at least fifty seals had been found. By 1868, the Royal Irish Academy learned from a Dr Frazer that there were now sixty-one seals but he believed that they were relatively modern, probably dating from the fourteenth or fifteenth centuries, or even later.

But the mystery of how the seals got to Ireland still remains. A few of the seals are to be found on the top shelf of a glass case in the National Museum of Ireland in Dublin. With them are four seals which the museum's catalogue says were 'bought at Canton, 1864', and were ordered by Dr Frazer for comparison.

At our request, they were examined for the first time in many years by Jan Chapman, an orientalist from Dublin's Chester Beatty Library. To begin with, she noted that the fact that the seals were made of porcelain was very unusual, since they are usually carved from minerals. Their size, too, surprised her, for most Chinese seals, including some on other shelves in the museum are much larger. She was, however, able to identify the porcelain itself as the product of a factory situated near one of China's main trading ports, Amoy. Although the factory started making porcelain in the twelfth century, Miss Chapman believes the seals found in Ireland date from the early eighteenth century, which is when the factory exported porcelain of that type. But, beyond that, she can shed no light on the mystery. All the seals were, it is true, found east of a line drawn from Lough Foyle to Cape Clear, and it may be that they entered Ireland at Cork. But this is too vague a pattern to be of any real use, and the Chinese seals of Ireland remain as puzzling as they were in Fort's day.

THE LOCH NESS
MONSTER

Although many countries around the world have claimed a monster of their own, the classic one remains the Loch Ness monster in Scotland.

Loch Ness slashes like a great scar north-eastwards, almost severing northern Scotland from the rest of Britain: twenty-four miles (39km) long, it can be a daunting place. Sheer mountains rise 2,000 feet (600m) from the loch side. The water, always dark and murky, can be whipped into impressive storms. The depths reach 900 feet (275m), perhaps 1,000 feet (300m). Inverness lies at the northern end, Fort Augustus at the southern. Urquhart Castle stands out as the greatest landmark halfway along on the northern side. It was here on the northern bank of the loch in 1933 that a monster was not only seen but also photographed.

Hugh Gray, the man who took the photograph, swore a statement about the circumstances in which the picture had been taken.

Four Sundays ago, after church, I went for my usual walk near where the Foyers river enters the loch. The loch was like a mill pond and the sun was shining brightly. An object of considerable dimensions rose out of the water not so very far from where I was. I immediately got my camera ready and snapped the object which was then two to three feet above the surface of the water. I did not see any head, for what I took to be the front parts were under the water, but there was considerable movement from what seemed to be the tail.

Earlier that year, a flurry of sightings had appeared in the local and national papers. One day in September, the Reverend W E Hobbes of Wroxeter had arrived at Miss Janet Fraser's Halfway House tea shop to find the place empty. All the guests were upstairs looking at the monster. Joined by the new arrival, the group watched the creature disporting itself about half a mile out in the loch. They gave what was to become an almost standard description of the monster: two low humps and a tail which splashed about making a disturbance on the surface, a snake-like head and neck which stood well out of the water and seemed to be looking round, a large shining eye.

This was only one of more than fifty sightings that had the newspapers streaming north for copy to bury the gloomy news of unemployment and depression which was otherwise dominating their pages. Almost everyone noticed the V-shaped wash and the considerable speed which the monster produced when it moved. Some noticed a powerful tail and in August, Mr A H Palmer, who saw it at only a 100-yard range, reported a gaping red mouth, 1 foot or more across and short horns or antennae on the head. All witnesses that year were sure the creature was large, at least twenty feet (6m) long.

The worldwide publicity has produced a steady stream of monster-hunters to the loch, which only recently has eased off.

Undoubtedly the champion eyewitness is Alex Campbell, who was the water bailiff of Loch Ness for many years.

My best sighting was in May 1934 right off the Abbey boathouse. That morning I was standing at the mouth of the River Hawick looking for what we call a run of salmon. I heard the sound of two trawlers coming through the canal from the West. Suddenly there was this upsurge of water right in front of the canal entrance. I was stunned. I shut my eyes three times to make sure I was not imagining things – the head and the huge humped body were perfectly clear. I knew right away that the creature was scared because of its behaviour. The head was twisting about frantically. It was the thud, thud of the engines that was the reason for its upset. As soon as the bow of the first trawler came within my line of vision, that's when it was in its line of vision too, and it vanished out of sight, gone. I estimated the length of the body thirty feet at least, the height of the head and neck above water level as six feet, and the skin was grey.

Despite many organized efforts, the best evidence still seems to turn up by chance. Peter and Gwen Smith from Luton were holidaying round the loch. Gwen was idly gazing across at Urquhart Castle with a view to taking some shots for the family movie. 'Suddenly,' she recounts, 'this thing came vertically up out of the water, more or less where I was looking. I started filming and of course, I caught it just as it was going down. We stood for a minute and then it came up again and I started filming again. And then a third time.'

Her husband watched the whole thing through binoculars.

The head rose up at least the height of a man [he said]. It was a good foot thick across the neck. The head seemed to me strangely rectangular. I watched it actually turn its head through ninety degrees as though it was looking directly at us or directly away from us. The last time it came right next to a youth who was in a boat. It came up very confidently as before, then, suddenly, seemed to change its mind and withdrew very quickly as it perceived the boat. I am convinced, if only because of the enormous length of the neck that it was no animal we are familiar with.

The film, though clear enough, adds little to earlier photographs of the animal.

In August 1986, three teenaged girls working for the summer at the Loch Ness Hotel, Drumnadrochit, were standing near Urquhart Castle. It was near midnight. The loch was quiet. But they claim that when they looked out over the water, they saw a dark shape in the middle of the loch.

'It had a large hump at one end and a smaller hump at the other,' said Catriona Murray. 'At first we thought it was an island, but then we realized there are no islands in that part of Loch Ness.'

Catriona's companion, Sharon Boulton, was equally astonished. 'It kept appearing and disappearing,' she said, 'and, despite its massive size, we could not hear a sound. It could not have been an illusion because we all saw it.'

The girls tried to rouse the occupants of a nearby house, but no one stirred. Instead they stopped a passing milk lorry and its driver obligingly shone his headlights over the water. But there was nothing unusual to be seen: just the glinting water, unruffled by humps.

Most ambitious of all the schemes to find definitive proof of Nessie's existence came in 1984, when a huge tubular trap, eighty feet (25m) long and made of fibreglass, was airlifted into the loch. But patience was not rewarded. The trap – designed merely to detain the monster for photography and examination by a zoologist – was never sprung.

Other researchers took to the air in the Goodyear blimp *Europa*, but its crew of twenty-five failed to spot anything out of the ordinary as they cruised above the loch at a stately thirty-five miles per hour.

Theories advanced to explain the monster's elusive nature and its reasons for taking up residence in Loch Ness have become weirder and wilder. 'Is Nessie a Giant Squid?' asked a writer in Britain's journal of strange phenomena, *Fortean Times*. Meanwhile, in 1983, monster-hunter Eric Beckjord explained his new idea to reporters:

> I am beginning to think of it this way: you need a pair of polaroid glasses to see the laminations on your car windscreen.
>
> What if there is a monster and it has quasi-or pseudo-invisibility? The human eye cannot register the whole spectrum of light. We cannot see infra-red.
>
> Maybe Nessie's coat has some sort of colour that doesn't show up too good on most people's retinas. That would explain a lot.

Yet it would be wrong to suggest that little has changed. At Loch Ness the heyday of monster-hunting seems to be over. In addition, the publication, in 1983, of *The Loch Ness Mystery Solved* by Ronald Binns and R J Bell cast serious doubt on many now 'taken-for-granted' beliefs and sightings. They challenge many of the accepted 'facts' about the monster. Here are a couple of examples of Binns' and Bell's well-argued 'demolition jobs'.

The first concerns the idea, much loved by Nessie's 'biographers', that eyewitness accounts of monster sightings can be traced far back into history. Binns and Bell decided to go back to the original sources of these tales, and what they found convinced them that, 'under scrutiny, the legends of Loch Ness all vanish into thin air'.

For example, a neolithic carved stone found near the loch is said to portray the monster, when in fact it carries a Pictish design common throughout Scotland. Frequently quoted references to sightings in 1520, 1771 and 1885 come from what the authors call 'an eccentric letter which appeared in *The Scotsman* on 20 October 1933'. They add that the letter-writer 'failed to supply either his address or any specific references to the chronicles or publications wherein his weird and wonderful stories could be found'. References to a Loch Ness monster in the works of a Greek historian, Dio Cassius, who wrote a history of Rome in about AD200, or to an article apparently containing a woodcut of the creature in the Atlanta *Constitution* for November 1896 turn out not to exist. Even St Columba's encounter with a 'water beast' in the River Ness, reported in a life of the saint written in AD565, is persuasively dismissed on the grounds that the *River* Ness is some way from the loch and is separated from it by another lake; the 'water beast' is merely one of a cast of many obviously mythical creatures introduced into the story to show that Columba possessed magical powers.

The authors' second target is Alex Campbell, the water bailiff of Loch Ness, whom they believe was altogether biased when, in his capacity of part-time journalist, he incited readers into sharing his passionate belief in the existence of the monster.

So how do Binns and Bell interpret the hundreds of monster sightings? Since they believe that no single theory can explain them all, they offer quite a variety, among them swimming deer ('horned monsters') otters (at least two of the rare sightings on land turn out to contain, they say, 'only a marginally exaggerated description of an otter'), floating tar barrels (left over from road improvements), tree trunks ('single-humped monsters'), and wakes of the many boats that criss-cross the loch. Other sightings they ascribe to mirages. Alex Campbell was far from being the only person to have seen them: the authoritative six-volume *Bathymetrical Survey of the Scottish Fresh-Water Lochs,* published in 1910, devotes a special section to mirages seen at Loch Ness. The authors of *The Loch Ness Mystery Solved* add that the summer of 1933 was particularly fine – ideal mirage conditions.

Binns and Bell were not the only investigators at work. In April 1984 perhaps the most formidable of them all, Steuart Campbell of Edinburgh, published an article in the *British Journal of Photography* to mark – in a devastatingly back-handed way – the fiftieth anniversary of the taking of one of the most famous of all Loch Ness monster photographs. Known as 'the surgeon's picture', it had been snapped in April 1934 by a London gynaecologist called Robert Kenneth Wilson.

Wilson's story was that he had been driving along the lochside road early in the morning, when he noticed 'a considerable commotion on the surface, some distance out from the shore, perhaps two or three hundred yards out. When I watched it for perhaps a minute or so, something broke surface and I saw the head of some strange animal rising out of the water. I hurried to the car for my camera . . .' He said he took four photographs, but two of them turned out to be blank when they were developed by the local chemist. One was bought by a newspaper, which published only the section showing the 'monster'.

Steuart Campbell managed to locate the full print, by then extremely tattered, and looked carefully at both pictures. Wilson had claimed that he had been 'some hundred feet above the loch' when the pictures were taken and that the 'monster' had been 'between 150 and 200 yards from the shore'. But using the prints, and calculating the angle from which the pictures must have been taken, Campbell calculated that Wilson had, in fact, been very much nearer the water than he had said. Campbell also showed that the 'monster' must be only twenty-eight inches (70cm) high, observing, 'That is a rather small monster!'

Finally, Campbell suggested that the photographs probably show an otter. In one – the frame usually published – its tail is visible; in the other, its head. Commented Campbell: 'It can hardly be an accident that this second picture, which might have revealed the true nature of the object, is out of focus.' There seemed, in short, to be a distinct element of hoax about the whole thing. This revealing analysis shook one of the main photographic pillars of support for the existence of the Loch Ness monster.

Campbell later moved on to a re-examination of the most famous piece of motion picture evidence, the so-called 'Dinsdale film'. This was taken on 23 April 1960 by Tim Dinsdale, an aeronautical engineer who was on a lone investigation of the monster. On the last morning of his trip, Dinsdale was in his car, rolling down the road near the Foyers Hotel, when he saw a puzzling object about three-quarters of a mile out in the loch. It was large, dappled, and 'a distinct mahogany colour'. Dinsdale slammed on his brakes, jumped out and located the object with his binoculars. Now it looked like a living creature – with humps. He started to film, pausing only to rewind the motor of his clockwork cine camera. With only a few feet of film left, he made a desperate dash to the lochside in the hope of a closer shot, but, to his exasperation, by the time he got there the object had disappeared from view.

Shortly afterwards, with good scientific principles in mind, Dinsdale persuaded the owner of the Foyers Hotel to take a dinghy with an outboard motor on to the water and to follow the course taken by the mysterious object. The two sequences could then be compared.

Later, the film was analysed by experts at JARIC (The Joint Air Reconnaissance Intelligence Centre), a leading British photographic interpretation unit. The centre's Report Number 66/1 set the seal on the mystery, for the experts opined that the object was not a boat – it had been moving too fast to have been a dinghy with an outboard motor, and was not painted in the bright colours of a power boat. The report's conclusion brought joy to monster-hunters: 'One can presumably rule out the idea that it is any sort of submarine vessel for various reasons which leaves the conclusion that it is probably an animate object.'

Some twenty years later, in the *Photographic Journal*, Steuart Campbell took another look at the report, and discovered what he took to be a crucial flaw. Dinsdale had said that he had not only paused during filming but had also had to stop so that he could wind up his camera. Campbell suggested that he had done this at least twice. This of course meant that the film did not show one continuous sequence. JARIC, however, appeared not to have taken this into account and, by mistakenly contracting the timescale, had reached the wrong conclusion about the speed at which the object had been travelling. When the pauses between shots had been added to the overall timings, the object and the hotel-owner's dinghy, which Dinsdale had filmed for comparison, were found to have been moving at a similar rate. Campbell therefore arrived at this no-nonsense verdict: 'The only mystery about the film is why it should ever have been thought that it showed anything other than a boat, and why JARIC did not reach the right conclusion.'

The arguments, of course, will continue, in the pages of learned journals, in books, in the lochside pubs far into the chilly Highland nights, and on the shores of the great lake itself during long, hopeful vigils. The monster-hunters, assailed as they increasingly are by the carefully researched doubts of the sceptics, can bask in one certainty: the world wants Loch Ness to have a monster. While there is a chance, however faint, that such a creature may exist, the search is sure to go on.

ARTHUR C CLARKE COMMENTS:

The evidence for something in the Loch is overwhelming; whether it is an animal new to science is another matter. If you want my personal opinion – on Mondays, Wednesdays and Fridays I believe in Nessie. . . .

FIGURES IN A
LANDSCAPE

One hot summer's day in 1932, George Palmer, a civilian pilot, was making a leisurely flight from Las Vegas, Nevada, to Blythe, California, a small town inland from Los Angeles. As he neared Blythe, Palmer scanned the desert 5,000 feet (1,500m) below, looking for emergency landing sites as pilots do in difficult country. Suddenly, as he neared the winding Colorado River, about eighteen miles (29km) from his destination, the giant figure of a man swam into view.

Palmer had only seen it for a moment, and was well aware that the desert sun can play tricks on the most experienced of pilots. So he turned and made another run across the stony bluffs near the river's edge. And there it was, a giant lying on his back, drawn in stones upon the desert pavement. Palmer guessed that the body was about 100 feet (30m) long. And nearby, the astonished pilot could see another vast figure: a four-legged animal like a dog or horse.

Alerted by Palmer, the Los Angeles Museum sent its Curator of History, Arthur Woodward, to investigate, and when he reached the plateaux or *mesas* near Blythe, Woodward found not one group of figures, but three. This was a major archaeological find on his own doorstep, and Woodward's report barely conceals his excitement:

> The first one we visited consisted of a 'trinity' of a man (spread-eagled and lying partly in a huge circle, which from its nature appears to have been used as a dance ring), a long-legged, long-tailed animal, and a small serpentine coil which may have represented a reptile. The man in this case was ninety-five feet long from the crown of the head to the bottom of his feet. The dance ring was a hundred

and forty feet in diameter. The animal was thirty-six feet in length from the tip of its nose to the base of its tail. The serpentine coil was twelve feet in diameter.

The next mesa we visited had a single figure, that of a man upon it. The outline was ninety-eight feet long. The torso was over seventeen feet wide. The arms were outstretched over a span of seventy-four feet. The third mesa had a 'trinity' similar to the first one, save that here the artists had outdone themselves as creators of Herculean monsters. The man in this case was a hundred and sixty-seven feet in length. Each hand had the normal number of fingers and each foot the requisite number of toes.

But the strangest thing about the desert giants was that no one had reported them before, despite the fact that the area had been 'fairly well covered', as Woodward puts it, 'by hundreds of wandering prospectors, surveying crews and many others afflicted with the *Wanderlust*'. This was mainly because the Blythe figures, drawn on the desert before the age of aircraft, were almost impossible to detect on the ground, and were clearly designed to be seen *from the air*.

More than 4,000 miles (5,400km) further south, pilots in southern Peru had made a similar puzzling and spectacular discovery. As the local airline began to open up the country, aircrew and passengers were amazed to discover that the desert between the Ica and Nazca valleys, more than 200 miles (320km) south of Lima, was criss-crossed with a vast 'picture book' of lines, geometrical figures and drawings of birds, insects and animals. Not only was their scale extravagant – some of the lines ran for miles, unswervingly straight over plateaux and mountains, others formed giant enclosures like runways – but they too seemed to have been laid out to be viewed from the sky.

In the face of these discoveries, American archaeologists of the 1930s began to ask questions: who had drawn the pictures, what did they depict, and what were they for? It was easy to ask the questions, but it would prove to be far more difficult to arrive at any satisfactory answers.

*

THE NAZCA LINES

The Nazca lines of Peru offer a profound challenge to archaeologists, but research in laboratory and desert has brought a new
understanding of their purpose. Theories that the lines were
runways for alien spacecraft or tracks laid out for pre-Columbian
athletics meetings have long been laughed out of court.

Anthony F Aveni, Professor of Astronomy and Anthropology
at Colgate University in the United States, led a team which
began an elaborate survey of the lines in 1977. Earlier, he and
a colleague had studied the extraordinary *ceque* system of the
Inca capital, Cuzco. This was a network of forty-one 'invisible
lines' radiating out of the city. Each was punctuated at intervals
by a *huaca*, or sacred place. Unlike the lines, these *huacas* actually existed, and the investigators found that many of those at
the end of the *ceques* marked places near which water could be
found. The system also operated as a gigantic agricultural
calendar: each *huaca* signified a different day in the farmer's
year, and some *ceques* pinpointed where the sun would be on
important dates, thus signifying when, for example, the crops
should be sown. The *ceques* were also used as ritual paths by
pilgrims.

The Nazca lines were probably laid out 1,000 years before
Cuzco was built. Were they, Aveni wondered, forerunners of
the *ceque* system? To find out, six expeditions laboured under the
desert sun; volunteers followed the lines for miles across
the pampa; aerial photographers produced a photo-mosaic;
and the triangles, trapezoids and spirals were meticulously measured. The results were fascinating. Like the spokes of a vast
wheel, many lines radiated from centres, each of which took the
form of a natural hill or a mound on which a rock cairn had been
constructed. These centres reminded the investigators of the
huacas of Cuzco.

Many of the Nazca lines, like their invisible counterparts at
Cuzco, turned out to be associated with water. Some opened up
into vast trapezoids, two thirds of which were aligned with water
courses with their 'thin ends' pointing upstream. The astronomical studies added extra weight to the theory. The lines that

intersected the part of the horizon through which the sun travelled in the course of a year tended to cluster around one particular area – the region where the sun appears in late October, a time especially important to the Nazca farmers, for this is when the dried-up rivers flow again with water. This suggests that the Nazca lines, like the *ceque* system, formed a giant agricultural calendar.

The survey also revealed that the lines had been used as pathways and established that they have many of the characteristics of the old Inca roads. Aveni speculated that workers might have used them to travel from one river valley to another and that the paths might have had some sort of ritual use.

This is how Professor Aveni summed up his findings:

> To be sure, our argument has proceeded by analogy, but whatever the final answer may be to the mystery of the Nazca lines, this much is certain: the pampa is not a confused and meaningless maze of lines, and it was no more intended to be viewed from the air than an Iowa wheatfield. The lines and line centers give evidence of a great deal of order, and the well-entrenched concept of radiality offers affinities between the *ceque* system of Cuzco and the lines on the pampa. All the clues point to a ritual scheme involving water, irrigation and planting; but as we might expect of these ancient cultures, elements of astronomy and calendar were also evident.

Although the question of why the lines were built is the major mystery of Nazca, there is another intriguing enigma still to be resolved: how did the Indians of at least 1,000 years ago draw the birds, insects, and animals that make up the huge 'picture book' of Nazca? The outlines are difficult to make out on the desert floor, yet from the air their precision is flawless.

In August 1982, a small group of enthusiasts assembled at a location far to the north of the 'giant scratchpad', a landfill site near West Liberty, Kentucky. Joe Nickell of the University of Kentucky, an experienced investigator of mysteries, planned to work out how the vast drawings of birds, insects and animals that probably predate the larger Nazca lines were actually inscribed onto the desert. Maria Reiche, the stalwart investigator whose study of Nazca began in the 1940s, had noticed an important clue in the course of her painstaking mapping.

The draughtsmen of ancient times had made small-scale preliminary drawings of the figures on plots six foot (2m) square. They
had then enlarged them, section by section. There can be no
doubt that this was the method used: like the lines and figures,
these sketches have survived the centuries and can still be seen.

Maria Reiche was less specific about how the drawings were
scaled up, however. She suggested that the Nazca Indians could
have used a rope and stakes to make straight lines and circles,
but was vague about how they could have found the right
positions for the stakes that served as the centres of circles or
the ends of straight lines. Joe Nickell thought he might have the
answer, and called in two of his cousins to put his theory to
the test. They decided to try to reproduce one of the most striking
of the Nazca drawings, the giant 440-ft (135-m)-long condor.
Nickell wrote afterwards:

> The method we chose was quite simple. We would establish a center
> line and locate points on the drawing by plotting their coordinates.
> That is, on the small drawing we would measure along the center
> line from one end (the bird's beak) to a point on the line directly
> opposite the point to be plotted (say a wing tip). Then we would
> measure the distance from the center line to the desired point. A
> given number of units on the small drawing would require the same
> number of units – larger units – on the large drawing.

Maria Reiche had suggested that the desert artists had used a
standard unit of measurement known as the 'Nazca foot' – thirty-
two centimetres (12.68in) long. So, using the 'Nazca foot', a
wooden T-square to ensure each measurement they made would
be at right angles to the centre line, a supply of tennis-court
marker-lime for drawing the outline, and with an aeroplane
standing by for aerial photography, Nickell and his group (which
now included his father) set to work. The task took nine
laborious hours of plotting and pegging. Over a mile of string
connected the stakes, but the outline was unmistakable. After a
week's delay, due to rain, they traced it out with lime, and the
figure, 'possibly the world's largest art reproduction', could be
photographed in all its glory from the air.

Cheerfully, Nickell summed up. They had proved that:

the drawings could have been produced by a simple method requiring only materials available to South American Indians centuries ago. The Nazcas probably used a simplified form of this method, with perhaps a significant amount of the work being done freehand. There is no evidence that extra-terrestrials were involved; but, if they were, one can only conclude that they seem to have used sticks and cord just as the Indians did.

THE WHITE HORSES AND FIGURES OF GREAT BRITAIN

The origin of most of the fifty figures that adorn English hillsides is known. The regimental badges near Salisbury, for example, were made by soldiers stationed nearby during the First World War.

However, major mysteries, comparable to the riddles of the Californian Giants and the Nazca Lines, exist in the case of four British hill figures: two chalk giants and two horses, one white, the other red.

The White Horse of Uffington

The White Horse is at the village of Uffington in Berkshire, and is such a local landmark that the whole area, the Vale of the White Horse, takes its name from it. Most of the other British white horses were inspired by it, but the Uffington horse differs from them in one crucial respect: it is the only truly ancient white horse now in existence – all the other horses look as modern as the thoroughbreds stabled in the racing establishments at nearby Lambourn. This is because they are in the style of the eighteenth-century painter George Stubbs, whose equine pictures were popular with the clergymen, doctors and farmers who cut many of the hill figures. The Uffington White Horse is a strange, stylized and disjointed creature, its head is skeletal and beaked, its body thin and elongated, with only two of its galloping legs attached to its flanks. It looks more like a dragon than a horse and the nearby Dragon Hill where St George is said to have killed the dragon has led some people to identify it as that mythical creature. But the earliest reference to it, in a twelfth-century *Book of Wonders*, clearly describes it as a horse with a foal – though what has become of the foal remains one of Uffington's many mysteries.

There are many other references to the White Horse of Uffington in ancient documents. In a cartulary or book of monastic documents relating to the Abbey of Abingdon in the reign of Henry II, a monk named Godrick is said to own land *juxta locum qui vulgo Mons Albi Equi nuncupatur* (near to the place which is popularly known as the Hill of the White Horse). A fourteenth-century manuscript classes it as a marvel second only to Stonehenge. In more modern times, Thomas Hughes, author of *Tom Brown's Schooldays*, wrote a novel set in Uffington and containing much folklore about the White Horse, and G K Chesterton an epic poem full of rolling cadences and rather muddled history. But none of these writers can solve the mystery of White Horse Hill: the horse is certainly ancient, but no one knows exactly how old; it gallops across the Berkshire Downs, but no one knows why it is there.

There have, of course, been many theories. In the seventeenth century John Aubrey and the topographer, Thomas Baskerville (1630–1720), believed the horse was cut by the Anglo-Saxon leader Hengist (his name means 'stallion') twelve hundred years before. Others thought it was commissioned by Alfred the Great, in whose kingdom of Wessex Uffington is situated, to celebrate his victory over the Danes in AD871. More recently, archaeologists have suggested it was the totem of a horse cult. It has even been 'identified' as an ichthyosaurus.

Certainly, the inhabitants of the Vale of the White Horse must have held it in high esteem, for chalk figures must be regularly cleaned or 'scoured' if they are not to disappear again beneath the encroaching turf. From the seventeenth century onwards, historians recorded the curious ceremonies that accompanied the scouring. Known as the Uffington 'Pastime', it was a festival intended to celebrate the horse after a hard day's work of restoration. Thomas Hughes describes the last 'pastime' held in 1857, which was a colourful country fair visited by lords and ladies, gypsies and mountebanks. It suggests that earlier ceremonies may have had a more serious ritualistic purpose, with the horse, perhaps, as an object of worship.

In the face of all this conjecture, one noted archaeologist, Professor Stuart Piggott, has analysed the problems of establishing at least one fact about the White Horse. Piggott has a special interest in the problem: his family came from the Vale and he now lives there himself. His great-grandfather farmed at Uffington; his grandfather, as a boy of ten, was taken to the 1857 'pastime'.

In 1931, in a review article in *Antiquity*, Piggott discussed attempts to set a date for the cutting of the White Horse. One was a very simple technique which had first been suggested in 1740 by a writer who called himself Philalethes Rusticus. Rusticus, and others after him, noticed a stylistic similarity between the Uffington Horse and horses portrayed on coins from the early Iron Age. These early Iron Age horses shared many of the peculiarities of the White Horse, notably the disjointed legs and the beaklike jaws. The coins were minted in Britain some time in the first century BC and they imitate a coin of Philip of Macedon, who had died two centuries earlier. On one side of Philip's original coin is a chariot drawn by two horses and driven by a charioteer. It had long been noted that the design was copied again and again, with the result that 'the chariot degenerated on the British examples to a wheel . . . , the charioteer to a group of pellets and the horse (in the latest stages) to a jumble of dumbbells and crescents'. Halfway through this process of degeneration, the horse on the coins begins to bear a striking resemblance to the Uffington White Horse. There are several such coins from the Uffington area preserved in the Ashmolean Museum in Oxford and elsewhere. And, to reinforce the point, Piggott also recalled how horses on two early Iron Age buckets were in the same artistic tradition. The coins, particularly, allowed him to agree to a fairly precise date for the horse: it was unlikely that so massive a work would have been undertaken during the Roman occupation of Britain, and therefore suggested it was cut in the Celtic Iron Age during the first century BC.

*

The Cerne Giant

An equally puzzling figure stands on a hillside above the picturesque village of Cerne Abbas in Dorset. He is called, quite simply, the Cerne Giant, because, as with the White Horse of Uffington, nothing is known about his origins, and even his name is lost. Yet he is an imposing fellow, 180 feet (55m) long from head to foot, brandishing a knobbly club 120 feet (37m) long in his right hand, as he marches across the hillside away from the village. Unlike the white horses, the Giant is drawn in outline only: his body is made of the hillside turf and the shape and anatomical details are marked out by trenches one to two feet (30–60cm) wide.

The most striking feature of the Cerne Giant is that he is the most blatantly sexual of all the British hill figures. Indeed, his phallus is thirty feet (9m) long, and is so prominent that he has been nicknamed 'The Rude Man of Cerne'. Inevitably, there have been many attempts to bowdlerize him over the years: one of the first was in Hutchins' *History of Dorset* of 1774, where the engraver has stripped him of his manhood. More recently, one letter to *The Dorset Magazine* said, 'Propriety demands that he don a loincloth', and there was even an attempt to provide him with a figleaf of sacking and paper. Fortunately, the Giant has survived in all his glory, much to the delight of archaeologists, small children and old ladies who, apparently, always seem to be standing in the most embarrassing place on the figure when they ask their guide exactly where they are.

Not surprisingly, the Cerne Giant has been taken to be the symbol of a fertility cult, but the few clues to this are vague. One curious phenomenon is that at dawn on 1 May the sun rises directly in line with an observer standing at the base of the Giant's phallus. Whatever this may mean, plenty of legends are associated with him, some of which suggest the vestiges of fertility rites. Girls who fear they may lose their husbands or boyfriends walk round him, hoping his influence will help them prolong their relationship, and others visit the Giant for luck in the week before their marriage. People who live in the Cerne district think that if a barren woman sleeps or makes love in the Giant's phallus she will bear children. It may also be significant that maypole dancing was a regular feature of the village's May Day celebrations, and that the site of the maypole was a rectangular enclosure called the Trendle or Frying Pan a few yards up the hill, above the Giant's Left arm. May Day frolics were certainly associated with fertility; indeed, one sixteenth-century writer, Philip Stubbs, wrote: 'I have heard it crediblie reported by men of great gravity that, of an hundred maides going to the wood, there have scarcely the third part of them returned home again as they went.'

But folklore is a notoriously unreliable guide, and modern theories about the Giant's identity depend on one crucial factor: the date when he was first drawn. The village of Cerne Abbas lies in an area scarred with the remains of ancient forts, henges and camps, and this has led some scholars to claim that the Giant must be a very old man indeed, cut perhaps in prehistoric times. But others think differently, and suggest that, by archaeo-logical standards, he may be quite 'modern', dating from the seventeenth century. They have come to this conclusion by sifting through the reports of the surveyors, tax collectors and topog-raphers who have chronicled the changing landscape of Britain over the centuries.

It is odd, if the Giant is ancient, that he is not mentioned in any document written before 1751. In that year, the Reverend John Hutchins, author of a guide to Dorset, wrote to Dr Lyttleton, Dean of Exeter, about a 'gyant delineated on the side of the Hill, facing the town, of vast Dimensions. . . .' It is stranger still that detailed surveys of the area, notably in 1356 and 1617, should have missed him. There is also nothing in the one set of documents that could hardly have ignored his presence, the parish records. Another telling argument advanced by the modernists is that it is hardly likely that so phallic a figure could have survived in a place like Cerne where there was an impor-tant monastery established in the sixth century AD.

Hutchins was certainly convinced of its modernity. In his letter to Dr Lyttleton he wrote: 'I have heard from the Steward of the Manor it is a modern thing. . . .' Moreover, both Hutchins and local legend agree that the Giant is, in fact, a lampoon, but they are divided on the question of his identity. The locals say he was cut in 1539 when the monastery was dissolved, and that he depicts Thomas Corton, the corrupt last abbot. The Giant's obscene appearance represents his lust, the club his desire for revenge, and the direction of his feet shows he is on his way out of the area. Hutchins, on the other hand, though he later decided the Giant was ancient, said that it ridiculed a local landowner, Lord Holles, whose servants rebelled against him, killed his son, and cut the figure on the hillside to mock him. However, there is no real evidence to connect either the abbot or Lord Holles with the Giant. The eighteenth century delighted in follies, and drawings of primitive men in early seventeenth-century books look very like the Giant, all of which reinforce the case for his modernity.

If, however, the Rude Man of Cerne is ancient, then he may portray a god. The question is, which one?

The first candidate is Nodens, a Celtic god thought to have been worshipped by the Durotriges, the tribe that inhabited Dorset before the Roman invasion of Britain in AD43. The theory stems from a remarkable discovery made just thirteen miles (21 km) from Cerne during the Second World War. A ploughman was ploughing a Celtic fort called Hod Hill near Blandford Forum when he discovered a hoard of objects, including a bronze handle, probably from a skillet or bowl, depicting a naked man. No sooner had the handle been identified by experts as Celtic and the man as Nodens, than the handle's then owner, Bernard Pickard, realized that he had seen him, or someone very like him, before: on the hillside at Cerne. Certainly there are marked similarities: the man on the handle faces forward but his feet are in profile, his nipples are clearly delineated, and in his hand he carries a knobbly club. There are differences too: the figure on the handle has wings and he holds a hare to symbolize his role as god of hunting, and his club is in his left hand, while the Giant's is in his right. Despite this, Bernard Pickard claims the handle provides enough evidence to say that the Cerne Giant may be Nodens.

The rival candidate from the ancient world is Hercules, as championed by Professor Stuart Piggott. Part of the evidence Piggott cites is very circumstantial indeed, consisting of two cryptic quotations from old documents. The first comes from a statement by the antiquarian William Stukeley in 1764 that 'the people there give the name of Helis' to the Giant. The second crops up in a twelfth-century account of a famous visit to Cerne made six hundred years before by St Augustine. The visit did not go well, for Augustine and his followers, who had come to convert the villagers to Christianity, were chased from the place and cows' or fish tails were tied to their clothes. The débâcle was reported by a later chronicler, Walter of Coventry, who mentions in passing that the god Helith was once worshipped in the area. Piggott points out the obvious similarity between the names Helis and Helith, and claims that they may have derived from the name Hercules, by way of the ancient version, Helethkin.

There is good reason for believing that Hercules was an important god in Roman Britain. Roman emperors had an egotistical tendency to identify themselves with great mythical heroes, and, in AD191, the Emperor Commodus managed to establish a cult that worshipped him as the incarnation of Hercules. The cult flourished in Britain, and portrayals of Hercules on an altar found at Whitley Castle, Northumberland bear a close resemblance to the Cerne Giant. Furthermore, Stuart Piggott goes on to speculate that the Trendle, the curious earthwork above the Giant, may have served as a country sanctuary for the Hercules cult. The giant would therefore have been cut in about AD191 as an icon or as a sign to summon the faithful to the hillside temple.

With so many theories, and so little evidence to go on, only new information will help provide the key to the identity and function of the Cerne Giant, One useful step may be to establish whether the Giant looked different when he was first cut. Although he was apparently scoured every seven years, the ravages of the weather or the encroaching grass can soon change or obliterate parts of chalk figures. Indeed, before a scouring in 1979, the Giant had become overgrown and indistinct, and could have disappeared in a few years if its owners, the National Trust, had not called in a firm of building contractors to restore him.

There is a scientific technique for discovering whether ground has been disturbed in the past. It is called resistivity surveying, and has already helped archaeologists in their search for lost features of hill figures. To conduct a resistivity survey, a scientist walks over the area he wishes to examine, carrying a set of electrodes on a frame. At regular intervals, he sticks the electrodes into the ground and passes an electric current through them. With a meter, he measures the soil's resistance to electricity. The basic principle is that soil which has been disturbed is looser and drier than the undug ground beneath, and is more resistant to the electric current. As a result, the disturbed areas give a high resistance, while that of untouched land is low.

The exciting part comes back in the laboratory: now the points where resistance is high can be plotted and joined up, as in a child's puzzle book, to see if they form a recognizable pattern. The technique is still in its infancy, and may do no more than pinpoint rocks or rabbit holes just below the surface, but it can also yield remarkable results.

THE LONG MAN OF WILMINGTON

An early resistivity survey revealed some intriguing 'lost' features of Britain's other great chalk giant, the Long Man of Wilmington near Eastbourne in East Sussex. Like the Cerne Giant, the Long Man is cut in outline, in trenches two foot four inches (71 cm) wide. He is 231 foot (70.1m) tall, his legs look rather athletic, but his face is blank and his body quite sexless. The most striking thing about him is that he holds a staff about 240 foot (73m) long in each hand. Even less is known about his early history than the Giant's, because no document before 1799 mentions him. A sketch made in that year shows the Long Man with a rake in his right hand and a scythe in the other, like a labourer setting out for the fields. But by 1825, if a local guide-book of the time is to be believed, the Long Man merely carried two staffs, suggesting that if they existed in the first place the rake and scythe-blade had been obliterated.

Certainly, the detailed shape of the Long Man may have been changed over the years, notably by a restoration in 1874, when he was given a permanent outline of 7,000 bricks. Mr K W E Gravett of the Sussex Archaeological Society decided to carry out a resistivity survey to discover whether the tops of the staves had in fact disappeared. Gravett and his companions, working on the steep slopes of Windover Hill, found it an arduous task, but the results of their two-day survey were unexpectedly rewarding. Their meter registered points of disturbance, not only at the tops of both staves, but also above the Long Man's head. When they joined up the points, the outline of something very like a rake appeared on the right-hand staff, a 'scythe-blade' on the other, and, on his head, a 'feather' or 'plume'. It is a fascinating discovery, suggesting the 1799 sketch may be the most accurate portrayal of the Long Man, but, even if the resistivity findings are verified by excavation, they fail to solve the central question of his purpose. In the hope of establishing whether the Cerne Giant's appearance has altered, we commissioned a resistivity survey from Anthony Clark of the Ancient Monuments Laboratory in London's Savile Row. Clark was the first full-time geophysicist to be employed in British archaeology, and was therefore uniquely qualified to do the work. If the Giant turned out to be carrying a hare, then the case for identifying him as the Celtic god Nodens would be strengthened; if, on the other hand, something like a lion skin were to emerge, Professor Stuart Piggott's theory that he is Hercules would win the day.

The survey began in July 1979 and, after two days' work, Dr Clark and his assistant, Alistair Bartlett, were already excited: their instruments showed that the ground round the Giant's arm and left hand had indeed been disturbed. When computer analysis revealed the precise outline of the disturbance, they were astonished: it looked exactly like the lion skin depicted on Roman statues of Hercules. David Thackray, the archaeologist responsible for the care of the Giant, thought the findings convincing: 'He has so many features which Hercules has from portrayals of the Roman period. He has the club, the great virility, the superhuman size, and now the lion skin . . .'

The Red Horse of Tysoe

The final mysterious British landscape figure is the Red Horse of Tysoe, which, at the moment, can be seen neither from the ground nor the air. It was once so prominently situated above the village of Tysoe in Warwickshire that the whole area was known as the Vale of the Red Horse, and the creature itself was dubbed 'The Nag of Renown'. The Horse was red because it was cut, not from chalk, but from the loamy soil. Now it has vanished, and the search for it has become something of a personal crusade for two local men, Kenneth Carrdus and Graham Miller, both retired schoolmasters.

Carrdus and Miller spent long hours in libraries and record offices before establishing, to their satisfaction, exactly where the Red Horse had been before its destruction by a pub landlord in 1800. The documents they had consulted led them to a slope near Tysoe called The Hangings. After several years and a dry summer, Miller photographed a patch of vegetation on The Hangings that had turned a different colour from its surroundings. The patch formed the head, neck and back of a gigantic horse. Later, aerial pictures revealed not only the ears, legs and tail, but also the outlines of two other horses: clearly there had been a succession of Red Horses cut at different times. Carrdus and Miller also chanced upon a map drawn in 1796 with the symbol of a horse on the spot they had found. According to their measurements, the Red Horse of Tysoe measured 200 feet (64m) long and 250 feet (76m) high. The problem was that many people could not clearly see the Horse's outline in the photographs and, despite a resistivity survey commissioned by Carrdus which confirmed his findings, some, though by no means all, archaeologists remain unconvinced. Carrdus and Miller, however, are satisfied that they have found what they believe to be the largest Anglo-Saxon work of art in Britain. Until they can convince everyone that it is there, the Red Horse of Tysoe will remain 'lost' beneath the young larches and Scots pines that today cover The Hangings. In the meantime, Carrdus and Miller, undaunted, are searching for another vanished giant, said to have been cut on Shotover Hill near Oxford.

BLYTHE'S FIGURES

With so many of the riddles of the British hill figures still un-
resolved after more than 200 years, it was perhaps too much to
expect that archaeologists in the Americas would come to definitive conclusions about the drawings on their own landscape in
a mere half century. The figures at Blythe in California are still
a puzzle, although members of an expedition to them from the
National Geographical Society in 1951 did, at least, come up
with a theory. To the expedition leader, anthropologist Frank
M Setzler, the presence of four-footed animals at two of the
Blythe sites was a clue to their date. They looked like horses,
and horses meant the figures were either very ancient or relatively modern, since the native American horse died out 10,000
years ago and its successor had not been introduced by the
Spaniards until 1540. There was little erosion of the figures so
Setzler opted for their modernity, and turned to Indian folklore
for an explanation. He found a legend of a strange child called
Ha'ak who grew to maturity in three or four years. When she
began to eat their children, the Indians tried to kill her, and this
deed was finally done by another strange figure called 'Elder
Brother'. In Arizona, Setzler discovered a shrine depicting the
overthrown Ha'ak, and concluded that the tradition had passed
from tribe to tribe, and that the giants had been drawn between
1540 and 1850 by local Indians as a similar shrine. But this is
one man's theory, and no one has explained why the Indians
should have designed figures which, as Setzler graphically put it,
'only Gods or birds could grasp'.

ARTHUR C CLARKE COMMENTS:

*My earlier comments on circles and standing stones apply even
more strongly here (see page 111). The 'Nazca Lines' are
certainly puzzling and impressive, but they may represent not
much more than man's age-old desire to leave some record of
his existence – 'Kilroy was here' on a landscape-filling scale. The
contemporary artist, Christo, has been doing exactly the same
sort of thing with his fifty-mile-long constructions.*

And as for the figures of animals which can only be appreciated from an aerial vantage point – why should there be any mystery about this? Men have always peopled the sky with gods, and seen all manner of strange beasts in the patterns of the stars.

From this, it is only a short step – and a good deal of tedious but not difficult labour – to reproduce those patterns on the ground, perhaps in the hope of receiving celestial benefits.

Sorry, Herr von Däniken. The simplest explanation is often the right one....

INSIDE
INFORMATION

One Saturday morning in the summer of 1974 Mrs Lesley Brennan lay on the sofa at home watching an old movie, *The Nevadan*, on television. Suddenly the film, she says, was interrupted by a newsflash announcing that there had been a serious explosion in the large chemical plant at Flixborough, in Lincolnshire. Many people had been killed and injured.

Irritated though she was at the interruption to the adventures of the Nevadan, Mrs Brennan registered the story particularly, because it was local. The Flixborough Nypro plant which produced caprolactam, a basic material of nylon, covered a sixty-acre site twenty miles inland from Mrs Brennan's home at Cleethorpes, near Grimsby, on the east coast of England. Shortly afterwards, around noon, two friends, Janice and Peter East, came in from work and Mrs Brennan told them the news. They then forgot about the incident until they were watching the early evening television news.

Mrs Brennan says: 'We sat laughing, because they said it had happened at teatime. We sat there saying: "Silly reporters. Got it wrong again. It was midday, dinner time, not teatime, it happened." Anyway, next morning we got the paper, *The Sunday People*. It said the accident happened at five o'clock in the afternoon.

'I went ever so cold. I really went funny. We went out and got another paper and that said teatime too. My friends said, "You told us at dinner – twelve o'clock."' In fact the Nypro plant had blown up at 4.53pm in the afternoon of Saturday, 1 June 1974, killing twenty-eight people and damaging nearly

2,000 factories and shops. By chance, though the site was remote, a Yorkshire Television camera team happened to be in the area, and filmed some graphic scenes within minutes. The event took place about five hours after Mrs Brennan had claimed to have heard about it from the newsflash. The two friends confirmed the story immediately afterwards to Mr Robin Furman, who then wrote an account for the *Grimsby Evening Telegraph*.

Grimsby, as it happens, already held a place in the history of precognition. It was a Grimsby woman, Sandra MacDonald, who claimed to have foreseen the dramatic sinking of the Royal Navy submarine HMS *Artemis* in 1971. Then seventeen years old, Sandra had gone out with a number of the sailors from *Artemis* when the boat had paid a 'courtesy' visit to Grimsby. At the Mecca Dance Hall the submariners made an exotic addition to the squad of lads from the local fishing fleet. They made a big impression on the girls of Grimsby, and then, as sailors do, they moved on.

Three days later, Sandra MacDonald came running downstairs after a terrible nightmare in which she had seen the submarine sinking in a port or dockyard. 'I saw it disappearing under the water. There were people running all over. Then for some reason there were three men that were in this compartment, and I knew they were trapped. It was Doug and Taffy and another man I didn't know. In my dream one of them died.' Sandra told the story to her mother, and also to a number of friends. 'Well then, a week later, I came home from Tiffany's and my Mum said, "I've got bad news for you. The submarine's gone down. And there's three trapped." I just broke down and sobbed.'

Artemis had in fact sunk at her moorings at Gosport in Hampshire because she had been wrongly ballasted. It was ten and a half hours before the three trapped men were rescued from the watertight compartment to which they had retreated. But, contrary to Sandra MacDonald's dream, they all survived, including the two she had dreamt of. There seems little doubt from the array of testimony collected by Dr Keith Hearne that Sandra had indeed reported her dream in quite precise detail to a number of friends as well as her mother in the days before the sinking took place.

Across the Atlantic in the summer of 1976 the Teton Dam in eastern Idaho failed on 5 June, killing eleven people and causing damage on a massive scale. Dr Lucille Wood-Trost, who lived in the area, took the opportunity to ask through local radio and newspapers whether there had been any precognition of the disaster. She had eighteen replies. One woman, the wife of a man who had worked on the dam, had had a persistent dream that her neighbour's goats were being washed away in a flood and drowned. The dream recurred at least three times, despite the fact that in real life the goats were never normally near the water. But the day before the flood, the neighbour moved them to pasture on an island in the middle of the Snake River. They were all lost. Another woman, who had not lived in Idaho for nineteen years, dreamed the night before of going back to visit her relatives. As they crossed the Snake River Bridge, 'Huge waves began to come over it. They finally snapped the bridge in half.' The bridge did indeed break in the real flood the following day. Both dreams were confirmed by the women's husbands.

Sensations of premonition and clairvoyance – seeing across time and space – are probably the most universal of the mind's 'strange powers'. Even among the upmarket readership of *The Times*, more than half of the respondents to a questionnaire admitted to at least one personal experience of prerecognition – having 'an impression, hunch or vision concerning events you did not know about or expect, but which turned out to be true'.

It is important in assessing such experiences to try to separate them from the mind's extraordinary powers of visual imagination. Everyone dreams at night, many have a fantasy life more vivid than their mundane reality. The mind will absorb clues to the future. Frequently perceptions of imminent death can be ascribed to a friend or spouse unconsciously noticing some telltale signs of sickness or decline. The hidden logic of the mind draws its fatal conclusions.

Professional clairvoyants, the Genuine Gypsy Rose Lees, the suburban practitioners operating through the small ad columns of newspapers, rely more consciously on small signs and giveaways among their clients. Professional magicians use the same techniques on stage in mind-reading and clairvoyance acts. If necessary, and if the effort is worth it for professional or even criminal intent, the clairvoyant may, like the medium, indulge in some prior research. It has been a lucrative field for at least a hundred years on both sides of the Atlantic. But when the clutter of avarice and fraud has been cleared away and all cases with a known rational explanation disposed of, there still remains an extraordinary body of challenging testimony to consider.

War has inevitably produced the most intense premonitions of imminent death. Wing Commander George Potter from Bushey in Hertfordshire developed a terrifying facility for fore-seeing deaths among his comrades during the relentless RAF campaigns against Rommel's German troops in the Western Desert in 1942. Once he saw the commanding officer of a torpedo aircraft squadron drinking in the officers' mess. 'Gradually I saw his head and shoulders moving in a bottom-less depth of blue-blackness. He had eye sockets but no eyes, the flesh of his face was dully blotched in greenish purplish shadows, with shreds peeling off near his left ear.'

The CO died within two days, shot down off Benghazi – the 'blue-blackness' of the Mediterranean had claimed him. Wing Commander Potter had other premonitions too, but with thirty or forty million casualties in the Second World War and the universal tensions and stresses of those six years of conflict, it is inevitable that nightmares and hallucinations, anxieties and apprehensions, should have, on statistical grounds alone, produced what seemed like premonitions fulfilled.

However, the war was over when one of the most striking of such incidents occurred to Air Marshal Sir Victor Goddard of the Royal New Zealand Air Force. In January 1946, he was in Shanghai. Goddard's friend George Alwyne Ogden, the new British consul, decided to give a cocktail party on the night before he was due to fly home. It was a crowded occasion. Suddenly, through the hubbub, the Air Marshal heard a voice behind him say, 'Too bad about Goddard. Terrible crash.'

The speaker was an English naval officer, Gerald Gladstone – later Admiral Sir Gerald Gladstone. The two men knew each

other. Goddard turned. And Gladstone froze. 'I'm terribly sorry
... I mean, I'm terribly glad.' Then he began to entreat Goddard
not to fly, saying he had had the most vivid, involuntary vision
of Goddard in a Dakota plane in a snowstorm. It had come over
mountains in a storm and then crashed in the evening on a
'rocky shingly shore'. There had been two civilian Englishmen
and a girl on board as well as the crew.

Goddard relaxed, for although he was indeed due to fly on
to Japan in a Dakota – Lord Mountbatten's personal plane – he
was taking only his military crew, certainly no passengers. Only
a few minutes elapsed, however, before a messenger came in to
the party with a radio signal for the consul: Ogden was asked
to go to Tokyo at once for an urgent meeting. He asked Goddard
to take him along. Then an English reporter, Seymour Berry of
the *Daily Telegraph*, begged a ride. Reluctantly, Goddard agreed.
Just as the party was ending came another message. A secretary
was needed in Tokyo. Could Ogden bring one with him? The
girl chosen was Dorita Breakspear.

The party in the Dakota, call-sign *Sister Ann*, took off for
Tokyo the following morning. It was a long flight. The radio
went down. By three in the afternoon there was snow. Goddard
registered that time was beginning to tick off Gladstone's premonition – a Dakota, two men and one girl civilian passengers,
failing light, and snow. Then, as they came over the Japanese
coast in ten-tenths cloud – mountains. It was clear they were off
course. Fuel was low. What were they to do?

They decided to look for an emergency landing. Below the
clouds, as they came down, was a howling snowstorm. The first
thing they could make out was a small fishing village and the
only flat area in sight a stretch of 'rocky, shingly shore'. Out at
sea the waves were mountainous. There was no alternative to
an emergency landing on the beach. Goddard, by now certain
that fate had caught up with him, watched as the pilot tried
three times to land. The plan was to come in with the wheels
down, then retract the undercarriage to stop *Sister Ann* sticking
in the shingle and cartwheeling. On the third pass the Dakota
hit the ground. There was no time for any action on the undercarriage. The plane slewed across the beach to the sound of

tearing metal. Ogden was thrown out of his seat. Then silence. After a few moments Goddard realized he was still alive. So was Ogden. So was the girl, Dorita Breakspear, and Seymour Berry and, indeed, the whole crew. Villagers ran down to help them out of the wreckage, all unscathed. The premonition had been fulfilled in every respect. Except the last.

The frisson that follows violent, random, sadistic death despatches its vibrations rapidly through any community. In the damp autumn of 1979 the people of England's largest county, Yorkshire, were experiencing perhaps more acutely than any peaceful community in modern times, the tremors from a series of frightful killings. Already twelve women were dead and four others had barely escaped with their lives. The last murder, with knife, hammer and screwdriver, had been as horrific as the previous eleven, though the public had not yet been told the dreadful details. Still, enough was known to make every woman in the county careful about going out after dark. Firms organized special cars to take their staff home at night; university clubs and societies cancelled meetings unless they could provide coaches or escorts to take girls back to their homes; the night life of Bradford, Leeds and Huddersfield was at its lowest ebb. In the charged atmosphere, naked fear was dominant as the police seemed no nearer to capturing a murderer armoured by what seemed supernatural impunity.

It is not surprising, either, that there were presentiments and premonitions, clairvoyants who 'saw' the time and place of the next killing, dreamers who described the features of the 'Ripper', women who were certain that if they went out that night they would be the next victim. They all telephoned the police. And the police, already overwhelmed with reports from a frantic public, took note – and took such precautions as they could. The press and television dutifully and sceptically investigated the tips and visions that came the way of their news desks.

So it was in no great mood of expectation that a girl from the London office of the *Yorkshire Post*, Shirley Davenport, made her way to an address in south London one day in October 1979. She had been sent to interview Mrs Nella Jones who was claiming to have had a clairvoyant vision of the Yorkshire killer.

Miss Davenport is an experienced reporter. She knew that whatever Mrs Jones said would never get in the paper: it might inspire a 'copy cat' killer; it might merely add further tangles to the jungle of information already smothering the police. Nevertheless, she made careful note of what Mrs Jones had to say, went back to the office and wrote it up. The story was duly 'spiked' and never published.Three months later Mrs Jones came up with more information. Again Shirley Davenport noted it, but without writing it up. At the beginning of November 1980 Mrs Jones reported 'seeing' the next killing. It would be 17 or 27 November, she said.

On the night of 17 November the thirteenth victim died. Shirley Davenport was shaken. She went back through her notes, but still the paper refrained from publishing anything. The New Year of 1981 came, and then, at last, by a combination of luck and 'normal police work' the Yorkshire killer was caught. Ignoring the usual restraints, the networks fed the nation with every detail they could find about Peter Sutcliffe, killer of thirteen women. Shirley Davenport, sitting in front of a television set 200 miles away in London watched with growing astonishment.

Peter Sutcliffe was a lorry driver working for a firm called Clark Transport. Miss Davenport remembered that in the very first interview, a year and four months earlier, Mrs Nella Jones had said the 'Ripper' was a lorry driver called Peter and that she could see a name beginning with C on the side of his cab. Miss Davenport went for her notebooks. The January 1980 report was quite specific. The killer, said Mrs Jones, lived in a big house in Bradford, No. 6 in its street. It was elevated above the street behind wrought-iron gates, with steps leading up to the front door. In amazement Miss Davenport watched as the first pictures of Sutcliffe's home came up on the screen. It was No. 6 Garden Lane, Bradford. As the police and press milled about in the road, the house itself loomed above them in the dark. There were indeed wrought-iron gates. There were indeed steps up to the front door.

It has to be said that Nella Jones made a stream of predictions about the 'Ripper', some utterly wide of the mark, some, in her subsequent accounts, differing from her reported statements at the time. But Shirley Davenport says: 'It was still the most weird experience. It went far beyond anything coincidence or guesswork could possibly have provided. And you have to remember that for the previous two years all the public signs had been that the police were looking for a man who came from the north-east of England, a hundred miles away and who worked in an engineering plant.'

Premonition need not be doom-laden. Throughout the Western world, punters scouring the *Daily Racing Form* or the *Sporting Life* pray fervently every morning that some vision will be vouchsafed to them – preferably at a transparently attractive price, like thirty-three to one. And it does happen – Lord Kilbracken, the late English peer, claimed to dream of race horses with a clairvoyance worthy of *The Rocking Horse Winner*.

His successes began when he was an undergraduate at Balliol College, Oxford, in 1946, and still plain John Godley. He dreamed that two horses, Bindal and Juladin, were winning at Plumpton and Wetherby racecourses. When he woke up he checked the paper and the two horses were listed. That afternoon they both won. Within a month Godley dreamed of another double. He told his friends Kenneth Harris and Angelica Bohm. This time he decided to eliminate all scepticism by having the names of the horses, Baroda Squadron and The Brogue, witnessed and time-stamped by the Oxford Post Office. Again, both won.

Godley became Racing Correspondent of the *Daily Mirror* and the gift stayed with him sporadically for more than a decade, including a hefty win on the 1958 Grand National winner, Mr What, an outsider at eighteen to one.

The Grand National had provided another Fleet Street tale more than thirty years before, when the celebrated columnist, Hannen Swaffer, reported in the *Daily Graphic* on the morning of the 1921 race that his friend, Dennis Bradley, had had a dream. All the horses in the race had fallen except three, and the winner was a horse in tartan colours, Shaun Spadah. Though thirty-five horses started, events turned out precisely as Bradley had dreamed.

Peter Fairley, then Science Correspondent of Britain's Independent Television News, had a series of profitable visions of winners of England's classic races, though the horses' names seemed to come to him more through coincidence rather than dreams. Though not a betting man, he heard the name Blakeney four times on the morning of the 1969 Derby – none of them connected with the horse of that name which, to Peter Fairley's advantage, duly obliged at Epsom that afternoon at fifteen to two. Two years earlier he had backed a filly called Pia in the Oaks at one hundred to seven after receiving a letter from a lady called Pia and then reading a story about Pia Lindstrom, when previously he had never heard of the name. L'Escargot won for him at thirty-three to one after he had found out there was a horse of that name while eating in the eponymous restaurant in London's Soho. The run went on. 'But then, for no apparent reason, I seemed to lose the gift,' said Fairley.

Fairley himself was the recipient of the forecasts of a young Australian George Cranmer, who first dreamed of a horse called Foinavon winning the English Grand National in 1967 – he saw the jockey's colours. In one of the most dramatic and casualty-strewn races ever, Foinavon, the rankest of outsiders, picked his way through the fallen to win at one hundred to one. Then Cranmer reported seeing a horse carrying Ribocco's colours in the winning enclosure at the Derby. Unfortunately it was the wrong Derby: Ribocco came second in the 1967 English Derby at twenty-two to one, but went on to win the Irish Derby at five to two.

A building company director from Richmond in Surrey, England, had a bizarre experience when one of his customers came to see him in November 1947. The director, Mr M B Campbell of Campbell and Co., afterwards gave an affidavit of the circumstances. 'I certify that during the morning of 10 November 1947, Mr A S Jarman [the late Archie Jarman, a businessman and diligent psychical researcher called at this office and told me of a dream he had had the previous night relating to a horse winning a race, and the figures 2020. We looked together through the morning paper to see if these figures could be relevant to the statistical figures of a horse running that day, but could find nothing apt. The following morning Mr Jarman showed me a morning paper which reported that a horse named Twenty Twenty had won the 3.45 race at Leicester the previous day. He had not considered the names of the runners when trying to allocate the figures 2020 the previous day.'

It was certainly odd. Twenty Twenty was by a stallion called Rosewell out of a mare called Thirteen. It had won only one race previously in its career before taking the Stoughton Plate with Gordon Richards riding. Jarman, who lived in the seaside resort of Brighton in England, had, he said, seen himself standing between the sea and a race track. As the racing horses came towards him all except one veered away and disappeared into the sea. The lone horse, ridden by a man in a business suit, kept its course. 'Facing the stands', he recounts, 'was an enormous long white board supported on posts and on this appeared one after the other the figures 2–0 2–0. The horse and horseman had disappeared but they had evidently won the race and it was a popular victory. I felt a sense of elation and shared in the excited talk among the racegoers. That was the end of the dream.' To his eternal regret Jarman assumed that the figures had to do with the winner's previous form or number on the race card. He and Mr Campbell never thought to look at the horses' names. Jarman never again had a racing dream.

Peter Fairley, the man who really did have a winner, was instrumental in launching the two serious attempts to validate precognition – the British Premonitions Bureau in London and the Central Premonitions Registry in New York.

Fairley's London Bureau, set up through the *Evening Standard*, was the first systematic attempt to record premonitions, and to see how well they matched subsequent happenings. One event, the disaster of Aberfan, had precipitated the idea. On the morning of Friday, 21 October 1966, a huge mass of coal waste, loosened by incessant rain, moved down the side of a valley in south Wales and enveloped the Pantglas Junior School, Aberfan. It was one of the worst civil disasters in British history – 116 children died and twenty-eight adults. As television screens were cleared to follow the hopeless task of the rescue teams and the story drove everything else from the front pages of newspapers, it became apparent that many people felt they had had a warning of the tragedy. The most heart-rending of these came from a little nine-year-old girl, Eryl Mai Jones, who lived in the valley. The day before she had woken in the morning and said, 'Mummy, you must listen to my dream. I dreamed I went to school and there was no school there. Something black had come down all over it.' Eryl Mai Jones was one of the Aberfan victims.

Dr John Barker was struck by the number of accounts in the newspapers from people who claimed to have had some hint of the impending disaster. He persuaded Peter Fairley to send out an appeal through the *Evening Standard* for people to report these premonitions. There were sixty replies which Dr Barker felt warranted further investigation. Eventually he decided there were twenty-two which had, without doubt, been reported to at least one other person before the event.

Some were astonishingly close in detail. Mrs Monica McBean, working in an aircraft factory 200 miles away from the scene, had had a vision of 'a black mountain moving and children buried under it'. The vision was so distressing that she had to go to the ladies' room and sit down. She told one of her fellow workers why she was upset. That was half an hour before the Pantglas school was buried. A London woman, Mrs Sybil Brown, reported a nightmare in which a child was followed by 'a black billowing mass'. She woke her husband and told him, 'Something terrible has happened.' This was still five hours before the mountain of soil moved.

The accounts were vivid but, from a scientific point of view, Fairley and Barker felt it was difficult to make anything of premonitions which were known only after the precognized event had occurred. Thus it was decided to set up the British Bureau and later the American Registry. Peter Fairley decided simply to time and date-stamp reported premonitions, then devise a system for calculating their subsequent accuracy. From the moment the first article appeared in the *Standard*, reports had flowed in – hundreds in the first month. Fairley had struck a vein which, unlike the usual nine-day wonders of Fleet Street, showed no signs of decline. There were upwards of 1000 replies in the first year. Fairley moved to Britain's Independent Television channel, to *TV Times*, and the Bureau went with him. Still the flow went on, by phone and by letter, for almost a decade, when it was taken over by Mrs Jennifer Preston.

'We arrived at a way of assessing these premonitions,' said Fairley. 'We gave up to five points for the unusualness of the event, five points for level of detail – in other words, if you saw a plane crash with a tail fin sticking up with a white or red cross on it, then you could identify the airline – and eventually we gave five points for accuracy of timing – a possible total of fifteen.

'It began to emerge that there were two people, a rather jolly ballet teacher in North London and a night switchboard operator in the East End, who were undoubtedly scoring above chance. So we had them in for interview. And that is where everything started to go haywire. Immediately these people felt they were good at it, they lost it completely – they began to apply conscious thinking. That, along with other research I've done, has led me to conclude, first, that there *is* something in it and, second, that whatever it is, resides in the non-conscious part of the human mind.

'There seems no doubt to me that premonition is literally a flash of intuition, instantaneous, and very overpowering to people when it happens. They just *know* this event is going to happen. There is not a shadow of doubt in their minds. But I'm afraid that with every single person that looked interesting, the same thing happened – they lost it when they started to think they were good at it.

'Now there's a parallel to this in the alpha rhythms of the brain. Basically an alpha rhythm comes through only when the person being investigated is doing and thinking practically nothing. It disappears the moment they try to do something or to make some mental effort. If there is such a thing as premonition, I reckon it's in some way connected with the alpha rhythm part of the brain.'

Fairley himself felt that he lost his own ability to pick horse race winners for similar reasons. 'In the space of about three weeks one year – and not being normally a betting man – I made about £400. These were outsiders, all sorts of peculiar horses, not odds-on favourites. But I liked to laugh and joke about all this with my colleagues at ITN and they started to come up to me and say, "Got anything for the 3.30?" or whatever. And of course it began to go. The moment I applied any kind of conscious thought to it, the whole thing disappeared out of the window.'

The American Central Premonitions Registry was set up in 1968 in New York by Robert D Nelson and Stanley Krippner of the Maimonides Dream Laboratory in Brooklyn. They felt they had some immediate 'strikes' with people predicting Robert Kennedy's assassination later that year. But, as with the British Bureau, many of the Registry's successes seemed to vanish like fairy gold when subjected to investigation.

For more than half a century spectacular disasters of the air have provided some of the most vivid stories of premonition – the special horror of spiralling helplessly down from the skies, trapped inside some crippled aircraft, has been one of the staple dramas of twentieth-century newspapers.

The Chicago DC10 crash of 1979 was a lurid addition to the nightmare. Not only was it the United States' worst air death toll, with 273 people killed, but it was particularly engraved on public imagination by the chilling pictures, snatched by an amateur photographer who happened to be near O'Hare Airport, of the stricken plane plummeting to the ground. But one man, David Booth of Cincinnati, Ohio, believed he had been living with that vision for ten days before the crash actually happened.

He had dreamed quite clearly of a big American Airlines jet, a three-engined plane, apparently trying to land. The engines did not sound right. Then, in his dream, he saw the plane roll over and crash in a mass of flames. 'It was like I was standing there watching the whole thing,' said Booth, 'like watching television.' The next night the dream came back again with equal intensity. 'I did everything to stop sleeping from then on. I'd watch TV until 2am. One night I got drunk.' But for seven consecutive nights the dream recurred. Finally on Tuesday, 22 May, four days before the crash, David Booth decided he had to try to do something. He rang American Airlines. He rang the Federal

Aviation Administration. He rang Cincinnati Airport control. And he was taken seriously. 'It didn't sound like a prank,' said Cincinnati Airport official, Ray Pinkerton.

On Thursday, 24 May, Pinkerton's colleague, Paul Williams, talked to Booth for about three-quarters of an hour. 'What he described to me, I thought might be a 727, because I knew that American Airlines flew Boeing 727s. Another possibility was a DC10. He specifically identified it as an American Airlines aircraft with an engine on the tail. He described his vantage point as beside a gravel road running up towards a flat-roofed building. He described the plane at rather a low altitude which I took to be two to four hundred feet. It suddenly turned sharply and dived into the ground. He described in great detail the explosion. He became quite distraught, almost as if he was seeing death occurring.' But no one felt there was anything practical to be done.

On Friday, 25 May, American Airlines Flight 191, a three-engined DC10, crashed on take-off. With the engine breaking away, the plane turned over on its back and crashed in flames. Paul Williams said: 'I heard about the crash on Friday afternoon on my way home from work about 5pm. As I was listening to the description of the crash on the radio, it sounded like a replay of what I'd heard the day before from David.' David Booth's nightmares stopped. 'It was uncanny,' said FAA official, Jack Barker. 'He named the airline, he called the right type of plane – three-engined – he said the plane came in inverted, which it did, and of course he reported it to officials just four days before it happened.'

Williams reflects: 'Perhaps the most remarkable coincidence of the whole thing was the similarity of the manoeuvre the plane made. It's a very unusual manoeuvre for a plane to make before crashing. Most of them crash with wings horizontal. They run into some obstruction, or there is a mid-air collision. But the manoeuvre David described was very unusual. As a matter of fact, it's the only one I've ever heard of in a plane that size.'

From the early days of passenger aircraft there have been vivid premonitions reported. A certain Mrs G H M Holms, the wife of an Indian civil servant, had an unsettling dream while on holiday in Yorkshire. In the dream it was a cloudy day. Suddenly out of the clouds came the body of a man, shooting down at a terrific pace. 'He landed on his head a few yards from me, with a sickening thud,' she wrote. 'I heard something crack and said, "There goes his skull." The body rebounded and bumped into a tree. I saw some labourers hurry across the grass. They carried the body past me to a plastered thatched cottage, such as is never seen on the Yorkshire moors, with two or three apple trees round it.' Mrs Holms related the dream to her husband and a Welsh friend, M Riley.

Four days later, on 21 July 1930, there was a gruesome and unusual accident in Kent in which the occupants of a small plane, including Lord Dufferin and Lady Ednam, were tipped out as the aircraft apparently broke up. They landed on their heads in an orchard. Harold Ward, who lived at Leylands Orchard, Meopham, Kent, later told an inquest that he saw the plane turn over. Things that looked like small aeroplanes came from it.

'I did not realize what these objects were until they came lower. Then I saw they were human bodies. I rushed down the garden to the orchard. We searched and found four of the bodies. The other was found later.'

Mrs Holms's story would certainly have taken maximum points under Peter Fairley's grading system for timing, precision and unusualness. Unfortunately her two witnesses, her friend and her husband, were not asked to testify to the story until well after the event.

Three months later, when the celebrated airship R101, on a test flight to India, ploughed into the brow of a hill near Beauvais in France, bursting into flame and killing forty-six people, there were some well-attested premonitions. A Liverpool man, J S Wright had dreamed of the R101 crashing six months previously. His friend Mr G Coxon said they had considered reporting it to the War Office. 'Knowing, however, from past experience,' he wrote, 'how futile it has been to attempt to make any impression on a Government Department, we refrained from pressing the matter.'

Mr R W Boyd of Enfield, London, two days before the crash, told his fiancée, Miss Catherine Hare, of seeing R101 in difficulties, then crashing into a hilltop. He saw burning bodies falling from the aircraft and soldiers arriving at the scene on horseback. Many of these details – including the mounted soldiers – later appeared in newspaper reports and pictures. The glamour and the dangers of the great hydrogen-filled airships of the 1930s were so high in public consciousness, however, that it would perhaps have been surprising had there not been dreams and reports of a spectacular end for a vessel which had been the object of such immense ballyhoo.

There are many stories of statesmen being struck by premonitions. Abraham Lincoln dreamed he was walking through the White House and saw a flag-draped coffin. 'Who is it?' he asked. 'The President,' was the reply. Within days Lincoln was assassinated in Ford's Theater in Washington. Winston Churchill was repeatedly said to act on hunches or premonitions. On one occasion he ordered the kitchen staff into the shelter minutes before a bomb struck; on another he insisted upon getting into his car on the unaccustomed off-side, thus saving it from rolling over in a bomb blast.

Adolf Hitler was supposed to have scrambled out of a First World War trench, impelled by a dream of being buried, seconds before it was struck by a shell which interred and killed all his comrades. Canadian Prime Minister Mackenzie King acted on information about the future received, he seems to have thought, from dead politicians. Even Franklin Roosevelt consulted Jeane Dixon, the Washington 'seer'.

The loss of the liner *Titanic* provided a plethora of reported forewarnings. Almost a century on, it is still unnerving to read W T Stead's 1892 article in the London *Review of Reviews*. Stead, fresh from campaigning against child prostitution by buying a small girl for himself and thus jolting Victorian England into action, had turned his uniquely colourful style on the inadequacies of safety precautions at sea. He described in awful detail the fate of a great liner which struck an iceberg in the north Atlantic and went down with enormous loss of life. Twenty years later, Stead himself went down with the *Titanic*.

There was an epidemic of visions in that April of 1912. Whether it was the passengers singing 'Eternal Father, strong to save' in the second-class dining room two hours before the ship struck the iceberg; or Mr J Connon Middleton cancelling his trip after twice seeing a liner floating keel upwards in his dreams; or Mr Colin Macdonald refusing to take the job of second engineer, though it would have meant a promotion. The sea and ships are notorious for jinxes, superstitions, hunches – in fact, all the ills bestowed by the albatross upon the Ancient Mariner. But some of the *Titanic* stories are bizarre. Morgan Robertson's book, published fourteen years previously, described a liner called the *Titan*, of almost identical dimensions to the *Titanic*, being struck by an iceberg and sinking in the month of April, in the north Atlantic.

Dr Ian Stevenson, Professor of Psychiatry at the University of Virginia, who has analysed the *Titanic* cases, quotes an account from a lady in Stoke-on-Trent in England, Mrs Charles Hughes. She was fourteen years old in 1912. On the fatal night of 12 April she dreamed she was walking towards Trentham Park in Stoke: 'Suddenly I saw a very large ship a short distance away as if in Trentham Park. I saw figures walking about on it. Then suddenly it lowered at one end and I heard a terrific scream.' She went to sleep again after telling her grandmother what she had dreamed. The dream recurred. The girl's uncle – the grandmother's son – was Fourth Engineer Leonard Hodgkinson. He died on the *Titanic*. In all, Dr Stevenson has collected nineteen *Titanic* cases.

Rational explanations are often available, however. Premonitions may simply have been well-grounded fears: for all the stories of the 'unsinkability' of the *Titanic*, icebergs were the prime terror of the north Atlantic sea passenger, as unpredictable and threatening as electrical storms are to the air passenger. A plane crashes somewhere every day in our modern world and few people who fly are immune from all apprehension. Statistics suggest that someone, somewhere, is having a nightmare about a plane crash every night of the year.

Fakery is not unknown, like Tamara Rand's alleged prediction on television of the attempt on President Reagan's life – the tape was in fact recorded after the event. The human memory is notoriously unreliable. Details accrete like barnacles to the testimony of witnesses as well as dreamers – but after the event. Some of the most celebrated cases disintegrate under cool investigation. Yet a string of intriguing and extraordinary cases remain: the little girl at Aberfan, Admiral Gladstone and the Dakota *Sister Ann*, Peter Fairley and the horse races, David Booth and the Chicago DC10 crash, the Flixborough newsflash – even the ability of British trades union leader Clive Jenkins to envisage the front pages of unpublished editions of *The Times* and describe them to his family. All these would suggest, if ever they are indubitably substantiated, that not only unusual powers of the human mind exist, but also a warp in our ideas of time itself.

ARTHUR C CLARKE COMMENTS:

It is hard for the non-mathematical layman to realize that even the most amazing examples of dowsing, telepathy or precognition could be due to nothing more than chance – which, it has been said, does not merely permit coincidences, but compels *them to happen. Given enough time, even the most incredible coincidences will occur; we can all give examples of this from everyday life. Here is my favourite:*

In December 1969, I flew into Paris to address a UNESCO conference when I noticed a Berlitz guide book lying on one of the seats. Instantly, the thought flashed through my mind: 'I wonder what's happened to Charlie Berlitz? I haven't seen him for years.' (This, incidentally, was long before he'd struck gold in the Bermuda Triangle.) I took another three or four steps, and a voice behind me said: 'Hello, Arthur.' Guess who ...

This incident still astonishes me – yet it shouldn't. In the course of a busy lifetime, many similar events must occur, purely by coincidence. Nevertheless, they give one an odd sensation somewhere at the top of the spine, and tend to induce a semi-mystical belief that there's a lot going on in the universe that We ... Don't ... Understand.

MYSTERIES FROM
EAST AND WEST

This chapter is about three mysteries which have long fascinated us. Two of them, Spontaneous Human Combustion and the ability of eastern fakirs and pilgrims to withstand the pain of hooks and knives skewered into their flesh, are mentioned in our earlier books, but only briefly. We felt there was little new to say about them, and so, reluctantly, we moved on to consider phenomena upon which researchers *had* shed new light.

Later, we found that we had been mistaken. A letter from an English doctor convinced us that we should reopen our investigations into Spontaneous Human Combustion; while the answer to the hook-hanging mystery lay virtually under our noses. It came from a distinguished professor of physiology who had conducted his experiments no more than a mile from Arthur C Clarke's home in Colombo, Sri Lanka. He also had much to tell us about fire-walking. A set of extraordinary photographs brought back from the Arctic in 1984 reminded us of the third mystery.

But first we must travel to the East.

SRI LANKAN SUPERSTITION

When it comes to investigating the supernatural, the West now has no monopoly. The East, from whence so many mysteries have been reported by generations of marvelling travellers, has begun to produce its own psychical researchers. Few have been more assiduous or successful than two sceptics from Sri Lanka: one an outspoken maverick and eminent psychical researcher,

Abraham Kovoor, who devoted his life to the banishment of superstition which he believed reached to the heart of Sri Lankan life; the other a respected professor of physiology who believes he can explain the most puzzling feats of the Oriental yogis – the ability to walk on fire and to hang from hooks without suffering serious injury.

Fortune-tellers still flourish throughout the island, even in the Fort of Colombo, the city's business district. Under the shady colonnade outside the Colombo Apothecaries store, for example, queues form early in the day at the stall of astrologer and palmist Miss Kosala Guneratna, who thoughtfully provides newspapers for her waiting clients to read. Near by, at 66⅓ Chatham Street, another astrologer, Mr B Wettasinghe, uses a pocket calculator to compute the future. Throughout the Pettah, the city's teeming market area, more exotic seers ply their trade. In Jamahattha Street, Mrs P Thiyagarajah gives 'light readings' by holding up a soot-blackened saucer to the sunlight and interpreting the patterns made on the surface by the dancing rays. Strangest of all, perhaps, are Rajah and Ranee, the psychic parrots, who hold their consultations on the pavement outside a Hindu temple. Upon payment of one rupee, the parrots' keeper fans out a pack of cards on the pavement in front of their wicker cage. Then he releases one of the birds, which scurries out and picks one of the cards. On it, according to the parrot-keeper, his client's fate is written.

Many Sri Lankans consult astrologers before making important decisions. Patients have been known to postpone operations because the stars seem unfavourably aligned, and the horoscopes of prospective marriage partners are compared minutely to ensure compatibility. An ill-starred future can even mean the cancellation of marriage plans. Often, the times of important events are ordained according to the planetary conjunctions – even the opening ceremony of the futuristic Arthur C Clarke Centre for Modern Technologies was carried out to a precise astrological schedule.

In the country districts, belief in demons is widespread, and *Kattadiyas*, the local variety of witch doctor, are hired to impose or exorcise curses. In one elaborate ceremony, regularly performed in the villages, the *Kattadiya* entices the evil demon from a 'possessed' person and, after a colourful wrestling ritual, traps it in an empty bottle which is then consigned to the depths of the Indian Ocean, out of harm's way.

Such strong belief in the forces of the supernatural enraged Abraham Kovoor. 'Superstitions flourish on the ignorance and credulity of people,' he proclaimed, and he made it his business to debunk the beliefs of the 'gullibles', as he called them. Once, in India, he pretended that water from a railway station tap came from the holy river Ganges, and was delighted when 'many miraculous cures' were attributed to it. And he issued this challenge to the magicians and psychics:

> He who does not allow his miracles to be investigated is a crook, he who does not have the courage to investigate a miracle is a gullible, and he who is prepared to believe without verification is a fool. If there were a single person with supernatural powers in any part of the world, I would have become a pauper long ago because I have offered an award of one lakh [100,000] Sri Lanka rupees to anyone who can demonstrate any one of the twenty-three items of miracles mentioned in my permanent challenge under fraud-proof conditions. Though this open challenge was published all over the world some fifteen years ago, I have not lost a single cent. Instead, I have gained a few thousands of rupees, the forfeited earnest deposits of contestants who failed to turn up in the end.

When Abraham Kovoor died in 1978, the reward was still on offer, and few claimants now come forward to be tested by his successor, Carlo Fonseka. Instead, Fonseka, Professor of Physiology at the University of Colombo, has been able to concentrate upon finding a rational explanation for those two Eastern mysteries which have fascinated and baffled travellers from the West since earliest times: fire-walking and hook-hanging.

FIRE-WALKING

Fire-walking is regularly performed in Sri Lanka, both as a tourist attraction and as a religious ritual at festivals such as the annual pilgrimage to Kataragama, the island's holiest shrine. To conduct his investigation, Carlo Fonseka visited every fire-walk he could find and, with the eye of a trained medical man, watched the devotees as they crossed the burning coals. He wanted to answer a simple question: How can people walk on fire and not get burned? At each fire-walk, Fonseka began by measuring the distance travelled and the surface temperature. The longest fire-bed he found, at Kataragama, was eighteen feet (5.5m) long, while many were very much shorter. They were between four and seven feet (1.2 to 2m) wide, and the embers three to six inches (8 to 15cm) deep. Fire temperatures varied from about 300° to 450°C. More crucially, he timed the pilgrims as they crossed the coals and counted the number of steps they took. At Kataragama, the year the professor made his investigations, 100 walkers were on the fire for a mere three seconds on average. The fastest rushed across in only 1.5, and even the slowest traverse took just 6 seconds. Usually, walkers made it in ten steps, with the soles of their feet barely touching the coals – 0.3 seconds was the average time. These findings prompted Fonseka's first conclusion:

> At this stage an obvious question poses itself: is the immunity of fire-walkers from burns due to the shortness of the duration of contact between their soles and embers in taking a step? . . . If so, is it reasonable to suppose that those who get burnt as a result of fire-walking are in fact like the children little Alice in Wonderland had heard of, who got burnt all because they would not remember the simple rule that '*a red hot poker will burn you if you hold it too long?*'

But this could not be the whole answer: the casualty ward of the Kataragama hospital was grisly testimony to the fact that fire-walkers can suffer massive burns even after coming into contact with burning coals for only a few seconds. One British clergyman who braved the fire-pit – and ended up in the burns unit – later described the experience: 'It was like animals tearing at my feet,' he said.

Carlo Fonseka had also noticed another factor:

> Examination of the feet of the men who frequently do fire-walking showed that the epidermis of the soles of most of them was thick and rough when compared with that of habitually shod people. On being asked, most of them said that they never use any kind of foot-

wear. Two obvious questions immediately suggested themselves: (1) are thick, rough soles more resistant to heat than thin, smooth ones? and (2) does habitual barefootedness increase the resistance of the soles to heat?

Back at the Medical Faculty, the professor knocked up an ingenious but simple apparatus, consisting of a forty-watt lightbulb in a metal cylinder. Volunteers, among them several experienced fire-walkers, were recruited for an experiment. Each of them simply put the sole of his foot on the top of the apparatus. Then Carlo Fonseka switched on the bulb and timed how long they were able to withstand its heat. The results showed a clear difference between the people who usually wore shoes and those who went round barefoot and whose soles had thickened as a result. In fact, the unshod 'guinea pigs' felt no heat at all for an average of twenty-nine seconds and could keep their foot above the bulb for over one and a quarter minutes, while those with soles softened by years of wearing shoes sensed the heat after only six seconds and were yelping in pain after thirty-seven. Further tests showed that people with cold, wet feet could withstand the heat for even longer.

To confirm his hypotheses, Carlo Fonseka then ordered cartloads of logs – the *Vitex pinnata* regularly used in fire-walks. Next, he built a series of fifteen fires and carefully reproduced the conditions that obtained at Kataragama and other similar festivals. None of the laboratory walkers suffered burns, although the surface temperature of the fire-pit reached up to 500°C, but those with the softest feet had to skip speedily across the coals to avoid pain, while those with soles roughened by a lifetime of going barefoot were able to stroll across. The professor was delighted. Not only had his theories been borne out, but he could also dismiss as 'mumbo-jumbo' the widely held idea that the ability to walk on hot coals was a supernatural power or a reward from divine authority for a good and moral life. 'Abstinence from meat, alcohol and sex is unnecessary to walk unscathed on fire,' he decided, and, in the interests of science, the fire-walkers at the Medical Faculty defied religious convention by taking hearty swigs from a bottle of arrack, the potent local spirit, and devouring pork cutlets.

HOOK-HANGERS

No sooner had Carlo Fonseka published the results of his fire-walking experiments in the *Ceylon Medical Journal* than a challenge from one of his own medical students sent him once more in search of fakirs and holy men. The student published an article in the island's *Daily Mirror*. Though the headline – HANGING ON HOOKS: WHAT IS THE EXPLANATION? – was rather bland, what he had to say was provocative in the extreme – at least to a rationalist professor of physiology.

He had been to religious festivals and was amazed by the pilgrims who atoned for their sins by hanging from ropes attached to their bodies by razor-sharp hooks embedded in their skin. The devotees' ability to withstand pain and to survive their ordeal without any apparent ill-effects seemed to the student to defy medical science. 'Under normal conditions,' he wrote, 'these devotees are susceptible to pain, bleeding, neurogenic shock, tetanus, gas gangrene and bacterial infection of wounds.' Yet none of these problems affected hook-hangers, nor did the hooks ever tear their flesh, even when the full weight of their bodies was suspended from ropes. He declared hook-hanging to be a miracle, for there were, he said, seven inexplicable mysteries about this 'fantastic feat of faith'.

Carlo Fonseka was not convinced. He was ideally placed to investigate, for in Sri Lanka there are professional hook-hangers who hire themselves out for displays and tourist shows. To them, a scientific experiment at the Medical Faculty was all in a day's work. From the many experts on offer, Professor Fonseka chose 'a young rationalist-minded volunteer named N C Jayasuriya' as his 'guinea pig'. Jayasuriya proved to be just his man for the job and, in three long sessions of carefully supervised investigation (for hook-hanging, while not miraculous, can be highly dangerous to the uninitiated), became known as 'the Hero on Hooks'.

Carlo Fonseka examined each of the student's seven 'mysteries' in turn. His findings can be summarized in a series of questions and answers:

Question: Why does the hook-hanger appear to suffer no pain? *Answer*: Because he has volunteered to undergo the ordeal. The right mental attitude is vital. Soldiers wounded in battle often say they feel no pain, and this may be because being wounded means they will be out of the combat zone for a time. For devotees, ecstasy and the feeling that they are purging their sins are powerful anaesthetics, but even Mr Jayasuriya, who apparently 'spurned divine aid', suffered no agonies, simply because he had chosen to take part. In fact, he chattered happily to passers-by as he hung from the hooks during the experiments.

Question: Why do the hooks not make him bleed? *Answers*: They do, but only a little. There are three reasons. Firstly, piercing the flesh releases the hormone adrenaline, which constricts the blood vessels in the skin and the superficial tissues into which the hooks are inserted. Secondly, the body has a natural mechanism (known as the 'extrinsic mechanism') for stopping bleeding from damaged tissues, which quickly comes into play and releases a chemical to clot the blood. The third factor is perhaps the most important of all: before the hook is inserted, the hanger's assistants firmly pinch the place where it is to go. This puts the surrounding blood vessels out of action, and pressure from the rope to which the hook is attached ensures that they stay that way.

Question: How do they avoid tetanus, gas gangrene and infected wounds? *Answer*: They don't always. The problem is that the devotees are seldom examined later, but there is evidence that some wounds do become infected. (During Fonseka's experiments the hooks and the wounds they produced were scrupulously wiped and sterilized.) Tetanus and gangrene can be discounted, for they are very rare, especially in the kind of people who practise hook-hanging, who are usually young and in good physical shape.

Question: Why doesn't the hook-hanger faint during his ordeal? *Answer*: People usually faint when they are in great pain or when they are emotionally upset. The hook-hanger is not in pain and, far from being upset, is happy to be doing penance in this spectacular way. (Mr Jayasuriya, delighted to be of help in the understanding of a 'miracle', did not faint either.)

Question: Why don't the hooks tear the hanger's back?
Answer: Because he hangs from several hooks. One would certainly tear his flesh, but several hooks distribute his weight and spread the load. Thus, if a devotee weighs 120 lbs (54kg) and uses six hooks, each one will have to bear only twenty pounds (9kg) – healthy human tissue can take the strain.

Carlo Fonseka is not only a rationalist: he is also a realist. He knows that however energetically he debunks the idea that hook-hanging and fire-walking are paranormal phenomena, people in his own country and abroad will probably continue to regard them as miracles. However, he continues his campaign undaunted, believing 'that it is intellectually degrading to continue to hold primitive beliefs which have become inconsistent with knowledge'. Indeed, so dedicated is he to his cause, that he has himself often walked on fire, each time emerging from the pit triumphant and, predictably, unburnt.

THE HUMAN CANDLES

Gruesome mysteries may require gruesome solutions. Thus it came about that a university professor, David Gee, could be found in his laboratory in Leeds fabricating a ghoulish test. First he rolled up a chunk of human body fat until it resembled an eight-inch (24cm) candle. Carefully he wrapped the 'candle' in a layer of human skin. Lastly, the whole object was clothed in fabric – dressed as though it were living flesh. Then Professor Gee applied a flame to the end of it.

He was ready to attempt to solve a mystery which has fascinated doctors and scientists for more than two centuries, and intrigued writers from Charles Dickens to Captain Marryat. Can human beings, apparently spontaneously, just burst into flame and melt away?

Professor Gee himself had been called to a case in Leeds in November 1963, when he was a young forensic scientist. He had found the remnants of an elderly woman, almost totally burned away apart from her right foot. Yet all around was undamaged combustible material. The hearth rug itself was intact except where the body had fallen. There was a tea towel, still neatly folded and scarcely singed, only a foot away from the body. The floorboards had burned through, but again only in the spot where the woman had fallen.

The young Dr Gee was intrigued. He knew that temperatures of 250°C or more were needed to make the human body burn. The precise Inquisitors of the Catholic Church had discovered that whole cartloads of wood were required to burn the heresy from recalcitrant souls and incinerate the bodies that had harboured such vice. Meaner allocations of fuel merely charred and roasted the sinner. In modern times, the annals of forensic science repeatedly demonstrate how futile it is for murderers to try to destroy the corpse of a victim by fire. Yet there are constant reports from unimpeachable sources of people being spontaneously, and for no apparent reason, consumed in flames.

A doctor from Aberdeen, Mackenzie Booth, recorded an astonishing case in which an old soldier had burned quietly away in a hayloft in Constitution Street in the middle of the city:

> What struck me especially was the fact that, notwithstanding the presence of abundant combustible material around, such as hay and wood, the main effects of combustion were limited to the corpse, and only a small piece of the adjacent flooring and the woodwork immediately above the man's head had suffered. The body was almost a cinder, yet retaining the form of the face and figure so well, that those who had known him in life could readily recognize him. Both hands and the right foot had been burnt off and had fallen through the floor among the ashes into the stables below. The hair and scalp were burnt off, exposing the bare and calcined skull. The tissues of the face were represented by a greasy cinder retaining the cast of the features, and the incinerated moustache still gave the wonted military expression to the old soldier.

Dr Booth was baffled.

Two years later, an American doctor was actually to witness 'spontaneous combustion' taking place. He was visiting a patient on the outskirts of the little town of Ayer, Massachusetts, when a girl rushed in begging him to come to her mother, who was being burned alive. The incident was only 200 yards away in some woodland. He arrived to find the woman's body still burning at the shoulder, along the trunk and down the legs.

'The flames reached from twelve to fifteen inches above the level of the body,' he reported. 'The clothing was nearly all consumed. As I reached the spot, the bones of the right leg broke with an audible snap, allowing the foot to hang by the tendons and muscles of one side, those of the other side having burned completely off.' Yet, bizarrely, except where the body had actually been burning, the mother's clothes were untouched. A woollen skirt, a cotton vest, a calico dress, underclothes, had all survived in parts unburnt. All around, the ground was untouched apart from a few charred leaves under the corpse, and her straw hat, slightly scorched, a few feet away. The woman had been out in the woods, clearing stumps and under-growth, and had indeed started a fire which might have caught her clothing. But that in no way seemed to Dr Hartwell to explain the human incendiary which he had seen before his very eyes.

Both these cases are just over a century old. Yet incidents keep recurring which confound the results of another 100 years of research into the properties of flame.

Fireman Jack Stacey was called to an incident in a run-down part of Vauxhall, South London, at Christmas 1967. A fire was reported. When the fire engine arrived, the crew found some down-and-outs awaiting them. They had been using an old building. Inside was the body of another vagrant. Said Mr Stacey, 'It was still alight. There were flames coming from the abdomen. They were coming out of a four-inch slit in the abdomen. It was a bluish flame. It seemed as though the fire had begun inside the body.' The building itself was undamaged, although there was charring of the woodwork underneath the victim.

At the end of 1985 the BBC showed a programme in which a police officer, John Haymer, testified to a strange death in

South Wales in 1979. When he arrived at the house he was immediately struck by an orange-red glow in the main room.

> The walls were generating heat. The window and lightbulb were covered in an orange substance. The lightbulb was bare because the plastic shade had melted. The settee still had its loose covers. The carpet was largely undamaged.
>
> On the floor was a pair of human feet clothed in socks. They were attached to the lower portion of the body. This was clad in trousers, undamaged as far as a distinct burn line. From the trousers protruded the calcined bone. And just beyond the knees, this disintegrated into an amorphous mass of ash.

The debris was all that remained of the elderly man who had lived in the house. Haymer was puzzled enough at the almost total destruction of the body, but what was even more baffling was the lack of damage elsewhere. The TV set was still on, though its plastic control knobs had melted. The grate itself was undisturbed, with unburnt firewood still in place. No cause of death, no source for the fire was ever found. Haymer, a sober individual who had investigated many deaths and had never flirted with the paranormal, believes to this day that the case defies rational explanation.

These modern cases of bodies reduced to ash in unscorched surroundings are the more incomprehensible to investigators because the technology of consuming a corpse in fire is now well understood as a result of the advancing fashion for cremation in both Britain and America. Crematoria have become remarkably sophisticated and automated, now that most people choose to have their earthly remains rapidly obliterated. The ovens which do the job operate at temperatures of at least 800°C and, even after an hour or more, quite large fragments of bone will remain. Rarely is there the complete reduction to ash which is a feature of the 'spontaneous combustion' cases.

These burnings are not usually witnessed, and there is only circumstantial evidence as to how long the process takes. But even in modern times there are cases of the most spectacular and horrible form of 'spontaneous combustion' when people burst into flames in front of friends, families or passers-by. These are the cases which have truly horrified, rather than merely intrigued, those unfortunate enough to see them – a man so angry during a dispute with a neighbour that he simply exploded into flame; in 1973 a baby who was suddenly alight in his pram; the six Nigerians in 1965 all consumed in a fire which hardly damaged their room. These dramas have all surfaced in the newspapers with neither explanation nor serious investigation.

However, in the winter of 1985 there was a dreadful incident in Cheshire, which was investigated at first hand by police, fire officers, a forensic chemist working for the British Home Office, and by the prestigious Shirley Institute in Manchester. A seventeen-year-old student, Jacqueline Fitzsimon, was walking down some stairs with a group of friends at Halton College of Further Education, Widnes, when she suddenly burst into flame. Although three staff members quickly arrived on the scene and smothered the flames, Jacqueline subsequently died.

Witnesses under oath at the inquest described the events of that February morning in apocalyptic terms. Two girls, Carina Leazer and Rachel Heckle, had passed Jacqueline on the stairs. Carina told the coroner that she noticed a strange glowing light above Jacqueline's right shoulder. It appeared in mid-air and then seemed to fall down her back. Two men, both mature students, were also on the stairs. John Foy, aged thirty-four, who worked for a chemical manufacturer, described hearing Jacqueline cry out. They turned to see her on fire. 'She was like a stunt man on TV,' he said. 'The flames simply engulfed her.' He and his companion, Neil Gargan, had seen no sign of smoke or smouldering as they passed the girl just a few seconds before. They helped put out the fire. Jacqueline herself only complained that she had burnt her finger trying to put out the flames, though there was melted nylon all over her back. She died in hospital.

Initially there seemed to be a fairly simple explanation. Jacqueline was a cookery student and had been working in the cookery room where a number of gas cookers were in use. She had finished her work early and had stood about talking to friends. The assumption was that she had perhaps leaned against a cooker where the gas ring was still on, her white catering jacket had started to smoulder and then, when she went out to the stairway, the increased oxygen and air-flow had fanned it into flame.

Slowly, however, doubts began to build up about this straightforward theory. There had been plenty of people about and no one had noticed any sign of scorching or smouldering on Jacqueline's back. Indeed, she had walked down the stairs linking arms with two friends, and they had not noticed anything. Then the cookery lecturer, Robert Carson, swore that all the rings had been turned off an hour before the end of the study period. 'In any case,' he told the coroner, 'in twenty years I have never seen a catering jacket on fire.' Next, the Home Office chemist, Philip Jones, described how he had been unable to make a smouldering catering jacket burst into flames, even when it was exposed to a strong air-flow. The Shirley Institute report also acknowledged that they could not get a smouldering catering jacket to flame. If it was directly ignited the whole thing burned within twenty-five seconds. Yet all the evidence indicated that a considerable time – several minutes – had elapsed between Jacqueline's departure from the cookery room and the fatal conflagration on the stairs.

The jury's verdict was 'Misadventure'. But few people either among the witnesses or among those who had attended the inquest, felt that they had heard a satisfactory explanation of why a seventeen-year-old girl should, without warning, be consumed by fire while walking downstairs arm-in-arm with friends one February morning.

The most relentlessly investigated case of modern times was the death of sixty-seven-year-old widow, Mary Reeser, in St Petersburg, Florida, in 1951. Her son, Dr Richard Reeser, had last seen her sitting in an armchair reading as he left for an evening out. When he returned there was nothing left of the chair except the metal springs. Of his mother there remained only her left foot, bizarrely unscorched, a few pieces of backbone and, apparently, a skull shrunk to the size of a baseball. The room was covered in oily soot, and a pair of candles twelve feet (3.5m) away from the body had melted. Yet newspapers and linen only inches away were intact. The room was stiflingly hot.

The local fire chief, Jake Reichert, confessed that it was the 'most unusual case I've seen in my almost twenty-five years of police work'.

Dr Wilton Krogman of the University of Pennsylvania reported the circumstances. He noted that not only was it peculiar that the fire was so localized and yet had clearly generated great heat, but also that there was an odd absence of smell. 'How could a hundred and seventy pounds of mortal flesh burn with no detectable or discernible smoke or odor permeating the entire apartment building?' Krogman remarked on the shrunken skull, 'I have experimented on this using cadaver heads,' but no similar effect had ever been produced.

Arson specialist Edward Davies was despatched by the National Board of Underwriters to analyse the death. He could find no cause.

More than thirty years later two investigators, Joe Nickell and John F Fischer, reworked the evidence for the *Journal of the International Association of Arson Investigators* and came to the conclusion that Mary Reeser had taken sleeping pills and had probably set herself and the chair alight with a cigarette. They dismissed the shrunken skull as it was reported only by Dr Krogman, who did not claim to have seen it for himself.

However, the great heat, the undamaged flammable material all around, the unburnt foot all remain as imponderables in Mary Reeser's death.

Ever since the drive towards 'science and enlightenment' began three centuries ago, there have been repeated attempts to explain a phenomenon which has regularly attracted the attention of journals and physicians.

Pierre-Aimé Lair produced an '*Essai sur les Combustions Humaines*' for the Paris medical publishers Crapelet in 1800. Most of the examples he cited were culled from the British *Annual Register* and the *Transactions of the Royal Society*. He describes the expiry of Grace Pitt from Ipswich, who died in April 1744. She was found by her daughter, who threw two vases of water over her. All that remained was what Lair described as a carpet of ash with some white cinders. He also cites the 1779 report by a surgeon, Muraire, from Aix-en-

Provence. A widow, Marie Jauffret, 'small, fat and fond of the bottle', had burnt away to a cinder, leaving 'one hand, one foot and the bones of the skull' unconsumed.

Lair was primarily concerned to show that over-indulgence in 'spiritous liquors' was responsible for spontaneous combustion. His theory was that most of the victims he recorded had been fat and addicted to alcohol. The alcohol, he opined, would build up in their tissues until finally they exploded into flame – rather, one assumes, like burning brandy on a Christmas pudding.

This prognosis – popular, naturally, among temperance campaigners – remained the favoured solution for the best part of a century, while the list of victims of the 'heavenly fire' steadily increased.

There are now hundreds of cases, many photographs, reliable witnesses, medical and forensic testimony, all demonstrating that human beings can be reduced to ash. Many show the most grotesque features of 'spontaneous combustion' – a hand or a foot left behind without a mark. Invariably, although there are signs of great heat, combustible materials near the body have been untouched. Usually there is no obvious source of fire – certainly not sufficient to generate crematorium levels of heat. Sadly for Pierre-Aimé Lair and his successors, there is by no means always evidence of an addiction to strong drink.

It was against this background that Professor Gee of Leeds began his ghoulish but necessary experiment with a human candle. Gee knew that human body fat, even when melted down in a crucible, will only burn at a temperature of about 250°C. However, a cloth wick in liquid fat will burn like a lamp when the temperature is as low as 24°C. With this in mind, Gee constructed his human candle wrapped in layers of cloth. He then set a bunsen burner at one end. It took about a minute for the fat to catch fire. As his report dispassionately records:

> Although the bunsen was removed at this point, combustion of the fat and cloth proceeded slowly along the length of the roll, with a smoky yellow flame and much production of soot, the entire roll being consumed after about one hour. In the experiment the draught of air from an extractor fan was arranged so that combustion proceeded in a direction opposite to the flow of air.

Another forensic professor, Keith Mant, summed up the current state of scientific thinking in the 1984 edition of *Taylor's Principles and Practice of Jurisprudence.*

> It seems that the probable course of events in these cases is that the victim collapses, for instance from a heart attack, or from carbon monoxide poisoning, and falls so that part of the body comes into contact with a source of heat such as a small domestic fire. This part of the body, usually the head, is thus ignited, and adjacent body fat when melted soaks into the layers of clothing, which, the victim being an old lady, are likely to be present in abundance. The clothing, acting as a wick, melts the next zone of adjacent fat, and the process is repeated along the length of the body. If floorboards beneath the body are ignited, they will be burnt through, and the sudden increase in draught which results will considerably raise the temperature and incinerate the rest of the body. By the time the lower legs are reached there is less fat and few, if any, layers of clothing, so the process ceases.

The scenario is as plausible as the evidence allows. But for the sceptic there remain ample imponderables. Can such great heat be generated as to pulverize bone too, and yet not burn surrounding combustibles – cloth, paper, even hay and straw? What about flames coming out of the victim's stomach? What about those fearful cases where people catch light suddenly in front of friends and passers-by? What about the shrunken skull?

The manifestations of the heavenly fire still throw up questions which have not yet proved amenable to the inquests of the laboratory and the bunsen burner.

ARTHUR C CLARKE COMMENTS:

The Strange Powers *television programme devoted to fire-walking and religious rituals such as hanging on hooks was broadcast in Sri Lanka (where much of it had been filmed) on 17 October 1986. I had rather hoped that my – and still more, Professor Carlo Fonseka's – 'debunking' of fire-walking would promote the ire of the professionals. Not a bit of it. In fact the only local criticism I received was from Mr A C B M Moneragala of Kelaniya (not far from Colombo, and the site of a famous Buddhist temple). He complained that we didn't do a thorough enough job of rationalizing, and enclosed an article he had published in the* Ceylon Daily News *for 16 October 1981, entitled 'Natural Pain Killers'. This discussed the recently discovered natural opiate, beta-endorphin which the body appears to produce in direct proportion to the severity of the pain suffered.*

To quote from Mr Moneragala's article:

> *Apparently, powerful and awesome religious emotions are able to release this natural narcotic ... controlling both physical and mental pain ... In the presence of death and in the fearsome havoc of the battlefield beta-endorphin is released into the limbic area of the brain and gruesome injuries and death are faced with apparent indifference ... [When] one of Napoleon's generals had his legs badly shattered by a cannonball they were amputated on the battlefield itself, without an anaesthetic and then thrust into a cauldron of boiling tar to be disinfected. All this time the general showed no sign of pain. His only antidote was his cigar which he smoked continually during this ghastly butchery ...*

I have little doubt that some such explanation is correct – and quite marvellous. All we have to do now is to explain the explanation. And that is a matter of no small importance, for it may lead to results of immeasurable value to the human race – the Conquest of Pain.

As for the 'human candles', in the Introduction to Arthur C Clarke's Mysterious World *I classified mysteries into three categories, according to our current level of understanding:*

> *Mysteries of the Third Kind are the rarest of all, and there is very little that can be said about them ... They are phenomena – or events – for which there appears to be no rational explanation; in the cases where there are theories to account for them, these are even more fantastic than 'the facts'.*
>
> *Perhaps the quintessential M3K is something so horrible that – even if the material existed – one would prefer not to use it in a television programme. It is the extraordinary phenomenon known as Spontaneous Human Combustion.*
>
> *There have been many recorded cases, supported by what seems to be indisputable medical evidence, of human bodies being*

consumed in a very short period of time by an extremely intense heat which has often left the surroundings – even the victim's clothing! – virtually untouched. The classic fictional case is in Dickens' Bleak House, but there are dozens of similar incidents in real life – and probably a far greater number that have never been reported.

'The human body is not normally a fire hazard; indeed, it takes a considerable amount of fuel to arrange a cremation. There seems no way in which this particular mystery can ever be solved without a great deal more evidence – and who would wish for that?

Well, since I wrote those words, more evidence has – tragically – become available. And I am indebted to Dr Geoffrey Diggle of Croydon for reference to experiments that suggest that, in his words, 'this previously baffling phenomenon has now been elucidated and shown not to require any preternatural explanation. In other words, the M3K had graduated to an M1K!'

I am still not completely convinced, despite the experiments which have been conducted in attempts to solve this bizarre mystery. I know of nothing else in the whole range of 'paranormal' literature that gives me such a feeling of unease. Some of the evidence seems beyond dispute – yet, if accepted, it hints that there are forces in the universe of which we know nothing. And even that there may be something in the old horror cliché: 'Such knowledge is not meant for Man . . .'

Here is a somewhat lighter, perfectly genuine and possibly relevant item from the British Medical Journal *for 12 December 1964.*

> *I recall a case referred to me many years ago. The patient was a parson who became alarmed when he noticed that his breath took fire every time he blew the altar candles out. I performed a Polyagastrectomy for a duodenal ulcer causing pyloric stenosis, following which he was able to carry out his duties in a more decorous fashion – I am, etc., Stephen Power, Royal London Homeopathic Hospital.*

*

THE SHIPS IN THE ICE

No picture in this book has a more compelling fascination than the photograph of a dead sailor who had been buried beneath the Arctic ice for 140 years. The hands, manicured, immaculate as though they had just recently scrubbed the planked and caulked deck; the eyes open as if in life; the teeth shining. Only the forehead and nose show the blackening of frost. The corpse is as perfect as that of the baby mammoth found in the Soviet north just five years before. It seems as if only some special stroke of lightning from out of the tundran sky would be needed to reanimate the young man in his icy coffin.

These pictures (brought back from Beechey Island in Canada's Barrow Strait, far beyond the Arctic Circle, in the summer of 1984) are, however, merely the latest clue to the greatest enigma of Arctic exploration – the fate of Sir John Franklin and his ships after they entered the northern ice in the summer of 1845.

The dead seaman is Petty Officer John Torrington. He was only nineteen years old when he sailed with Franklin to try to find the North West Passage from the Atlantic to the Pacific, which had eluded explorers for two centuries. Professor Owen Beattie of the University of Alberta, who exhumed Torrington and also Able Seaman John Hartnell, said: 'The bodies were extremely life-like, with skin almost normal and hair intact. It was a very touching experience. We felt very close to a moment of history.' Professor Beattie was leading the latest of scores of expeditions which have tried to solve the Franklin mystery. At one time, in the summer of 1850, there were no less than ten ships searching for Franklin. Bodies have been discovered, cairns, even messages left behind, but the two ships *Erebus* and *Terror* have never been found, and many of the clues merely seem to add to the mystery.

Franklin was already sixty years old when he left Britain in May 1845. The ships had provisions for three years, as it was expected that they would be imprisoned in the ice for at least one winter, perhaps two. After calling on the west Greenland coast, they were last seen by the whaler *Enterprise* leaving Melville Bay. None of the 129 crew of the two ships were ever seen alive again. But the deaths of Torrington, Hartnell, and Marine William Braine so early in the expedition – they appear to have died of either scurvy or lead poisoning – less than a year after they set sail, only add to the puzzles of a baffling expedition.

Subsequent expeditions found two messages left behind on King William Island. One reported that *Erebus* and *Terror* had wintered in 1846–7 at Beechey Island. The second message read:

> April 25 1848. HM's ships *Terror* and *Erebus* were deserted on 22nd April, 5 leagues NNW of this, having been beset since 12 September 1846. The officers and crew, consisting of 105 souls, under the command of Capt. F. R. M. Crozier, landed here in Lat 69 37 42 N Long 98 41 W.
>
> Sir John Franklin died on 11 June 1847, and the total loss by deaths in the expedition has been to this date 9 officers and 15 men.
> *Signed* James Fitzjames, Captain HMS *Erebus*
> F. R. M. Crozier, Captain and Senior Officer.

and start on tomorrow, 26th., for Back's Fish River.

Later, more than a dozen bodies were found further south at Starvation Cove.

Then, bizarrely, further north and facing out to sea, an extraordinary catafalque was discovered – a full-size ship's boat, mounted on a massive sledge with iron-shod runners, and, in it, two bodies, equipped like some Chinese emperor for the afterworld. Each had a double-barrelled gun with one barrel loaded and cocked. With them were calf-skin slippers, edged with red silk ribbon. One skeleton was wrapped in furs. There was a complete set of dinner plates with Sir John Franklin's crest and silver knives, forks and spoons with the crests or initials of five of *Erebus*'s officers and three of *Terror*'s. There were books, towels, soap, silk handkerchiefs, and 'an amazing quantity of clothing'. And all this facing back towards the frozen sea. What was the meaning of this extraordinary caravanserai, setting out so caparisoned after three years alone in the Arctic? Why was the mighty sledge-boat facing back towards the sea? Why had nine officers died – such a high proportion? Above all, what had happened to the ships? Not a nail or a plank has ever been found in all the years of searching for Franklin.

Could it possibly be true that the ships were seen high and dry on an iceberg off the Newfoundland banks, as three mariners aboard the brig *Renovation* reported in April 1851? This was 2,000 miles away from where the ships were abandoned. It seems unthinkable. But then one of the ships searching for Franklin, the *Resolute*, was found sailing like the *Mary Celeste* in Baffin Bay, 1,000 miles from where she had been prematurely deserted by her crew. The *Resolute* was picked up and taken to New London, Connecticut, where she was refitted and returned, courtesy of the United States Congress, to the British Admiralty. And there is little reason to doubt the evidence of the voyagers aboard the *Renovation*, which was in passage from Limerick in Ireland to Quebec in the spring of 1851.

The first account appeared in a letter from John S Lynch published in the *Limerick Chronicle*:

> The icebergs we met with were frightful in size. I do not exaggerate when I say that the steeple of Limerick cathedral would have appeared but a small pinnacle, and a dark one compared to the lofty and gorgeously-tinted spires that were on some of them. We met, or rather saw at a distance, one with two ships on it.

Later, Lynch was interrogated by the Admiralty. He told Captains Herbert and Boxer, RN, who were investigating, that the *Renovation* had been off the Newfoundland banks.

> We came in view of one iceberg, on which I distinctly saw two vessels, one certainly high and dry, the other might have her keel and bottom in the water, but the ice was a long way outside of her. I examined them particularly with the spy glass; one, the larger, lay on her beam ends, the other upright. I said to the mate that they were part of Sir J Franklin's squadron. He said very likely, and that it would be a good prize for whoever would fall in with them. My reason for supposing them to belong to Sir John Franklin's squadron was there being two ships on one iceberg, they appearing to be consorts, and having no appearance of being driven on the berg in distress, as the rigging and the spars of the upright one was all as shipshape as if she had been laid up in harbour; also the one on her beam ends had no more appearance of a wreck than a vessel with her topmast struck and left by the tide on a beach, no loose ropes hanging from any part of her.

The captain of the *Renovation* was sick at the time and would not countenance going any closer to the iceberg. But Lynch was quite clear that he had not seen an optical illusion: 'Having seen them in different positions and minutely, I can have no doubt upon the subject at all.'

Later, the second mate of the *Renovation*, Robert Simpson, was questioned. He produced a vivid sketch, which was published in the *Nautical Magazine* of 1852, and confirmed the details of Lynch's account. He estimated the ships' size as between 4,000 and 5,000 tons for the larger and perhaps 100 tons less for the smaller. Both the rig and the deck array of the ships coincided with the appearance of *Erebus* and *Terror*.

It seems clear that all Franklin's crew perished in the vain attempt to reach the Canadian mainland at Fish River. The details of his attempted route, which indeed was accepted as proof of the existence of the North West Passage, are now clear. Professor Beattie may soon, from his analysis, know what caused Petty Officer Torrington's death – possibly lead poisoning from the early tinned food cans. But what happened to *Erebus* and *Terror* themselves is as mysterious as it was 140 years ago. The sledge-boat on King William Island remains one of the eeriest wrecks in all history.

THE GREAT SIBERIAN EXPLOSION

The civilized world certainly had no excuse for ignoring perhaps the greatest and most mysterious explosion that has ever taken place on earth. In London, on that last day of June 1908, it was possible to read the small print in *The Times* at midnight. In Stockholm, perfectly sharp scenic photographs were taken in the middle of what should have been the admittedly brief northern night. In Heidelberg in Germany, bright shining clouds persisted till morning and in Holland it was quite impossible to take normal astronomical observations because of the brightness. The scientific instruments too gave plenty of notice. Half a dozen traces in London and other parts of England gave gigantic hiccups as first one shock wave and then a second, which had travelled completely round the world, shook the recording pens. Even in America the vibrations were felt. In European Russia, which was even closer to the event, the bright nights went on well into July and an extraordinary photograph was taken of the main street of the town of Navrochat at midnight which looked as though it was exposed in full sunshine.

Certainly some very powerful happening had taken place. A woman did write to *The Times* asking for an explanation; some golfers from Brancaster in southeast England also wrote to say they could have managed a round on the links at 2am, and the director of the British Association drew attention to the hectic graphs recording the shock waves. But the world then entirely put aside, for nearly twenty years, what had in fact been one of the most cataclysmic events in all its history: an impact that, if the earth had been just a quarter of a day further on in its spin, would have wiped out St Petersburg or, at a slightly different angle, London, or, half a day on, New York.

Today, nearly a century later, it is still far from certain what it was that came hurtling out of the great interplanetary spaces and dashed itself against the earth in the remote and forested regions of far Siberia.

All the exotic phenomena of modern astrophysics have been considered in connection with the mystery. Was it that most demonic of manifestations, a black hole? Could it have been 'anti-matter' which the Nobel prizewinner, Paul Dirac, postulated lay somewhere out in the universe, that would annihilate anything it touched? Was it, as some argue, a crippled spaceship exploding as it entered the earth's atmosphere? Could it, thirty-seven years before the Hiroshima and Nagasaki bombs, have been an atomic blast? But, except for a few notes and reports by local people and papers in Siberia, all investigation had to wait half a generation while Europe fought a war, and Russia divested herself of a tsar, installed the Bolsheviks, and slowly and bloodily removed Admiral Kilchak and the White Russian forces who had taken possession of the vastnesses of Siberia.

KULIK'S SEARCH

Only in 1921, with Lenin in power determined that the new Soviet Union should be a force in the scientific world, did the first faltering enquiries begin. The new Soviet Academy of Sciences commissioned a remarkable scientist called Leonid Kulik to collect information about meteorite falls on USSR territory. A friend gave Kulik a newspaper clipping describing the event of June 1908. This said that a huge meteorite had landed near Filimonovo junction on the Trans-Siberian Railway.

> Its fall was accompanied by a frightful roar and a deafening crash. The driver of the train stopped in fright and the passengers poured out of the carriages to examine the fallen object but they were unable to approach the meteorite because it was burning hot.

This one clipping, almost all of it fanciful – though an alarmed train driver had indeed stopped to have his locomotive and carriages examined – was to launch Kulik on a twenty-year quest. But when he died, killed by the Nazis during the Second World War, he had still not come to any clear conclusion as to the cause of the explosion.

Kulik began by gathering eyewitness accounts and collating other meteorologists' reports. The local papers of Irkutsk, Tomsk and Krasnoyarsk had all reported the event. *Sibir*, the Irkutsk newspaper, described it as 'a most unusual phenomenon of nature'.

> In the village of Nizhne-Karelinsk in the northwest high above the horizon, the peasants saw a body shining very brightly (too bright for the naked eye) with a bluish-white light. It moved vertically downwards for about ten minutes. The body was in the form of a 'pipe' (i.e. cylindrical). The sky was cloudless, except that low down on the horizon in the direction in which this glowing body was observed, a small dark cloud was noticed. It was hot and dry and when the shining body approached the ground it seemed to be pulverized and in its place a huge cloud of black smoke was formed and a loud crash, not like thunder, but as if from the fall of large stones, or from gunfire, was heard. All the buildings shook and at the same time, a forked tongue of flame broke through the cloud. The old women wept, everyone thought that the end of the world was approaching.

This village of Nizhne-Karelinsk, Kulik was eventually to discover, was 200 miles (320km) away from the centre of the explosion.

A local meteorologist named Voznesensky had collected reports of the phenomenon and plotted the likely point of impact. Almost unbelievably, the crash had been heard 500 miles (800km) away from its centre, and at that distance the seismic instruments in Irkutsk had registered a crash of earthquake proportions.

Kulik read of a 'fiery heavenly body', a 'flame that cut the sky in two' and a 'pillar of smoke'. One eyewitness account by Il'ya Potapovich was sent to Kulik:

> One day a terrible explosion occurred, the force of which was so great that the forest was flattened for many versts along both banks of the River Chambe. My brother's hut was flattened to the ground,

its roof was carried away by the wind and his reindeer fled in fright. The noise deafened my brother and the shock caused him to suffer a long illness.

Kulik's correspondent went on:

As Il'ya Potapovich told this story, he kept turning to his brother who had endured all this. The latter grew animated, related something energetically in Tungusk language, striking the poles of his tent and the roof and gesticulating in an attempt to show how his tent had been carried away.

Another witness, like Potapovich a Tungus from the Evenki people, was Vasiley Okhchen. He related how he and his family were asleep when, together with their tent, the whole family went flying into the air. He went on:

All the family were bruised but Akulina and Ivan lost consciousness. The ground shook and an incredibly long roaring was heard. Everything round about was shrouded in smoke and fog from burning, falling trees. Eventually the roar died away but the forest went on burning. We set off in search of the reindeer which had rushed away. Many of them did not come back.

A woman of Vanavara, called Koso Lapova, had been on her way to the spring for water.

I saw the sky in the north open to the ground and fire pour out. We thought that stones were falling from the sky and rushed off in terror, leaving our pail by the spring. When we reached the house, we saw my father Semenov unconscious lying near the barn. The fire was brighter than the sun. During the bangs, the earth and the huts trembled greatly, and earth came sprinkling down from the roofs.

There were tales of horses bolting with their plough in tow, of a man who felt his shirt burning on his back. Yet, miraculously it was to turn out that an impact which would have killed millions of people had it landed on one of the great cities or inhabited areas of the world, had not caused the death of a single person. Dogs and reindeer, and no doubt much wildlife, died. The local people's flour stores and houses were destroyed. The forest was flattened but no humans were even seriously injured. The event had taken place in one of the few parts of the earth where its effect on humanity could be almost negligible. Had it even crashed into the sea there would have been tidal waves as great as those which followed the Krakatoa eruption of 1883 that swamped huge areas and cost the lives of 36,000 people.

From all these accounts and newspaper reports and the assessment of the local Siberian meteorologists, Kulik still had only a vague idea of where this most awesome of explosions had taken place. And so in 1927, with the backing of the Academy of Sciences, he set out from Leningrad to see if, nineteen years after the happening, he could find the spot where the Tunguska meteorite, as he believed it to be, had fallen.

Kulik's odyssey was to last more than ten years, but, at last, after an epic series of journeys, worthy of the great explorers, he was to find the centre of the Tunguska explosion.

By March 1927, he had left the Trans-Siberian railway at Taishet and set off by horse and sledge over the snow towards the village of Dvorets on the River Angara. After a fortnight he reached Vanavara, the last settlement before he had to plunge in the uncharted Siberian forest, or taiga, as the Russians can it, a vast, dark and fearsome prospect in the 1920s.

Finally, in the middle of April, the men reached the River Mekirta. It was a moment of wonderment. For as Kulik stood on the south bank and gazed towards the north, he saw the first extraordinary signs of the cataclysm that had now obsessed him for six years. On the north bank, there were a number of little hillocks above the general lie of the land. These little knolls stood out starkly against the sky. They had been stripped bare of trees. As Kulik got nearer he could see the great trunks of the fallen pines. Weirdly, they all lay like some annihilated regiment with their tops facing uniformly towards the southeast. Kulik knew that he was seeing the outmost victims of what must have been an enormous blast. Eagerly he climbed the highest of the ridges he could see, the Khladni Ridge as he was to call it. There was the most incredible sight. Stretching as far as he could see, at least twelve to sixteen miles (20–25km), was utter devastation. The huge trees of the taiga lay flat. Pines, firs, deciduous trees; all had succumbed. The sharp outlines of the winter landscape etched it like a plate. And again, this bizarre and unbroken regimentation. Slowly, as he surveyed the scene from the ridge, realization dawned on Kulik. Despite this devastation of almost unimaginable proportions, twelve miles or more of flattened forest stretching to the horizon, the trees still lay in only one direction. The centre of the blast must be even further away. The Tunguska explosion had been vast, beyond even the wildest reports that had filtered back to St Petersburg.

Kulik was anxious to press on to find the point from which the blast had originated but Potapovich and Okhchen, the two Tungus, flatly refused to go on. Kulik was forced to return to Vanavara to find new companions, and it was not until June that, using rafts to transport his equipment along rivers where the ice had melted, he managed to get back to Khladni Ridge. From there, following the line of the fallen trees, he pushed steadily north and west, until one day he came to a natural amphitheatre in the hills and pitched camp in the bottom of its bowl. The bowl was less than a mile across, so the next day Kulik set out methodically to survey the tops of the surrounding hills. He had to work his way almost completely round the circle before he could be certain of what he had found: all the fallen trees faced outwards. This 'cauldron' as he called it, was the very centre of the Tunguska blast.

Among all the tribulations that were to follow, this discovery at least was to remain unchallenged. Whatever had caused the mighty Tunguska explosion – and Kulik now knew it had devastated thirty-seven miles (60km) in one direction alone – this was the epicentre. His own account conveys his excitement.

> I pitched my camp and began to circle the mountains around the Great Cauldron. At first I went towards the west, covering several kilometres over the bare hill crests; the tree tops of the windbreak already lay facing west. I went round the whole cauldron in a great circle to the south, and the windbreak as though bewitched, turned its tree tops also to the south. I returned to camp and again set out over the bare hills to the east and the windbreak turned its tree tops in that direction. I summoned all my strength and came out again to the south almost to the Khushmo River; the tops of the windbreak had also turned towards the south.

There could be no doubt. I had circled the centre of the fall. With a fiery stream of hot gases and cold solid bodies, the meteorite had struck the cauldron with its hills, tundra and swamp and, as a stream of water striking a flat surface splashes spray in all directions, the stream of hot gases with the swarm of bodies penetrated the earth, and both directly and with explosive recoil wrought all this mighty havoc.

This first account makes almost heart-rending reading. For in his moment of triumph Kulik started to make assumptions that were to involve him in enormous and unrewarded labour and leave him at his death still unaware of the true nature of the explosion, still less what had caused it.

Almost immediately, in the Cauldron, Kulik thought he spotted places where the fragments of his meteorite must lie.

He wrote:

The area is strewn with dozens of peculiar flat holes varying from several metres to tens of metres across and several metres also in depth. The sides of these holes are unusually steep, although flat sides are also encountered; their base is flat, mossy, marshy, and with occasional traces of a raised area in the centre.

The expedition's stocks, however, were so low by now that there was no time to investigate further. They set off back, living as best they could off the land.

KULIK'S SECOND EXPEDITION

Kulik had returned to Leningrad after his first expedition with his astonishing news about the size of the great explosion and he had no trouble, even in times of turmoil and austerity in the Soviet Union, in persuading the Academy of Sciences to finance further exploration.

It was this expedition that was joined by the cameraman Strukov from Sovkino and was thus to provide the vivid and engrossing film record we still possess. Strukov seems to have had all the virtues of the great documentary cameraman. When Kulik's boat overturned in some swirling rapids and the leader only just escaped with his life, Strukov kept filming. When the expedition reached its most difficult traverses, Strukov was there first to record it. The small human incidents, the cumbersome struggle to continue scientific work under mosquito veils through clouds of swarming insects; it is all there. And when the moment came to film the first great panorama of destruction, he gave us epic sweeping shots.

This second expedition was beset with difficulties. Several members suffered from boils and vitamin deficiencies and had to go back. There was Kulik's accident. The magnetic survey seeking iron meteorites was unproductive and the party returned to Leningrad with little to show for their efforts except the graphic and exciting film. This was sufficient, however, to launch a third and much larger expedition the following year.

KULIK'S THIRD EXPEDITION

Once again the pictures provide an evocative record: the long horse-drawn baggage train, the exhausting task of manhandling boats across swamps and around rapids and shoals, above all the huge labour of cutting trenches and draining the 'peculiar holes', which was Kulik's main objective. The group stayed all the summer of 1929, then through the winter into 1930, saw Krinov, the deputy leader, lose a toe through frostbite while on a trek back for supplies, and another member go down with appendicitis. They put together a much more detailed picture of the devastation without greatly altering the impression gathered by Kulik on his pioneering journey. But of a meteorite they found not a trace. Slowly it was becoming apparent that this site was like no other on earth. Always before, fragments, large or small, often in their thousands, had been recovered from the ground. But at Tunguska there seemed nothing left whatever of the fireball itself. Kulik's team members were already beginning to suspect that their labours in the 'peculiar holes' in the swamp were futile. Krinov took a photograph of the tree stump they found at the bottom of one hole, proving it, at least, could not be a meteorite crater. But he hid the picture from Kulik. For the leader was now utterly dedicated to looking for a meteorite and he would consider no other possible cause of the explosion.

On this third long sojourn the team was also unable to carry out the aerial survey on which so much store had been set. The logistics proved beyond the capability of the Soviet fliers of those days. For more than eighteen months, Kulik and his helpers endured not only deprivation, but, in their principal goal, frustration too.

There now fell on the Soviet Union that dark era, known as the Great Terror. Literally no one was safe from denunciation, from exile or execution, as Stalin liquidated all the old Bolsheviks, almost all the senior officers in the Red Army, thousands of old party members, and sent millions of ordinary Russians to experience for themselves the rigours of the Siberian taiga and tundra in that frightful 'Gulag Archipelago' which Alexander Solzhenitsyn has described.

THE FOURTH EXPEDITION

The sole task of any man in the Soviet Union of those days was to survive. For seven years the study of the Tunguska event was buried by more vital considerations. But in 1937, with all opposition to Stalin dismembered, the Terror seemed to ease a little and Kulik set off on his fourth expedition to Siberia with his main task to complete an aerial survey, and to search once again for fragments.

The most careful covering of the ground still produced not a sign of a meteorite, but the aerial survey of 1938 and the close examination of the trees, their burn marks, and the pattern of their fall did at last allow scientists to get some real impression of what had happened on that day in June thirty years before.

First, it seemed that the flying object had entered the earth's atmosphere and become visible somewhere over Lake Baykal and then travelled from southeast to northwest as it plunged downwards, though there was some suggestion that it might have changed direction.

What was beyond doubt after the aerial survey was the breath-taking extent of the destruction. More than 770 square miles (2,000km^2) was devastated, an area as big as Birmingham in England, or Philadelphia. Yet within this enormous blitz, there were some very odd features. Right in the middle quite a large number of trees were left standing, though stripped of their branches.

Furthermore, despite all the diligent surveying, digging, boring, there was absolutely no sign that anything had actually hit the earth. There had been at least two blast waves, an explosion and a ballistic wave, there had been extensive though brief fires and some flash burns. But there was not a trace of impact damage. Curiously too, the new growth of trees seemed to be very much accelerated, compared with other young groups of trees in that part of Siberia.

The puzzle seemed greater than ever until, at the other end of the world, came the apocalyptic moment which changed so many things: the Americans dropped the atomic bomb on Hiroshima. The similarity between the pattern of destruction at Hiroshima and the damage caused by the Tunguska blast was extraordinary.

At Hiroshima the first American observers noticed that right in the centre of the blast there was relatively little damage. Similarly, the trees had remained upright in the centre of Tunguska. Also, at Hiroshima the plants seemed to grow more quickly, as had the trees in the blast zone in Siberia. There was the same 'shadowing' effect where favourable contours in the ground seemed to protect people and objects even quite near the epicentre. Above all, that sinister symbol which had entered mankind's nightmare – the mushroom cloud – seemed uncannily like the description that the Tungus had given of a pillar of smoke going up into the sky. The Russian scientists already knew that the Tunguska cloud must have gone very high into the upper atmosphere, for it had been seen from great distances. They also noticed with some awe that the Tunguska explosion had been perhaps a thousand times as powerful as the Hiroshima bomb.

The similarities were too close to ignore. Yet surely it was in-conceivable that an atomic explosion had occurred in Siberia

nearly forty years before the physicists of the United States
managed to create the first big bang at Alamagordo? But once
the thought was planted other evidence came to mind. The
blisters on the Tungus reindeer; were they radiation burns such
as the cattle of New Mexico had suffered when the first test
dust cloud hit them? Did the tree rings after 1908 show
signs of radiation? The American scientist W F Libby thought
they did.

And another strange symmetry with nuclear explosions has
emerged. When the Russian, American and British H-bombs were
tested in the 1950s it was noticed that they produced on the
opposite side of the earth extraordinary bright aurora lights and
disturbances in the ionosphere. Only in 1985, Arthur C Clarke
received a report from Mr Samuel Sunter of Victoria, Canada
who as a boy of nine, lived in Northumberland, England, when
the explosion took place.

> I saw, looking north east, on June 30th 1908, a large red ball of
> fire, about three times the size of a full moon. It looked just like a
> hole in the sky. On the other side of the hole, it looked like flames,
> just like looking into the fire box of a locomotive. But what made
> me afraid was a solid beam of light which reached right down to
> where I was standing. This made me afraid and I ran into the house,
> so I do not know how long it lasted after I first saw it. Even today
> I have a very vivid memory of it.

The weight of scientific opinion now favours the idea that it
was a comet which exploded above Siberia. Indeed, in the
summer of 1986, the American Geophysical Union held a special
session in Baltimore, Maryland, designed to alert the world, in
that year of Halley's return, to the catastrophic implications of
another comet arriving and colliding with earth.

The geophysicists have a special nightmare. Rocks and boulders – the debris of space – are swirling round the earth all the
time, running into our atmosphere and disintegrating. On average, a 1000-ton boulder bumps into us each month. Frequently,
especially in June, there are spectacular displays of shooting stars
at night as fragments burn up in the upper atmosphere. But what
the geophysicists fear is the arrival of a really large body weighing
perhaps 100,000 tons or more. They envisage its sudden appear-

ance, unanticipated, in the upper atmosphere. There would be a tremendous fireball, brighter than the sun; then a cataclysmic explosion. If this took place over a populated area, the destruction and loss of life would be enormous.

However, in September 1986, another natural disaster occurred, which some scientists felt might shed light on the mystery of Tunguska. In Yaounde, capital of the West African state of Cameroon, the authorities started to receive reports that in an area around Lake Nios, in the interior, hundreds of people had just fallen down dead. Officials who quickly arrived on the scene were confronted with an apocalyptic vision. The rolling green countryside was strewn with the carcasses of cattle, pigs and wild animals. Along the roads and tracks leading to the lake lay the corpses of people who had apparently been struck down as they walked or bicycled along. In the villages themselves around the lake, people had died by the hundred in their houses and gardens. In total, more than 1,700 people died, as well as herds of animals. It was soon apparent that a great cloud of poisonous gas was responsible. It had rolled down from the crater lake, fatally enveloping everything in its path.

In 1984 a geologist, A R Crawford of the University of Canterbury, New Zealand, suggested that a great gas cloud from within the earth might have been the cause of the Tunguska explosion. Tunguska, he wrote, 'might be a wholly terrestrial phenomenon ... Rather than being the only well-argued-for cometary impact on Earth, it may be the only modern example of a sudden very voluminous hot gaseous effusion.' Crawford noted that such gases were associated with diamond-bearing kimberlite pipes, a belt of which lie across Siberia.

Crawford belongs to a school of geologists which believes that the earth may be expanding, even pulsating like a heart, and that this may account for some of the fractures associated with plate tectonics. From these fractures in the earth's crust may emerge gouts of lethal and explosive gases.

Sixty years of research on the Tunguska site have still failed to come up with any convincing residue of extraterrestrial material, though there are plenty of exotic minerals in the little glass globules found in the Tunguska soil. It is a frightening but plausible concept that the big bang, which could have laid waste a city the size of Paris, might simply have been the biggest gas explosion the modern world has ever seen.

ARTHUR C CLARKE COMMENTS:

The whole subject of meteor – or cometary – impact has now become of great scientific and, surprisingly, political *importance. On the scientific side, it is now widely believed that the extinction of the dinosaurs (as well as a vast range of other creatures) some sixty-five million years ago was due to the impact of an asteroid or comet about five miles in diameter. Quite apart from the colossal immediate damage, the resulting smoke and airborne debris darkened the earth for months, killing off much of the planet's vegetation and the chains of life that were based upon it.*

But perhaps the most important lesson from Tunguska is that what happened once will *(not* may*) happen again. Almost all our planetary neighbours bear evidence of repeated bombardments from space. Mercury, Mars, the Moon, the satellites of Jupiter, show meteoric scars sometimes* hundreds *of kilometres in diameter. The only reason why it has taken so long to recognize such stigmata on our own planet is because weathering, and geological processes, have largely obliterated them.*

Early in 1980, American scientists produced evidence that the extinction of the dinosaurs, was triggered by the impact of a heavenly body far larger than the Tunguska object. Perhaps that gave us a chance to evolve; and perhaps a similar event will open the way to our successors.

It may not happen for a million years. Or it may happen, as I wrote in Rendezvous with Rama, *much sooner:*

> *At 09.46 GMT on the morning of 11th September, in the exceptionally beautiful summer of the year 2077, most of the inhabitants of Europe saw a dazzling fireball appear in the eastern sky. Within seconds it was brighter than the sun, and as it moved across the heavens – at first in utter silence – it left behind it a churning column of smoke.*

Somewhere above Austria it began to disintegrate, producing a series of concussions so violent that more than a million people had their hearing permanently damaged. They were the lucky ones.

Moving at fifty kilometres a second, a thousand tons of rock and metal impacted on the plains of northern Italy, destroying in a few flaming moments the labour of centuries. The cities of Padua and Verona were wiped from the face of the earth; and the last glories of Venice sank forever beneath the sea as the waters of the Adriatic came thundering landwards after the hammer-blow from space.

Six hundred thousand people died, and the total damage was more than a trillion dollars. But the loss to art, to history, to science – to the whole human race, for the rest of time – was beyond all computation. It was as if a great war had been fought and lost in a single morning; and few could draw much pleasure from the fact that, as the dust of destruction slowly settled, for months the whole world witnessed the most splendid dawns and sunsets since Krakatoa.

After the initial shock, mankind reacted with a determination and a unity that no earlier age could have shown. Such a disaster, it was realised, might not occur again for a thousand years – but it might occur tomorrow. And the next time, the consequences could be even worse.

But the Tunguska event, comet or no, spaceship, black hole, or anti-matter, remains unique. If it was indeed a comet, it is hardly a comforting thought. If a small comet, too tiny to see in the morning sky, can produce the destructive force of a twenty megaton bomb, what would a big one do? Worse, if the bomb doors of the solar system ever do open again, what chance is there that the great missile would again choose a target so conveniently barren as the remoteness of Siberia? Next time we can hardly be so lucky.

LIFE BEFORE
LIFE

Underlying the search for the strange powers of the human mind is the most fundamental quest of all – is death the end? Shall we live again? Have we, indeed, lived before? Hinduism and Buddhism, the two greatest religions of the East, claiming the allegiance of hundreds of millions, are founded on a belief in reincarnation – a conviction that we reappear on earth in a chain of linked existences. Death is merely a prelude to a new life.

Yet, despite the Christian creed of 'resurrection of the body', it has never been assumed in Western cultures that the dead return to live on this earth: 'life everlasting' was only to be expected in some heavenly abode beyond space and time – certainly not back in Balham or the Bronx. Today, however, surveys in the United States suggest that four out of every ten people believe in earthly reincarnation. In Britain, one in six of those who completed a questionnaire in *The Times* claimed to have had 'an experience which convinced you that you must have had a previous life or lives'. And a growing number of research workers are claiming to produce evidence – if not proof – of what those previous existences were, often with astonishing precision and with details of life centuries ago which, it seems, could not possibly have been acquired by normal means. Most of this evidence is produced by hypnotizing people and then 'taking them back' through childhood, through birth, and then through to their previous incarnation.

Whatever happens during hypnotic regressions, the subjects can appear to be actually living the part, even to the point of personal peril. When the first post-war ventures into past-life regression were being tried by hypnotists in Britain, they had some nasty shocks.

Henry Blythe, a West Country hypnotist who practised both privately and on the halls, discovered he had a subject, Naomi Henry from Exeter, who could reproduce the life of an Irish woman, Mary Cohen from Cork.

'What year is this?'

'1790.'

'Whereabouts in Cork do you live?'

'On a farm.'

'What is the name of the farm?'

'Greengates.'

'What is the name of the nearest village?'

'Grener.'

Carefully, in a number of sessions, Blythe took Naomi Henry through the various stages of a life which had apparently been spent milking the cows, marrying a violent husband and losing her children. Blythe suggested she was getting older, decade by decade, until she was 70.

'How much longer have you to live?'

'A woman said not long.'

'Have you any pain?'

'No, that is all gone.'

'Has the priest been to see you?'

Silence.

Blythe had by now interested the London *Daily Express* in the case, and there was a shorthand writer present. Still there was silence from Naomi Henry, whether in her Mary Cohen role, or as herself. Blythe describes what followed.

I was watching her closely, my fingers on the pulse of her left wrist. There was still no reply from Naomi, and suddenly I felt her pulse die away; her breathing stopped, every trace of colour left her face. She appeared to be dead. I bent closer to try and discover a trace of breath, but there was nothing. The atmosphere in the room was tense. I could feel the fear in my wife and the shorthand writer. Hurriedly, I spoke urgently, whispering into Naomi's ear: 'You are quite safe, I am with you. You are safe, safe, safe.' Slowly, her pulse began to beat again, her breathing resumed, some colour returned to her face. I estimate that about five seconds had elapsed. I heard a gasp of relief from the witnesses.

The incident was enough to deter the *Daily Express* from dabbling in such waters; they abandoned their investigation. Blythe, with some hesitation, continued his sessions with Naomi Henry, and even extracted another 'life' from her as Clarice Hellier, a Bristol girl at the turn of the century.

Hypnotist Arnall Bloxham extracted eleven former lives out of Ann Ockenden, a Midlands schoolteacher – nine of them as a man.

Anyone who has seen a professional hypnotist's stage show, such as the presentations throughout England for many years past by Martin St James, will not be surprised by uninhibited and fantastic performances under hypnosis. St James's victims respond spectacularly: ordinary coalminers at Batley Variety Club declaiming a pro-Tory political speech for twenty minutes on end without pause or repetition; housewives desperately tearing off their clothes, convinced they are on fire, until Martin St James intervenes in time to save their modesty; feats of unusual strength are commonplace; and there emerge hidden talents as singers and dancers.

The credibility of the 'past lives' of hypnotic regression subjects turns on the wealth of detail which they provide and which apparently they could not possibly have known by normal means.

In the autumn of 1952, Colorado businessman Morey Bernstein, who was also an amateur hypnotist, started a series of sessions which were to result in one of the most celebrated cases. His subject was Virginia Tighe, a twenty-nine-year-old who hailed from Madison, Wisconsin. In the course of six regressions, Virginia Tighe became Bridey Murphy, an Irish woman living in the first half of the last century. (Ireland seems to have a special place in the history of past life recall!)

The recorded tapes are impressive. The girl from Wisconsin is transformed into Bridget Kathleen Murphy, born 20 December 1798. She lives with her father, a Protestant barrister, in a secluded house outside Cork. She marries the son of another barrister – a Catholic, so there have to be two weddings. They move to Belfast and live in a cottage in Dooley Road. Bridey dies, it seems, in 1864. But it is the local detail which has marked out this case. Virginia Tighe had never been outside the United States. Yet, as Bridey Murphy she was able to name some family grocers, Farr and Carrigan, who had existed at the time. An 1801 map of Cork showed an area called the Meadows with a few houses round it, as Bridey had described. She referred to coins such as the tuppence, which seem only to have been used at the time of Bridey's 'life', used authentic words such as 'linen' for handkerchief, 'ditching' for burying. There is a theory that she had absorbed it all from a television film. But although American newspapermen also managed to find relatives and friends of Virginia Tighe of Irish extraction who might have given her the local colour and conveyed the beguiling accent, thirty years of investigation have not uncovered a conclusive, mundane explanation of Bridey Murphy as she emerged from Virginia Tighe during 1952 and 1953, in a sitting-room in Pueblo, Colorado, before witnesses including a sceptical, indeed hostile, husband.

Mrs Yvette Jones, of Warley, near Birmingham in England recently described being regressed by a hypnotist back to a life as a three-year-old child in the seventeenth century.

I seemed to be floating in a long dark tunnel, then found myself in a small paved courtyard. The hypnotist said, 'What is your name?' 'Mary –' I answered. There was a long pause, then '– Johnson.' 'Where are you?' 'In my father's garden in London.' '"What does your father do?' 'He is a cloth merchant.' 'In what part of London do you live?' The word 'Eastcheap' came to me, but for some reason I felt unable to say so. 'Who is on the throne?' 'King Charles,' I replied. 'Which King Charles, Mary?' I was silent. There was only one King Charles and he was married to Henrietta Maria.

'What are you wearing, Mary?' I became animated. 'Oh, a pretty green velvet dress and green velvet slippers, I said proudly. I was always well dressed because of my father's trade. 'My father calls me 'My little Lady Greensleeves.'

'What year is it?' I wanted to say 1643 but, again, felt tongue-tied. 'Are there any soldiers in the streets?' I began to tremble, suddenly afraid. 'There are many soldiers, they frighten me – they carry guns and pikes.' I had a mental picture of hard-faced men my father called Puritans.

'What religion are you, Mary?' 'We are Catholic,' I said – they told me later I'd pronounced it in the seventeenth century way – "Catholeek'.

The hypnotist then told me to come forward to the last day of my life. 'How old are you now?' 'I am four,' I said. Immediately my mouth was very dry and I was conscious of extreme thirst and high fever. 'What's the matter with you, Mary?' "Plague," was the only word I could utter, as my tongue stuck to the roof of my mouth. 'Have you any spots or boils on your body?' 'Yes,' I said, and indicated a swelling under my right armpit.

'How long have you been ill?' 'Three days," I replied. 'Are they giving you medicine to make you feel better?' 'Just cold water." I tossed restlessly in my chair, hot and thirsty.

I want you to come now to the very last moment of your life, Mary.' My head lolled to one side and once again, I found myself in the inky blackness of the tunnel which had no ending.

After I was 'restored' to the twentieth century, I felt strange for a while. Throughout the session I had been aware of street noises. My seventeenth-century self was real enough, yet I knew I was still living in the present.'

The dialogues between hypnotist and subject in the special circumstances of regression parallel what appears to be a by-no-means-uncommon spontaneous experience in normal life – when a person feels that he has not only been, impossibly, in a particular place before, but has actually taken part in events there: he feels he has lived the scene in a past life.

An Indian Army major, A D McDonough, from Worthing in Sussex, told of an incident on the North West Frontier, near Attock:

I reached a ridge which overlooked a precipitous drop into a densely wooded valley, shaped much like a horseshoe.

Suddenly, I found myself down in the valley, amid a large number of ancient Greek soldiers. The whole scene was a busy encampment. In the centre of the valley were three altars. But what attracted me most was a group of men at the head of the valley, looking up at something. I went over and found that it was a newly-cut inscription in Greek on the dressed surface of the rock, commemorating the death of one of Alexander the Great's generals. Now I never studied Greek, but I was able to read the inscription clearly and understand it. There was a tense atmosphere of sorrow in the vicinity.

A sudden blank and I was back in my place on the ridge, still gazing into the valley with a vivid recollection of what I had seen.

I determined, however, to explore that valley, and did so with the help of Indian coolies, for the whole place was densely covered in rank vegetation and jungle growth, and full of large fallen boulders. I headed for the place where the rock-cut inscription was, and after much labour in clearing rank vegetation, I exposed what was once a dressed surface, and on a part of it were traces of incised Greek letters; but the greater portion of the inscription had disintegrated and fallen off.

'till, there was ample evidence to convince me that this was the rock-cut inscription I had seen.

Major McDonough concluded that he had been at the spot where Alexander the Great's army had camped before fording the Indus River into India, in 329BC.

Another soldier, Alex Aiscough of Wallasey, Cheshire, related an experience during the retreat of 1918 in northern France: 'We were billeted at Quivelly, in the suburbs of Rouen. I knew nothing of Rouen.' Ainscough went into the city to get some of his favourite tobacco from the British army canteen. He then had half-an-hour to spare.

I decided to investigate the street and the old turnings off it. It was a warm evening, and my decision had hardly passed through my brain when a strange chill struck me. I seemed suddenly to become familiar with my surroundings. I was marching with seven other men at the head of a column. We were all clad in black chainmail, and we were all tall. In front rode three men on horseback, also clad in black mail. We were going to see the burning of Joan of Arc. Here comes the strange part of my experience. I followed the street and eventually came to the outside of some kind of market, and on the pavement were marks cut into the stones.

A tablet above stated that Joan of Arc had been burned on the spot.

But not everyone who feels themselves transported in time manages a brush with history's high dramas. Mrs W Barnard of Kenton, Middlesex, in England, was motoring in Ontario, Canada. 'As we approached Smith's Falls, I started to describe the town. My husband knew I had never been in Canada before, so he was surprised when I described a part of the main street, a grocer's shop, name of Desjardins, on one corner opposite a Royal Bank of Canada branch on the other corner. Our surprise was complete when we drove up the main street and saw the bank on one corner, and a grocer's shop on the other, exactly as I had said, except that the name on the grocer's shop was not Desjardins. My husband stopped the car and went into the grocer's shop. There he was informed that the last owner's name was Desjardins – thirty years ago.'

Sometimes, an experience of 'reliving the past' can be so overwhelming that it transforms a life. A BBC playwright, Ada Stewart, was in Scotland in August 1967, planning to visit the Flodden Field battle site in which James IV of Scotland was killed by the English army under the Earl of Surrey.

She had already taken a great interest in James, who had been something of an Arthurian figure among the more blackguard monarchs of the age. That night she was struck by a vision of the Flodden battle. She was on her back – 'staring up at what seemed like a tunnel of staves and blades, and beyond them, hands and merciless faces of men intent on killing me.

'My left arm I raised to cover my head, to ward off the blows. All the hate of the world was concentrated on me at that moment, and nobody was stopping it. I howled, a howl of pure animal terror as the blades thrust down upon me.' From that moment, A J Stewart was convinced that she actually had been James IV in a previous life, indeed that she *was* James IV.

She began to dress in all-black costume with white cuffs and ruffles. Her writing and speech assumed an antique style. She wrote an autobiography of James 'presented by A J Stewart', explaining some of the enigmas of the king, such as why he built the world's then biggest warship (apparently it was to attack London). She adopts, in the most matter-of-fact way, King James's supposed point of view in many aspects of daily life.

When she saw Van der Goes' picture of King James III and the future James IV she said, 'Oh, no. That's not the way it was originally. It was just my father and St Andrew. I had myself painted in later, as an act of penance, kneeling behind him. That is me in my coronation robes over my funeral black, with my poor lank hair in need of washing. If I remember correctly, there was a vine painted where I now kneel, because my mother was at that time pregnant.' This is one piece of autobiographical King James which has been shown to be wrong, courtesy of the Courtauld Institute's Stephen Rees-Jones, plus X-ray and infrared photography.

But it is the hypnotic regressions, rather than waking experiences, which compel the most serious investigation. Their vividness, the undoubted authenticity of the records (now many thousands of them on tape and film); the almost impossibly obscure information thrown up during such experiences – all these have compelled many people to take them as evidence amounting to proof of life after death and reincarnation on this Earth.

But the human mind is perhaps stranger than even these enthusiasts allow. A Finnish psychiatrist, Dr Reima Kampman, who worked up at Oulu, a port at the top of the Gulf of Bothnia on the edge of Lapland, determined to make a detailed study of the phenomenon of producing other personalities under hypnosis. He used a group of teenage secondary school students, all of them as mentally healthy as he could find. More than thirty were able to summon up, under hypnosis, multiple personalities. One thirteen-year-old conjured up no fewer than eight secondary personalities.

The first one was Bessina who lived in Babylon some 2,500 years ago. She was succeeded by some 'water-like' intermediate state, then came Ving Len in Nanking, China, around the year 100. The next one was Gunhild, the wife of a fisherman, who was born in Storviken, Norway, in 846. Then there was Dorothy, the daughter of an English innkeeper, born near Norwich in the village of Laughton in 1139. She was followed by Genevienne de Bonde in Paris at the end of the seventeenth century. Then came Emily Sunderland, an English lady and the wife of a member of the House of Lords, in 1743. After her came a Swedish peasant girl, Judith Martinson, born in the 1800s. Then Karolina Prokovjeff, the daughter of a Russian officer. She died from tuberculosis in Leningrad after the revolution.

Across the whole gallery of personalities, extending over thousands of years, the girl produced an astonishing amount of detail and description of everyday life. But it was the medieval English personality 'Dorothy' which was the most startling. 'Dorothy' gave what Kampman described as 'amazingly explicit' accounts of life in twelfth-century England, where her father had been an innkeeper: place names were accurate, distances were given in miles, contemporary events were reported correctly. At one point 'Dorothy' sang a song which she called the 'Summer Song'. Kampman was fascinated: why did 'Dorothy' here suddenly change from Finnish into a strange language that reminded him of English? Did the song really date back to the twelfth century? Professor Ole Reuter was called in. He quickly identified the language as Middle English. Even the words were recognisable. This was 'The Cuckoo Song', a canon song treasured by the British Museum as an extreme rarity.

The feat seemed impossible of rational explanation in a thirteen-year-old-Finnish secondary school girl who had hardly learnt any English at all in her normal life. It was not until nearly seven years later that the girl, now making a name for herself as a singer, was re-hypnotized by Kampman in the course of a follow-up investigation. An astonishing story unfolded.

Kampman took the girl, now nineteen years old, carefully and slowly back to the point where she might have come across 'Summer Song'. She recalled once going to the library and borrowing a pile of books, including *The Hound of the Baskervilles*. But she had to kill time until her bus came. Idly she had glanced at a book called *The Story of Music* and riffled through the papers.

Kampman's transcript reflects his astonished pursuit of the girl's hypnotic memory:

'Is there an English song or something very old?'
    'It was just there.'
    'Have another look at it.'
    'I cannot read that. I've had English at school, but I cannot read that.'
    'But are there words?'
    'Yes.'
    'And notes?'
    'Yeah, there.'

'Whereabouts at the library is that book?'

'I don't know. It was here on the table. I just started to look and I thought I'll look at some magazines, but the book was here. I'll have a look at it.'

'Is it in Finnish?'

'Yeah.'

'What is the story of it?'

'*The Story of Music.* So it says, yeah.'

'Who has written it?'

'Benjamin Britten. And Imogen Holst. I wonder [laughs] if that is a man or a woman.'

It took little time to establish that Britten and Holst had indeed produced a book called *The Story of Music,* containing 'The Cuckoo song'.

The source of 'Dorothy's' song was confirmed – as was the astounding reach of the girl's memory. In one unthinking glance she had, it seemed, absorbed a whole song in an obscure language – modernized medieval English, as it turned out – and reproduced it under hypnosis.

This is an extraordinary demonstration of the mind's capacity, under hypnosis, to reach unbelievably fleeting memories and impressions. Nearly 80 years ago members of the British Society of Psychical Research were investigating a woman who took on the persona of a medieval lady called Blanche Poynings. The investigators were spellbound:

'As presented to us, she was a lady of very distinct character, a great gossip, taken up exclusively with herself and her circle of friends and acquaintances, which was a very distinguished one. She was a great friend of Maud, Countess of Salisbury, and much of her talk was about that lady and her husband, the Earl. The Countess, she said, had been married three times, and she gave the names of her former husbands – Aubrey, and Sir Alan de Buxhall. She gave the names of the Countess's children by the Earl, and of her stepson, Alan de Buxhall, her own maiden name, Frances, and the names of the Earl of Salisbury's brothers.'

She described with much vigour how the Earl, who was a Lollard, threw the images out of his chapel, and especially an image of Saint Catherine. This image, when they were removing it, fell on one of the men and made his nose bleed. She described the three kinds of bread – simmel, wastel and cotchet – eaten by different classes, and gave some account of her way of life. Her favourite dish was lampreys stewed in oil. On the saga went, in immense detail, until the investigator, G Lowes Dickinson, had the idea of asking his subject: 'How can we confirm what you are telling us?'

'Read his will.'
   'Whose will?'
   'Wilshere's.'
   'Where is it?'
   'Museum. On a parchment.'
   'How can we get at it?'
   'Ask E. Holt.'
   'Where is he?'
   'Dead. There is a book. Mrs Holt.'
   'Do you know where she lives?'
   'No. Wrote a book. *Countess Maud* by Emily Holt.'

When woken out of hypnosis, the woman could recall nothing whatsoever of the book except the title and the fact that she had read it. But when G Lowes Dickinson tracked down the volume he 'discovered in it every person and every fact (with one or two trifling exceptions) which had been referred to in the supposed life of Blanche Poynings'.

Reincarnation was therefore ruled out, but the mind's astounding powers of recall in the state of suggestibility known as hypnosis had been demonstrated in a most impressive fashion.

This recall faculty has already attracted the attention of police forces around the world. The Israeli Police Scientific Interrogation Unit has been using hypnotism since 1973, and reports a significant improvement in memory recall in twenty-four out of their first forty cases.

Their most spectacular success followed a hideous terrorist attack when a bus was blown up in northern Israel: a number of passengers were killed and injured. The *Journal* of the Forensic Science Society carried a report from the police investigating the crime saying that they had been able to discover nothing of significance through routine questioning of the driver. So the man was hypnotized. He was then able to recall the smallest details of the long journey, in which many passengers had joined and left the bus.

'He remembered that at a certain bus stop a dark-skinned youth entered the bus, carrying a parcel. When the driver handed him his change he noticed a cold sweat on the young man's palm. Therefore, during hypnosis, he pointed out the youth as being a likely suspect. Although the driver faced the youth for only the short period of time needed to sell him a ticket, he was able to reconstruct an identikit portrait.' With the help of the picture a man was arrested, and confessed to the crime.

The New York Police have a permanent hypnotism unit consisting of a personable lady detective, Millie Markham, and Police Officer John Gaspar. A survey of the crime squads for whom they have hypnotized witnesses found that seventy per cent of their colleagues felt the information obtained was helpful – and ninety-one per cent felt it was accurate.

Early in 1982 two women in Manhattan saw a man shot dead in front of them; he had come to their aid when they were being mugged. Under hypnosis one of the women was able to provide a minutely-detailed description of the gunman, right down to the type of spectacle frames he was wearing.

'When we go into the hypnosis room, the only thing we have,' said Millie Markham, 'is the time, date, place of occurrence, subject's name and what information the detective on the case is looking for. Let's say he might want a licence plate number or a description of a person. We don't ask questions like, "Do you see the man there? Is he tall and skinny?" We say, "What are you looking at? Describe this to me." You don't say, "Describe the man to me," because you don't know if it's a man or a woman. Our questions are very open and no element of suggestion comes into them.' The squad has now achieved the acceptance of hypnotically-produced evidence as admissible in court.

The phenomenal reaches of memory are astonishing. Professor Erika Fromm, of the University of Chicago, was regressing a twenty-six-year-old patient for demonstration purposes during a psychology class. Suddenly, when she got Don back to 'three years old' under hypnosis, he astonished her by breaking into fluent Japanese. 'The students in my class crowded around, gaping. He talked on and on in Japanese for fifteen to twenty minutes. When I progressed him to age seven, he spontaneously reverted to English.'

It emerged that during the Second World War, Don had been interned as a two-year-old with his family in California. Japanese had been the language of the camp, but he had spoken none after his release at the age of four and was aware of knowing only three or four words.

Back in 1902 a Scottish doctor, Henry Freeborn, had been treating a seventy-year-old patient with pneumonia. In delirium she suddenly broke into Hindustani, apparently conversing with her *ayah* and asking to be taken to the bazaar to buy sweets. It was more than sixty-six years since she had left India where she had been born and had been looked after by a native servant. She was not aware of ever having been able to speak the language.

In a comment on the case in *The Lancet* of June 1902, Dr C A Mercier wrote: 'It is to be noted that it was not the forgotten language alone whose memory was so strangely revived. Her whole personality was transported back. She spoke to friends and relatives of her girlhood and asked that she might be taken to the bazaar.' Coleridge, Mr Mercier recalled, described a case in which an illiterate maid-servant, when delirious, had recited for hours in Greek and Hebrew, apparently acquired from a parson for whom she had worked years before and who had been in the habit of reading Greek and Hebrew books aloud to himself in her hearing.

This power of the mind to recall things of which there is no conscious memory – cryptomnesia – may be the key to many 'past lives' produced in hypnotic regression.

Memories can be etched on the mind, it would seem, in the most fleeting moment. An American doctor, Harold Rosen from Johns Hopkins Hospital in Baltimore, described how one of his patients under hypnosis started writing in a weird script. It was eventually identified as Oscan, an obscure, pre-Latin language, used only in western Italy up to the beginning of the Christian era. It was principally known through a 2500-year-old lead scroll known as the Curse of Vibia.

Rosen eventually established that the curse had been reproduced on one page of a book being used by someone sitting next to his patient in a library years before. One glance had apparently sufficed to engrave it indelibly on the man's mind, without his knowing.

There is a theory current among some parapsychologists that memories of past lives may be transmitted in the genes from parent to child, in the same way as the DNA pattern carries all the necessary information for the entire lifetime's bodily development.

Dr Ian Stevenson, who is one of the leaders of reincarnation research, rejects the gene theory. He says: 'A person can transmit to his descendants, by genetic pathways, only memories of events occurring to him before the conception of his children. It follows that scenes of an ancestor's death could not figure among the events transmitted by genetic memory. Yet approximately two-thirds of the children whose cases I have studied claim to remember the death in the previous life remembered.'

Stevenson is also dismissive of regression: 'Although widely exploited by lay hypnotists and even by a few psychologists who should know better, hypnotic regression to "previous lives" (with rare exceptions) generates only fantasies. This is why I prefer to study the apparent memories of very young children: these occur spontaneously, and the children's minds have not already been filled with normally acquired information.'

Stevenson has indeed devoted much of the past twenty years to investigating children who claim to have lived as somebody else in a previous life, mainly in India, the Far East, Alaska and Nigeria. There are obvious pitfalls in this approach: studying reincarnation in societies to whom it is a tenet of faith may be thought to load the dice a little; making inquiries through an interpreter must add to the hazards; also, children who conjure up an invisible friend are familiar in almost every family, no matter where they live. Sometimes these childish familiars stay around for years. They are usually superior in every way to the mere mortals in the family and particularly to the child itself.

H Fielding Hall, who collected together his fascinating researches in Burma in a book, *The Soul of a People*, became irretrievably enmeshed in the religious outlook and expectations of Buddhism. Nevertheless he records some beguiling tales: a little girl showing extraordinary ability as a puppeteer, while claiming to have been a travelling marionette man named Maung Mon: a boy with deeply marked hands who said they were scars inflicted on him in a former life by dacoit bandits. Ian Stevenson has succeeded in raising such stories, much beloved by the Oriental press, out of the realm of anecdote on to a slightly firmer plane.

One of his prime cases concerns Bishen Chand, the son of a railway clerk in Bareilly, in Uttar Pradesh, northern India. A local lawyer, K K N Sahay, had taken an interest in Bishen Chand before any attempt had been made to check the 'previous life identity' which the four-year-old Bishen Chand described. Sahay wrote it all down.

Bishen Chand had started asking about a place called Pilibhit, some thirty miles away, almost before he could utter any other words. Then he said he was the dead nephew of a man named Har Narain, of Mohalla Ganj in Pilibhit. He had lived next door to Sunder Lal, who had a green gate, a sword and a gun, and who held parties with dancing girls in his courtyard. He had studied up to class six and knew Urdu, Hindi and English.

Sahay determined to take Bishen Chand to Pilibhit to check the story. It is by no means clear that the pilgrimage was conducted on scientific principles, acceptable to the learned Western societies for psychical research, but it must have been a high day in Pilibhit.

First, Sunder Lal and the green gate were spotted. Then the house of the 'previous life' uncle, Har Narain:

'The boy recognized the building and the place where they used to drink wine, eat *rohu* fish, and hear the songs of *nautch* girls.' Out tottered a relative from the 'previous life', Babu Brij Mohan Lal, clutching a faded photograph. By now a sizeable crowd had gathered to oversee the next test. Could Bishen Chand spot himself and his 'previous life' uncle in the picture? Sahay must have held his breath. But all was well. 'Here is Har Nahrain and here I,' pronounced the boy, pointing to the photograph of a boy on a chair. 'This was most remarkable,' wrote Sahay, 'and immediately established his identity as Laxmi Narain, nephew of Babu Har Narain.'

By now the one-time Laxmi Narain had been joined by two 'previous life' schoolfellows, so that the caravanserai moved on to the old Government High School, Philibhit, and he correctly identified various classrooms. The classmates sneakily asked him to name his teacher. But by now, like the audience in some television game show, the crowd were shouting out the answers – it had been fat old Moin-ud-din of Shajehanpur.

'Previous life' Laxmi had clearly been something of a rake and the crowd, turning, demanded to know the name of his favourite prostitute. 'Padma,' said Bishen Chand, which the people certified as correct.

Then came the bizarre moment, frequently found in Indian reincarnation cases, and which outdoes even the improbable plots of Indian cinema – the boy was taken to meet his 'previous life' mother, still in this life. 'She put the following test questions,' recorded lawyer Sahay, 'and became convinced that he is the reincarnation of her late lamented son.' Laxmi Narain had died of fever at the age of 32.

Q. Did you fly kites?
A. Yes
Q. With whom did you contest [in kit flying]?
A. I contested with every kite that came in my range, but particularly I contested with Sunder Lal.
Q. Did you throw away my *achar* [pickle]?
A. I did throw away the *achar*, but how was it possible to eat worms? You wanted me to eat worms, hence I threw your *achar* away.
Note: (by K K N Sahay): The mother says that once her pickles got rotten and she had worms in her jars. She threw the worms out, but kept the pickles in the sun. Laxmi Narain threw them away, much to her annoyance.
Q. Did you ever enter into the service?
A. Yes, I served for some time in the Oudh Railway.
Q. Who was your servant?

244 Arthur C Clarke's Mysteries

A. My servant was Maikua, a black, short-statured Kahar. He was my favourite *Khansama* [cook].
Q. You used to sleep on a bamboo *charpoy* with no bleeding? [This question was put by B Balbir Singh of Killa, Bareilly.)
A. You never saw my bed. I had a good bed with an ornamental plank towards the head side and had a *qalin* [thick cover] on it, and I kept two pillows under the head and two under my feet.
Q. What did I teach at Pilibhit? [This question was put by Sita Ram, now a teacher of the Government School, Bareilly, formerly a teacher at Pilibhit.)
A. You taught Hindi.

Thus was the four-year-old Bishen Chand accepted as the reincarnation of the dead Laxmi Narain, though it hardly seems to have been to his advantage. He ended up an excise tax collector in the town of Rampur.

Another celebrated Indian case also left its heroine, Shanti Devi, languishing in obscure government service in New Delhi, still pining for the 'previous life family' she had re-found and was then obliged to abandon.

Shanti Devi, born in Delhi in 1926, started speaking of her 'husband and children' almost as soon as she could talk. She gave her husband's name as Kedernath, her own as Ludgi. They had lived in Muttra, hundreds of miles from Delhi, in a large, yellow-stuccoed house. 'I died giving birth to another child,' Shanti Devi told the family doctor. 'Our sons are still there in Muttra with their father.'

Eventually, the family decided to send a letter to the name and address that Shanti repeatedly mentioned in Muttra. Again, it must have been a disorienting moment for the widower Kedarnath in Muttra when he opened the missive from Delhi. A visit was arranged and Shanti succeeded in finding the house where her 'previous life husband' had lived. Again there was a meeting with the 'previous life mother' and, most usefully of all, the identification of the spot where some jewellery had been buried in the back garden. But, inevitably, Shanti had to turn her back on her 'previous life family' and return in her incarnation as a nine-year-old girl to Delhi, and to a spinsterly career in government service.

In the twenty-four years since Professor Ian Stevenson first published some of his evidence he has gathered stories, still mainly from the East, of infants with birthmarks that accord with knife and bullet wounds from the 'previous lives', unexplained phobias to water or aircraft, predilections for strange food, or surprising, untaught skills such as thatching – all of them, according to the children, founded on events in a previous incarnation.

One case in the West, however, does display some of the curious features of Stevenson's more remarkable Eastern reports. It was founded in tragedy.

Two little English girls, Joanna and Jacqueline Pollock, aged eleven and six, were walking home from Sunday church at Hexham in Northumberland, in May 1957, when a car mounted the pavement and crushed them against a wall. They were both killed.

Their father, John Pollock, though a Roman Catholic convert, had been a convinced reincarnationist for years. He seems to have believed that the accident was a judgement on him for his views, and also that the girls would be restored to him in a new incarnation. Less than a year later his wife Florence became pregnant; John Pollock immediately told her she would have twins, that they would be the way of restoring the dead girls to them.

Against predictions by gynaecologists, twin girls were indeed born in October 1958. John Pollock immediately noticed a thin white line on the brow of the second-born twin. The dead Jacqueline had carried an identical scar after a fall from her bike at the age of two. The same baby also carried a thumb-print birthmark on her left hip: so had the dead Jacqueline.

Florence Pollock did not share her husband's views and apparently held him to a promise not to discuss them with the children until they were into their teens. Nevertheless, she could not deny the steady sequence of events which seemed to confirm her husband's conviction. The family moved from Hexham within four months of the twins' birth. At the age of three the girls returned for the first time, and immediately seemed at home. 'We used to live there,' they said as they passed the Pollocks' former house. 'The swings and slides are over there,' – even though the playing field was still out of sight. 'The school's just round the corner,' they said, before they were within view of the school that the dead girls had attended.

The twins were not allowed to play with toys which had belonged to their dead sisters, but one day their parents relented. Jennifer immediately named two dolls. 'That's your Mary and this is my Suzanne' – the same names the dead girls had bestowed. One day in the yard of their new house at Whitley Bay, Northumberland, John Pollock found the two girls screaming with fright. 'The car. It's coming at us.' A car outside in the road had turned and was facing straight at them, though safely enough on the other side of the wall. By the time they were six, the phenomena had ceased and at thirteen the girls remembered nothing when they were told the story by their father. Appearing on Tyne Tees Television in 1981, John Pollock had lost none of his certainty. He simply said: 'We were fortunate to be chosen for a most wonderful revelation of the truth: that we can hope for another life on this earth.'

Like so many of the 'truths' which have been hijacked from Asia to Manhattan and Munich, Kensington and California, this one has been absorbed into show business. Should we live again, perhaps it is our proper fate to receive that beguiling invitation card – 'Come as you were' – and land up at the Los Angeles Reincarnation Ball, the annual gathering of Atlanteans, Pilgrim Fathers, various versions of Richard III, and Isabella of Spain, attended by four beautifully-muscled bearers – all convinced of their place in the past.

ARTHUR C CLARKE COMMENTS

Having lived one life in the past, and doing so again in the future, is a basic tenet of many eastern religions, including Buddhism. So it is not surprising that stories of reincarnation are common here in Sri Lanka.

Young children sometimes talk about their real parents and their other homes. They seem to recall previous lives, often in such detail that they not only provide copy for local journalists, but persuade researchers all over the world that there's a phenomenon worth investigating.

We interviewed a little boy, Ajith, who remembers drowning five years ago, and a five-year-old girl who thinks she's a man who was killed in a road accident...

But the story which most fascinates me is one that comes from my favourite place in Sri Lanka, the beautiful little bay of Unawatuna. It's a tragic reminder of Sri Lanka's bloody insurrection of 1971, when a captured rebel – a young man named Robert – leapt to his death into the sea. His close companion, Johnny, had already been killed.

Almost as soon as they could speak, twin girls who were not born until seven years later, claimed to be reincarnations of Johnny and Robert. Shivanthi recounts gruesome details of Johnny's death and Shiromi says she remembers leaping into the sea with her wrists wired together. Such stories are intriguing, but for them to be accepted as evidence of reincarnation, every detail must be checked by a trusted – and dispassionate – investigation.

We're all bombarded with masses of information, from radio, TV, movies, books. People who claim to have lived past lives may have unconsciously absorbed the facts and stored them somewhere in the recesses of their minds. So what these reports may prove is that our brains have a truly astonishing ability to store huge blocks of information and to reproduce them with complete accuracy. This seems to me almost as amazing, and as improbable, as reincarnation itself!

Yet I do not rule out the possibility of reincarnation: the evidence is certainly impressive. My main problem with the concept is that of information storage – so let me use computer technology to explain.

It's been estimated that the number of bytes needed to store a human body – and its memories – is somewhere between 10E14 and 10E16. Let's take the average – 10E15 or 1,000,000,000,000,000. Now, today's hard discs can easily contain a gigabyte (ie 1,000,000,000 bytes). So you would need about a million of them to store yourself! However, in another *twenty years, it could probably be done on a single disc, or whatever device they use in 2020. (I can see a new slogan for Star Trek – 'Boot me up, Scottie.')*

So, if reincarnation does occur, just what is the storage device, and what are the input/output mechanisms? I must confess, I'm unable to imagine them.

Anyway, let's leave the last word on the subject to a poet who expressed beautifully what everyone, reincarnated or not, may have felt from time to time:

> *I have been here before,*
> *But when or how I cannot tell:*
> *I know the grass beyond the door,*
> *The sweet keen smell,*
> *The sighing sound, the lights around the shore.*
>
> *You have been mine before, –*
> *How long ago I may not know:*
> *But just when at that swallow's soar*
> *Your neck turned so,*
> *Some veil did fall, – I knew it all of yore.*
>
> *Then, now, – perchance again! . . .*
> *O round mine eyes your tresses shake!*
> *Shall we not lie as we have lain*
> *Thus for Love's sake,*
> *And sleep, and wake, yet never break the chain?*
>   *'Sudden Light'   D G Rossetti*

PICTURE
ACKNOWLEDGMENTS

Plate section

Page i   Popperfoto
       ii   The Illustrated London News Picture Library
       iii   Popperfoto/Reuter
       iv   Popperfoto
       v   Nick Reid
       vi   The Hutchison Library/H R Dorig
       vii   The Hutchison Library
       viii (top) Popperfoto
       ix   Popperfoto
       x   Charles Flynn
       xi   Popperfoto
       xiii   Popperfoto
       xiv   (top) Nick Reid
       xiv   (bottom) The Hutchison Library
       xv   Bedfordshire Newspapers
       xvi   Fortean Picture Library

INDEX